London
e>>guide

London
e>>guide

In style • In the know • Online

www.elondon.dk.com

LONDON, NEW YORK,
MELBOURNE, MUNICH AND DELHI
www.dk.com

Produced by Blue Island Publishing

Contributors
Jonathan Cox, Michael Ellis, Andrew Humphreys, Lisa Ritchie

Photographer
Max Alexander

Reproduced in Singapore by Colourscan
Printed and bound in Singapore by Tien Wah Press

First published in Great Britain in 2005
by Dorling Kindersley Limited
80 Strand, London WC2R 0RL

A CIP catalogue record is available from the British Library.

ISBN 1 4053 0615 7

The information in this e>>guide is checked annually.
This guide is supported by a dedicated website which provides the very latest information for visitors to
London; please see pages 6–7 for the web address and password. Some information, however, is liable to
change, and the publishers cannot accept responsibility for any consequences arising from the use of this
book, nor for any material on third party websites, and cannot guarantee that any website address in this
book will be a suitable source of travel information.
We value the views and suggestions of our readers very highly. Please write to:
Publisher, DK Eyewitness Travel Guides,
Dorling Kindersley, 80 Strand, London WC2R 0RL, Great Britain.

Contents

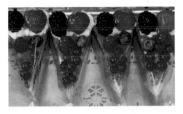

The only guidebook that's always up-to-date

Written by people who know London inside out, this guide provides in-depth information and reviews of the best the city has to offer. Listings are packed with great ideas and accompanied by stylish photographs, for a tantalizing foretaste of what's in store. Detailed practical information for each entry – including map references to the Street Finder at the back of the guide – take you directly to the heart of the action. So whether you live in London or are just visiting, to experience the real soul and pace of the city, you need this guide. Now visit the website...

top choice

- Spend the morning at a food or antiques market

- Stroll in one of the city's secluded parks or gardens

- Browse London's clothes shops for new ideas

- Discover small, independent art galleries

- Gain a new perspective on the classic tours and sights

- Find a bar to match your mood, be it mellow or loud

- Take your pick of restaurants, from fish'n'chips to French

feature

The one-stop website for all the city has to offer

Click onto elondon.dk.com for the latest, most complete news from and about places listed in the guide, plus travellers' reviews, features on hot topics, and an up-to-the-minute shortlist of London's most useful service providers, from the tourist board to dry cleaners to ticket agents. The website is only available to purchasers of e>>guide London (the unique password given below allows you access). And it's constantly updated. Every time you visit, you bring your guidebook bang up to date!

- Get the latest travel news and miss the crowds

- Check out the weather forecast and catch a cheap flight

- Book a hotel room that suits your budget and style

- Tap into what's on at Covent Garden and who's in at the Tate

- Browse reviews of the latest productions and secure tickets online

- Reserve a top table or seek out the best cheap eats

- Watch Oxford Street by webcam and plan your shopping trip online

reviews

>> password for access to website: **london48279**

top choices

London is one of the world's most cosmopolitan cities, and has recently gained renewed energy. Alongside its historic sights and monuments the city has superb modern architecture, bold street fashion, a vibrant arts scene, and restaurants and nightlife for every taste. This guide leads you to London's latest and best, opening with the top choices of what to do through the year and 24/7.

TOP CHOICES – *the year*

There's no doubt about it – London is ready to party. No matter what time of year you're in town, there's always something going on in this most international of cities. London's music and film festivals are second to none, and venerable British institutions such as the Chelsea Flower Show seem to become more exciting every year. Community celebrations too, such as Chinese New Year and Pride, have become bigger and slicker in recent years, attracting a wider cross-section of the population. However, don't miss out on the quirkier events that will give you insight into local life. Take advantage of Open Garden Squares Weekend to peek inside secluded gardens that are usually kept behind lock and key, and join in the free, family-friendly festivities dotting the summer calendar on the South Bank.

SPRING

Chinese New Year
www.chinatownchinese.com

The main celebration has outgrown Chinatown and moved to Trafalgar Square, which is decorated with lanterns and flowers. The entertainment includes traditional lion and dragon dances, and fireworks in Leicester Square. Food stalls spring up all along Gerrard Street. **Jan or Feb**

London Marathon
www.london-marathon.co.uk
More than 45,000 runners set off from Greenwich Park, and follow the Thames through Docklands and along Victoria Embankment to The Mall. You can join the party atmosphere in one of over 50 participating pubs, which open in readiness for the 9am start. **Apr**

SUMMER

Chelsea & Hampton Court Palace Flower Shows
Royal Hospital, Chelsea (Map 14 C4);
Hampton Court Palace • ⊖ Hampton Court; www.rhs.org.uk
The Royal Horticultural Society's Chelsea Flower Show is a slightly elitist occasion, but the show gardens – ranging from restrained, contemporary spaces to mystical landscapes – have universal appeal. In mid-summer, Hampton Court Palace hosts the world's largest horticultural event, with dazzling floral displays and temporary landscaped gardens in the palace's sprawling parkland. **May (Chelsea) & Jul (Hampton Court)**

Outdoor Concerts
Kenwood House (Map 1 C1; *see p108*),
www.picnicconcerts.com; Somerset House (Map 9 H3; *see p94*), www.somerset-house.org.uk; Holland Park (Map 6 D5; *see p170*), www.operahollandpark.com
What could be more magical than listening to music outdoors in a beautiful setting? On a balmy summer's evening, pack a picnic and throw down a blanket in the grounds of Kenwood House. Concerts feature big names in jazz, pop and classical music, and end with a fireworks display over the lake. In central London, the magnificent courtyard of Somerset House hosts concerts each summer. Recent super-chilled acts include Air and Bebel Gilberto. For something more classical, Opera Holland Park performs amid flowerbeds – a canopy ensures the show goes on whatever the weather. Check schedules on the websites. **Jul & Aug**

Open Garden Squares Weekend
http://myweb.tiscali.co.uk/london.gardens
A rare, fleeting opportunity to slip into some of London's secret gardens. More than 80 private squares – usually the preserve of privileged key-holding residents – open their gates to the public. Refreshments, live music and other entertainments are offered in some. Maps and full details are on the website. **Jun**

Coin Street Festival

Bernie Spain Gardens (Map 10 A4), www.coinstreetfestival.org
Ethnic diversity is celebrated with live world music, dance and art workshops at this free, community-based festival. Events take place over a series of theme days and weekends throughout the summer. **Jun–Aug**

Pride London

www.pridelondon.org
The gay and lesbian festival is one of London's largest, with flamboyant floats, dancers and, of course, drag queens. It begins in the morning with a parade through central London. In the afternoon, a massive party kicks off in a park, with live music and high camperie. **Jul**

The Proms

Royal Albert Hall (Map 13 G1), www.bbc.co.uk/proms
Launched over 100 years ago to promote musical appreciation among the masses, the Proms offer very cheap "promenade" (standing) tickets on the night, as well as prebooked seats for over 70 concerts. There is a big-screen link-up in Hyde Park. Securing a ticket for the famously high-spirited Last Night is tricky. **Jul–Sep**

Notting Hill Carnival

☺ Notting Hill Gate or Latimer Road (Map 7 E4),
08700 591111, www.nottinghillcarnival.co.uk
The famous Carnival still has a heavy Caribbean accent. Exotic floats and costumed dancers parade through the shabby-chic streets of Notting Hill, while throngs of revellers strut their stuff to calypso, salsa, R&B and hip-hop. Countless food stalls dish up rice'n'peas, jerk chicken and salt-fish patties. **Aug Bank Holiday Weekend**

Frieze Art Fair

Pavilion in Regent's Park (Map 2 B3), www.friezeartfair.com
London's newest and best contemporary art fair draws work from 150 galleries around the world, including big hitters Marian Goodman and Leo Koenig in New York, Jablonka Gallerie in Cologne and Galerie Yvon Lambert, Paris. The gathering is organized by international art magazine *Frieze* and lasts for four days. **Mid-Oct**

Open House Weekend

www.londonopenhouse.org
Over 500 London buildings, most of which are not usually accessible to the public, throw open their doors for just one weekend. The list of participating buildings changes annually, but each year's event includes a fabulous selection of grand mansions and contemporary houses;

public housing schemes by renowned architects; lavish government departments such as the Foreign Office; industrial buildings; theatres; church crypts and more. You have to book for some: check the website. **Mid-Sep**

London Film Festival

www.lff.org.uk
More than 300 films are screened during this two-week festival, at selected cinemas in central London. A diverse programme includes gala previews of big-budget movies, international and art-house features, and appearances by filmmakers, writers and actors. **Late Oct/Nov**

Somerset House Ice Rink

Somerset House (Map 9 H3; *see also p94*)
Glide around London's most beautiful ice rink, which is set in the courtyard of a Thames-side landmark and torch-lit in the evening. Hot chocolate and mulled wine are available at the Ice Rink Café. **Nov–Jan**

TOP CHOICES – *morning*

Rush-hour traffic aside, this is the best time to appreciate sights that are thronged later in the day. On a fine morning, the sun glistens on serene waterways and highlights the vivid floral displays in London's parks, where the relative quiet is punctuated by bird song. The city's atmospheric markets kick off early and are less crowded and combed-through than in the afternoon. Arrive at opening time with the professional dealers if you want to snap up the treasures. If the weather is unkind and paints the sky grey, you can still make the most of an early start by taking in a spot of culture. Beat the crowds to a famous museum, or attend a coffee concert of classical music. If all that sounds like a bit too much effort, linger over brunch in one of the most stylish parts of town.

An Early Swim
Serpentine Lido, Hyde Park (Map 8 A5);
Parliament Hill Lido • ⊖ Belsize Park or Kentish Town
Start your day with a splash in Hyde Park's mini Riviera. The south-west section of the Serpentine is reserved for swimming, and offers a sun deck and paddling pool as well. It opens at 10am. Afterwards, you can relax with an alfresco coffee at the Lido Café. For an earlier dip, try Parliament Hill Lido – a recently refurbished 60-m (100-ft) pool on Hampstead Heath. This one opens at 7am for free swimming until 9:30pm. It also has a terrace, café and paddling pool.

A Stroll around Little Venice
Blomfield Road, W2 (Map 7 G1; *see also p171*)
The picturesque area where three canals converge makes for a pleasant morning amble along towpaths. Brightly painted narrow boats line the Regent's Canal

between affluent Maida Avenue and Blomfield Road. Some boats are laden with splendid blooms in hanging baskets. There's a floating café in the triangle of water where the canals meet, but the best place for breakfast is Café Laville, which occupies a prime spot overlooking the canal on Edgware Road. The back of the restaurant opens up to command a spectacular view of the waterway and its colourful vessels.

A Boat Trip Upriver (Westminster Pier to Richmond, Kew or Hampton Court)
Thames River Boats, 020 7930 2062, www.wpsa.co.uk
For a relaxing day trip, follow the route of Henry VIII's Royal Barge from Westminster to the palace at Hampton Court, where the notorious 16th-century monarch bedded his many wives. You can disembark early at Kew for the Royal Botanical Gardens *(see p175)*, or Richmond for its deer park and large riverside pubs. However, going the extra distance is worth it, as the winding, willow-lined stretch of river between Kew and Hampton Court is especially picturesque.

Breakfast at Smithfields
Charterhouse Street & East Poultry Lane (Map 10 B2)
Catering primarily to the workers of Smithfield meat market, the Fox and Anchor, 115 Charterhouse Street, does a hearty "Full English" breakfast (fried bread, sausages, egg, beans and black pudding) from 7am. Wash it down with a Wadsworth ale or a stout. The Cock Tavern, set in the basement depths of the market, offers a similar line in fry-ups and beer from 6am, making it popular with all-night clubbers as well as night workers.

Brunch in Notting Hill

Dakota: 127 Ledbury Road; 202: 202 Westbourne Grove; Tom's Delicatessen: 226 Westbourne Grove (all on Map 6 D3)

Join the beautiful people gathering over Bloody Marys and eggs Benedict in cool Notting Hill. Airy, modern American restaurant Dakota has a terrific weekend brunch menu, while the French-style café in Nicole Farhi's lifestyle store, 202, serves blueberry pancakes, bagels and smoked salmon. Tom's Deli is a local institution, and all three have outside tables in summer.

Saturdays on Portobello Road

www.portobelloroad.co.uk *(see also p159)*

Get up early for some civilized antiques browsing before the melee is in full swing. The market officially opens at 5:30am, and most dealers have set up shop by 8am. Warrens of small stalls selling bric-a-brac and collector's pieces can be found in the arcades leading off the street. The café at kitchenalia shop Still Too Few (300 Westbourne Grove) is an excellent refuelling stop.

Sundays at Columbia Road Market

Columbia Road (Map 5 F4; *see also p161*)

From 8am to 2pm on Sundays, a short East End terrace is transformed into a verdant, vibrant strip of shrubs and flowers, enlivened by the cheeky patter of the vendors. There are some stylish shops among the storefronts, including Angela Flanders' perfumery at No. 96. Snack on fried prawns from Lee's Sea Foods (No.134), or stop for breakfast at local bistro Perennial (Nos. 110–12).

Browsing the British Museum

Great Russell St (Map 9 F2; *see also p98*)

On a fine day, sunlight streams through the curved steel-and-glass roof into the capacious Great Court at the centre of the "BM". The Court is huge and never

seems overly crowded, but that's not true of the museum galleries. Make the most of the relative quiet of a morning to peruse some of the highlights of the extensive collection: finely hewn Egyptian sculptures, reliefs from the Buddhist temple at Amaravati and, of course, the infamous Elgin Marbles.

A Walk in Regent's Park

www.royalparks.gov.uk (Map 2 B4)

Morning is the most peaceful time to enjoy what is arguably the most beautiful park in London. Before 11am you're likely to cross paths only with dog-walkers or pedestrians on their way to work. Seek out the glorious formal beds and classical fountains of the Avenue Gardens, Queen Mary's Gardens, for a riot of roses, and the Boating Lake, home to many unusual water fowl.

A Morning Concert at Wigmore Hall

From £10, including coffee, sherry or juice *(see also p122)*

Since this opulent yet intimate recital hall opened in 1901, some of the world's greatest musicians have played under its painted cupola. The Sunday Coffee Concerts are a civilized way to ease into the day. For a deeply relaxing experience, you can opt for a pre-lunch sherry.

TOP CHOICES – *afternoon*

Afternoons can be as busy or as lazy as you like. During the week, the pedestrian traffic in the centre thins out a bit after the lunchtime rush. This is the perfect time for a guided walking tour, to gain an informed perspective on the city. Many of London's cultural riches are free – the lunchtime recitals in a number of churches are a wonderful way to take in the beautiful architecture, and you can gallery-hop in hip Hoxton before hitting the bars. On weekend afternoons, the streets are thick with shoppers. If the crowds get too much, you may want to duck into a serene spa for some peace and quiet, or take part in time-honoured British rituals: go to a football match, tuck into a Sunday roast at one of the many excellent gastropubs, or take high tea at a chic hotspot or a grand hotel.

Summer Swimming at Brockwell Lido

Brockwell Park, Dulwich Road, SE24, 020 7274 3088, www.brockwelllido.com • ⊖ Brixton

A 15-minute walk from the Tube station, "Brixton Beach", as Brockwell Lido swimming pool is affectionately known, is a little summertime oasis. On any sunny day, the place gets packed by mid-afternoon, and especially at weekends, when the people-watching factor is at its most fascinating. Different social groups gravitate towards different areas of the terrace surrounding the big blue pool. Families with kids are at one end; topless bathers at the other. A gay enclave is easily spotted by the finest tans and tiniest swimwear. Everyone gets along fine, enjoying the sunshine and occasionally cooling off with a dip.

A Guided Tour

The Original London Walks, 020 7624 3978, www.walks.com

Get an insider's view of London on a walking tour led by someone in the know. The Original London Walks boasts leading archaeologists and historians among its guides and operates at least a dozen walks every day. Intriguing afternoon offerings include Legal and Illegal London (a tour of the Inns of Court) on Mondays and Fridays, and Christopher Wren's London on Tuesdays.

Sundays around Spitalfields

Spitalfields Market (Map 11 F1; *see also p161*)

This energetic part of town in and around Spitalfields Market, with cool stalls and food outlets, is abuzz on Sundays. Nearby, in Fournier, Fashion and Princelet streets, there are beautifully restored early 18th-century Georgian terraces, and Hawksmoor's Christ Church.

Lunchtime Recitals in London's Churches

www.stmartin-in-the-fields.org, www.st-james-piccadilly.org, www.stmarylebow.co.uk, www.stbrides.com; *see p226 for all*

For an uplifting lunchtime experience, attend a free recital at one of London's lovely churches. You could catch an up-and-coming soloist, a touring choir, or a student ensemble from one of the prestigious conservatories. St Martin-in-the-Fields in Trafalgar Square, where Handel once per-

To find more guided walks in London, check out ≫ www.elondon.dk.com

formed, has been hosting lunchtime concerts for 50 years. St James's (Piccadilly) and St Mary-le-Bow and St Brides (both in the City) are others. *(See also p169.)*

Off to the Football
Hackney Marshes • ⊖ Homerton · 020 8986 8615
Forget Arsenal, Chelsea, Spurs or even Fulham. To see what English football was about before corporate sponsors and inflated wages, head for Hackney Marshes on a Sunday. There you'll find 87 full-size pitches – the largest concentration in Europe. The quality of "footie" skills is patchy and diverse, but passions run as high as at any Premiership game.

A Sunday Roast
Recent years have seen a resurgence in the traditional English "Sunday Roast" – a joint of beef, lamb or pork, with roast potatoes, Yorkshire pudding, veg and gravy. London's gastropubs offer some good updated versions of the meal, which can be washed down with a decent ale or lager. Try the Lansdowne *(see p51)*; The House in Islington *(see p49)*; or The Lock Tavern *(see p152)*, which sources its meat from London's finest butchers.

Afternoon Tea
Sketch: 9 Conduit St (Map 8 D3), 0870 777 4488; Inn the Park, St James's Park (9 F5), 020 7451 9999; The Wolseley *(see p32)*
For alternatives to the chintz and hushed tones that accompany tea in the posh hotels, try The Parlour at Sketch, with its minimalist Louis XIV furniture and arty little pastries. For a more classic afternoon tea, book at The Wolseley. On a fine day, take tea at Inn the Park or the Orangery in Kensington Gardens *(see p170)*.

Revive at Porchester Spa
Queensway, W2 *(see p170)*
This original Art Deco spa offers pampering on a shoestring. Relax and revitalize in its Turkish hot rooms, Russian steam rooms, Jacuzzi and pool for under £20, or indulge in a body treatment from as little as £10. To save your blushes, there are specific days for men, women and mixed couples.

Sunday Double Bills at the Electric
Electric Cinema (Map 6 D3; *see p123*)
Don't wait for a rainy afternoon to slope off to the restored Edwardian splendour of the Electric Cinema. The Sunday Double Bill is excellent value. Book a 2-seater sofa to see the picture, and have brunch before the screening at the Electric Brasserie.

East London's Galleries
www.newexhibitions.com
Any afternoon between Thursday and Sunday is good for visiting the substantial clutch of contemporary art galleries in East London. Have a trawl through listings on the new exhibitions website, or pick up a printed copy (with map) at the first gallery you see. Aside from those in Hoxton *(see p162)*, check out

galleries near Victoria Park (nearest Tube: Bethnal Green), which primarily showcase up-and-coming artists from the UK and Europe. Look out for Vilma Gold, Wilkinson Gallery and the Showroom; and don't miss The Approach (art upstairs, pub downstairs). For contact info, *see p225*.

TOP CHOICES – *evening*

London notches up a gear in the early evening as everyone streams out of work and heads to the myriad pubs, bars and restaurants. A prevailing mood of fitting it all in before last orders gives evening London a very buzzy feel, as a 10 o'clock stroll through partying crowds in Soho will attest. Although central London is packed with entertainments, many Londoners prefer the less in-your-face vibe in neighbourhoods at the edges of the central zone. Clerkenwell, Islington and Notting Hill have great restaurants, pubs and cultural venues that are well worth seeking out, while in East London, you'll find a blossoming scene that caters to a hip, arty crowd. The city has an undeniable pub culture, but a quieter, more sophisticated London does exist; you just need to look a little bit harder to find it.

Down the Pub
See pp134–5 for our selection of the best pubs in the city
Old favourites for after-work drinks include Soho haunts such as the Coach & Horses (29 Greek St), the Dog & Duck (18 Bateman St) the Sun & Thirteen Cantons (21 Great Pulteney St), and Covent Garden's Lamb & Flag *(see p137)*, where patrons spill out onto the street on summer evenings. Clerkenwell Green (Map 10 A1) is another superb spot for an evening's drinking; the Three Kings, Crown Tavern, Horseshoe and Dovetail are all situated around a pleasant square. The last orders bell rings at 10:45pm, after which drinkers exit the bars either to head home or to move on to clubland.

Museum Late-Nights
Tate Modern *(see p111)*; V&A *(see p102)*
Having the cavernous converted Bankside Power Station to yourself is a real luxury, and that's pretty

much what you get on Friday and Saturday evenings, when Tate Modern is open until 10pm. The decorative arts museum, the V&A, is open until 10pm on Wednesdays, and on the last Friday of every month a special late event is staged: everything from high fashion to turntablists can be seen among the ancient art. It's truly atmospheric.

A Stroll in Hyde Park
☺ Hyde Park Corner (Map 8 C5)
With the late evening sun casting long shadows over the grass, this is a lovely time to take a walk in any of London's central parks. Hyde Park in particular draws strollers, picnickers and sporty types, who make use of long summer evenings for ad-hoc games of baseball or football. End your walk at the Blue Bar, across busy Knightsbridge *(see p142)*, or seek out the Nag's Head *(see p141)*, one of two great pubs on Kinnerton Street.

Greyhound Racing
Walthamstow Stadium *(see p126)*
"Going down the dogs" has made a comeback as a top night out, and "The Stow" – an Art Deco classic – is the place to go. Six greyhounds run 400- and 800-metre races, chasing a fake rabbit that zips along a rail; you can bet on any dog, but not the rabbit, alas. Punters quaff pints and eat scampi'n'chips in the Popular Enclosure, or sup wine and dine on steaks above the track in the Paddock Grill. Either way, the focus of the evening is on betting – but with stakes starting as low as 50p, the excursion need not cost you a mint.

Early Club Nights

www.clubinlondon.co.uk

The Social on Little Portland Street *(see p140)* was one of the first London venues to offer easy-going Sunday afternoon events. Now several club sessions kick off as early as 5pm every weekend. Check out 93 Feet East *(see p148)*, Cherry Jam *(see p141)*, the Notting Hill Arts Club *(see p144)* and Cargo *(see p146)*.

A Pint and a Play

Old Red Lion: 418 St John St (Map 4 A4); King's Head *(see p127)*; Orange Tree: 1 Clarence Street • Richmond

Dark, creaking spaces in the back rooms of pubs provide the most intimate of performance venues for up-and-coming playwrights, actors on the fringe of the fringe and even a big name sometimes. Islington has several theatre bars, including the Old Red Lion and the King's Head, the oldest theatre pub in London. In Richmond (about 30 minutes by Tube or train from central London), the Orange Tree is a wonderful theatre in the round.

Evening Cocktails

Fifth Floor Restaurant, Harvey Nichols (Map 14 B1); No.1 Aldwych *(see p136)*; Blue Bar *(see p142)*

With Harvey Nichols open until 8pm on Wednesdays, it would be a crime not to take advantage of the wonder-

ful bar at its Fifth Floor Restaurant. The hotel Lobby Bar at No.1 Aldwych is excellent for cocktails and classy snacks. For maximum style, though, saunter over to the Blue Bar in Knightsbridge, where celebrities socialize.

Oysters and Champagne

Bibendum Oyster Bar at The Conran Shop *(see p78)*; Randall & Aubin: 16 Brewer St, W1 (Map 9 E3)

Start your evening with a flourish! The Fulham Road Conran Shop is open until 7pm three nights a week, allowing an afternoon's shopping to drift seamlessly into an evening's light indulgence at the Bibendum Oyster Bar. Over in Soho, Randall & Aubin provides a vibrant, Parisian atmosphere in which to enjoy some crustacea and bubbly and set yourself up for a fun night out.

Great British Comedy

www.chortle.co.uk

London's comedy clubs are lively affairs, with the banter swinging between performers of all descriptions and frequently raucous audiences. The Comedy Store *(see p121)* and Jongleurs *(p128)* are established venues, but it's worth investigating the comedy pubs *(see website above)*, where the atmosphere is often a tad more spiky.

South Bank Promenade

From Waterloo Bridge to Shad Thames *(see also p164)*

The South Bank riverside path is relatively free of crowds on weekdays before sunset. Walking eastwards, you'll pass the National Theatre, Tate Modern and GLA building. At dusk, the city takes on a golden hue, with Canada Tower blazing orange on the eastern skyline.

Cutting-Edge Culture at the ICA

ICA, The Mall *(see p96)*

Occupying a regal John Nash terrace, the Institute of Contemporary Arts is a wellspring of the avant-garde within a stone's throw of Buckingham Palace. Two tiny cinemas feature art-house and foreign-language films. There are talks and music events in the evenings, and a lively bar that stays open pretty late.

TOP CHOICES – *night*

Glamorous, cultured, raucous, seedy... After dark, the metropolis pulses with nightlife in many guises. Soho is the nocturnal epicentre, with a high concentration of places to eat and drink. Pubs are packed to capacity, spilling out onto the narrow streets, and all-night cafés offer a ringside view of unfolding dramas. The pubs may close early (11pm), but, if you're prepared to pay a cover charge, the evening doesn't have to end there. Soak up the cool vibe at a quintessential jazz joint, catch a risqué cabaret, or head east for switched-on nightclubs. Londoners often counteract alcoholic excesses with a fiery curry, or a salt beef bagel at the all-night bakery in Brick Lane. For more refined entertainments, the arts complex on the South Bank may not be aesthetically pleasing, but it is unrivalled for cultural events.

The London Eye at Sunset

0870 5000 600, www.ba-londoneye.com (Map 9 G5)
Open 9:30am–10pm summer, 9:30am–8pm winter
A glass capsule on the world's largest observation wheel is the perfect vantage point for watching the sun set over London's landmarks, as you gently revolve at a speed of 0.26 m (about 10 inches) per second. From the top, at 135 m (443 ft), the view stretches 25 miles in every direction – as far as Windsor Castle. As darkness falls, illuminated buildings including St Paul's Cathedral and the Houses of Parliament create a romantic panorama.

Concerts on the South Bank

Royal Festival Hall, South Bank SE1 (Map 9 H4), 0870 401 8181
www.rfh.org.uk *(see also p129)*
As well as showcasing two resident orchestras, the London Philharmonic and the Philharmonia Orchestra, the 3,000-seat Royal Festival Hall, the smaller Queen Elizabeth Hall and The Purcell Room present a diverse programme of classical, contemporary and world music and dance. On Fridays at 5:15pm, in the Festival Hall Foyer, there's a free programme of "Commuter Jazz".

Candlelit Visits

Dennis Severs' House (Mon; *see p104*);
Sir John Soane's Museum (first Tue of month; *see p97*)
Two of the most curious and atmospheric houses in London both offer candlelit viewings. The aim is to recreate the mood of the past, when flickering yellow light and darting shadows characterised the ambience in these houses. In the light of a flame, Soane's classical sculptures seem to shimmer and shake, and the building seems even more labyrinthine. At Dennis Severs' House, the candlelight enhances an atmosphere already strong with scents of fruit and lavender, and the ghostly sound of voices, seemingly in the next room.

Clubbing in Shoreditch & Clerkenwell

Shoreditch and Clerkenwell currently have London's best concentration of dance clubs. At the hardcore techno and house end of the spectrum is Turnmills *(see p146)*. Fabric *(see p145)* charts a funkier path, with Craig Richards at the decks, joined by guests such as Roots Manuva. It also hosts regular live dance music nights. Club 333 *(see p147)* gets really wild on Saturdays, joining forces with its upstairs neighbour Mother for some trippy trance or jazz-inflected house rhythms. For an easy-going vibe and inventive musical concoctions, you can't beat Herbal *(see p147)*, especially on an Eastern Drum and Breaks night.

Late Night Jazz

Ronnie Scott's: 47 Frith Street *(see p121);*
Jazz Café: 5 Parkway *(see p127)*

Ronnie Scott's in Soho is the archetypal smoky jazz joint, with quirky, tiered seating, cramped tables, and photos of the legends who've played there covering every inch of wall space. Further north, in Camden, the Jazz Café is slicker and more spacious, the music is funkier and the food is better. At both, it's advisable to book a table.

DJ Bar-Hopping

Much of London's dance music scene is now concentrated in its DJ bars. Typically, such bars get going earlier than clubs, at around 9pm, and close at 2–3am. The music is eclectic, sometimes just creating a background vibe (as at the Medicine Bar and Lock Tavern, *see pp150 & 152*). These bars attract a clientele in their 20s and 30s. But at somewhere like Brixton's Dogstar *(see p154)*, the crowd tends to be younger, mostly 20-somethings, and the dancing is full-on at weekends.

Late Night Screenings at the Ritzy

Brixton Oval *(see p131)*

While most London cinemas have their final screenings

at around 9pm, the Ritzy keeps its lights on for an 11:30pm showing on Fridays and Saturdays. Its programme includes a good mix of mainstream, independent and international films.

Bagels and Curries on Brick Lane

Brick Lane Beigel Bake: 159 Brick Lane;
Café Naz: 46–8 Brick Lane, 020 7247 0234;
City Spice: 138 Brick Lane, 020 7247 1012;
Le Taj: 134 Brick Lane, 020 7247 4210 (Maps 5 F5 & 11 F1)

The yellow and red sign of the Beigel Bake marks a little gathering point throughout the day and night (it's open 24 hours) for everyone from cabbies picking up a quick snack to old Jewish residents of the area to clubbers getting a bite to eat in the early hours. You can buy a freshly baked bagel, with classic fillings such as salt beef and mustard or smoked salmon and cream cheese, for less than £2. Brick Lane is also famous for its curry houses. You'll find better Indian cuisine elsewhere, but the lively atmosphere along this narrow strip of road, with its bright neon signage, makes up for culinary shortfalls. As a stomach-filler after a few drinks, an inexpensive curry at somewhere like Café Naz, City Spice or Le Taj is just the ticket. *(For more on Brick Lane, see p160.)*

Espresso at Bar Italia

25 Frith Street W1,
020 7437 4520,
www.baritaliasoho.co.uk

Grab a seat outside this 24-hour Soho institution, sip a strong espresso and watch the circus go by. After the pubs and clubs close, it's jam-packed with people who want to keep the party going – or soak up the alcohol with a panini. You never know whom you might meet, but keep a firm grip on your bag or wallet.

The Whoopee Club

www.thewhoopeeclub.com

The producers of this arty burlesque extravaganza put on regular shows at venues around London, with themes such as Victorian valentines and 1940s film noir. Strippers in retro tasselled pasties, contortionists and camp cabaret acts perform and pose in postmodernist tableaux. The audience gets into the spirit too, sporting outfits that rival the stars' costumes.

restaurants

London's gastronomic scene is booming. The range of places to eat and the diversity of cuisines on offer are rivalled only by New York. The quality of cooking is something to write home about, too, especially at top-end restaurants. Prices are high if you want to sample the work of famous chefs, but there are excellent choices in all price ranges if you know where to look and what to order.

BEST BRITISH CUISINE	ROMANTIC SETTINGS	GASTROPUBS

Lindsay House
21 Romilly Street, W1
Superlative service plus Richard Corrigan's inventive British/Irish cuisine equals a gourmet's delight. *(See p26)*

The Cow
89 Westbourne Park Road, W2
You've seen the film, now hang out with the hip young things of Notting Hill in this characterful pub, which serves great food. *(See p160)*

Fish Central
149–51 Central Street, EC1
The setting may be sleek, but this City favourite serves up some of the best (and best-value) fish and chips in town. *(See p45)*

>> *www.toptable.co.uk is a useful site for listings, reviews and information about London restaurants.*

The Crown
116 Cloudesley Road, N1
Cheery, cosy and thoroughly relaxed, the Crown is the sort of place you go to for lunch and settle into for a whole afternoon. *(See p151)*

Rules
35 Maiden Lane, WC2
London's oldest restaurant is an atmospheric, Dickensian shrine to perfect roast meats, game and classic puddings. *(See p30)*

Andrew Edmunds
46 Lexington Street, W1
Cramped it may be, but there's something unbeatably romantic about this long-established, friendly Soho bistro. *(See p24)*

The Eagle
159 Farringdon Road, EC1
The pub that started the gastropub phenomenon is still a frontrunner. Tuck into great grills and chat with the Clerkenwell crowd. *(See p44)*

St John
26 St John Street, EC1
A stark former smokehouse provides a great setting for stripped-down "nose to tail" eating. It's carnivore heaven. *(See p46)*

Oxo Tower Restaurant, Bar & Brasserie
Oxo Tower Wharf, Barge House St, SE1
Sweeping views over the Thames provide a spectacular backdrop for fine dining. *(See p54)*

>> *Some gastropubs are more restaurant than pub, and have prices that reflect this. Be prepared to book.*

J Sheekey
28–32 St Martin's Court, WC2
With its faultless food, seductive decor and effortless service, J Sheekey oozes class. A perfect venue for a discreet date. *(See p31)*

Odette's
130 Regent's Park Road, NW1
Awash with gilded mirrors and candlelight, Odette's is a great spot for contemporary food combined with old-fashioned charm. *(See p50)*

The House
63–9 Canonbury Road, N1
The quality of food at this superb Islington gastropub puts most restaurants to shame. A must for weekend brunch. *(See p49)*

AROUND THE WORLD

Hakkasan
8 Hanway Place, W1
With an interior out of a design magazine and heavenly food, Hakkasan sets new standards for London's Chinese restaurants. *(See p27)*

Tsunami
5–7 Voltaire Road, SW4
Super-stylish and one of London's most exquisite dining experiences, with magnificent Japanese-influenced food. *(See p54)*

The Providores/Tapa Room
109 Marylebone High Street, W1
Pan-global fusion food at its most inventive. Snack and sip on the ground floor, or go for a full blow-out in the restaurant. *(See p35)*

>> *Brick Lane, in the East End, is good for a late-night curry (see p19). However, for authentic, ultra-cheap Indian food, hop on a train west to Southall, the heart of London's Punjabi community.*

Moro
34–6 Exmouth Market, EC1
Embracing the best of North African and Spanish cuisine, this ever-hip eaterie makes ta virtue out of simplicity. *(See p44)*

A QUICK BITE

Lisboa Patisserie
57 Golborne Road, W10
Come to this vibrant Portuguese place to sip strong coffee and nibble prime pastries. *(See p42)*

Patisserie Valerie
44 Old Compton Street, W1
Indulgent cakes and pastries to die for are the primary draws at one of Soho's oldest and best-loved classic cafés. *(See p26)*

Paul
20 Bedford Street, WC2
A little slice of Paris in London. Pop in to Paul for toothsome tarts, flans, *galettes* and salads, and plenty of Gallic bonhomie. *(See p29)*

>> *Conveyor-belt restaurants such as Yo! Sushi and Itsu offer a healthy form of fast food.*

Mô
23 Heddon Street, W1
Take tea and sample choice North African snacks in this Ali Baba's cave of a café, which is more Marrakesh than Mayfair. *(See p34)*

ON THE CHEAP

Navarro's
67 Charlotte Street, W1
Bright and bustling, Navarro's is one of the best spots in the capital to find authentic (and authentically priced) tapas. *(See p28)*

Viet Hoa
70–72 Kingsland Road, E2
Don't expect decorative frills; do expect culinary thrills. The Vietnamese food at this Hoxton canteen is the real deal. *(See p48)*

Café Emm
17 Frith Street, W1
Proof that it's possible to get good, filling fare in a lively Soho atmosphere without breaking the bank. *(See p25)*

Tas
33 The Cut, SE1
A lively vibe, contemporary setting, willing service, and affordable Turkish grills and meze. *(See p53)*

S&M Café
268 Portobello Road, W10
Superlative sausages, mash and gravy are served in various seasonings. First-rate comfort food at bargain-basement prices. *(See p42)*

>> *Gastropubs are pubs that serve good, sometimes excellent, modern cuisine*

Restaurants

Andrew Edmunds *modern European* 9 E3
46 Lexington Street, W1 • 020 7437 5708
Open lunch & dinner daily

Dark and discreet, this long-time Soho stalwart is a seductive spot for contemporary cuisine. The crowd-pleasing food embraces the classics, such as a perfect lamb steak with flageolet beans. Seating is a bit cramped, and the room can be noisy, but the service is breezily relaxed. **Moderate**

Bodean's *North American barbecue* 9 E3
10 Poland Street, W1 • 020 7287 7575
›› www.bodeansbbq.com Restaurant open lunch & dinner
Mon–Fri, noon–11pm Sat; diner open all day

Billing itself as "London's Original BBQ Smoke House", Bodean's is a classy US-style barbecue, featuring prime char-grilled steaks, racks of baby back ribs and smoked chicken. The ground floor is a casual eat-in/takeaway sports bar; the basement is more formal. **Moderate**

Donzoko *rare Japanese delights* 9 E3
15 Kingly Street, W1 • 020 7734 1974
Open lunch & dinner Mon–Fri, dinner Sat

This modest Japanese eaterie is one of Soho's hidden gems. It's a friendly, bustling *izakaya*-style joint (an informal pub-restaurant), with a counter along one side and a long menu taking in all the greatest hits of Japanese cuisine. The aubergine fried with garlic and soybean paste is sublime. **Cheap**

Mar i Terra *superior Spanish* 9 E3
17 Air Street, W1 • 020 7734 1992
›› www.mariterra.co.uk
Open lunch & dinner Mon–Fri, noon–11pm Sat

Spanish food can move with the times. The décor here is clean and contemporary; the service cheery and unfussy. The menu lists Iberian classics alongside more unusual delights, such as stuffed peppers with crab, and Catalan grilled vegetable salad. **Cheap**

Wong Kei *legendary cheap Chinese*
41–43 Wardour Street, W1 • 020 7437 8408
Open noon–11:30pm daily (to 10:30pm Sun)

A capacious restaurant with oddly decorated rooms on many floors, Wong Kei revels in its reputation of having the rudest service in Chinatown. And yet it continues to pull in the punters thanks to a lively atmosphere, seriously low prices and unexpectedly fine roast meats. Great fun with a crowd. **Cheap**

The Sugar Club *European fusion*
21 Warwick Street, W1 • 020 7437 7776
》www.thesugarclub.co.uk
Open lunch Tue–Fri, dinner daily

For almost a decade, this pioneering fusion restaurant has stood in the top echelon of London dining. Astonishingly inventive dishes include pan-roast sea bass on *harusame* noodles, and Jerusalem artichokes with spicy *harissa* broth and *hijiki* seaweed. **Expensive**

ECapital *Chinatown oasis*
8 Gerrard Street, W1 • 020 7434 3838
Open noon–11:30pm daily (to midnight Fri & Sat)

Few Chinatown restaurants offer distinctive cuisine, but ECapital is an exception: here you'll find a rare high-quality offering of rich-sweet-oily food from China's east coast. It's worth asking the staff to translate the Chinese menu to find the most interesting dishes, such as "lion's head meatball casserole". **Cheap**

Café Emm *hearty international fodder*
17 Frith Street, W1 • 020 7437 0723
》www.cafeemm.com
Open lunch & dinner daily (to 11:30pm Fri & Sat)

It's hard to beat Café Emm for value, atmosphere and good, filling grub. Dishes include cajun potato skins, deep-fried brie, hearty lamb shanks, calamari, pecan pie and tiramisu, and all come in huge portions, served up by smiling staff in a fun environment. **Cheap**

Restaurants

Lindsay House *modern British*

21 Romilly Street, W1 • 020 7439 0450
>> www.lindsayhouse.co.uk
Open lunch & dinner Mon–Fri, dinner only Sat

Irishman Richard Corrigan is a real chef's chef – while many of his peers play the media game, he sticks resolutely to fashioning imaginative dishes in the kitchen. The results show just how good creative British/Irish cuisine can be in the right hands.

The restaurant, set in a 1740s Georgian townhouse, is as understated as the man himself. Ring the bell to be let in, and you'll be shown to one of various small dining spaces. The gracious staff might be serving up globe artichoke, Cornish crab and parsley dressing, followed perhaps by saddle of rabbit, black pudding, polenta and confit garlic, and then glazed apple turnover with caramel and prunes to finish. If your wallet can bear the strain, consider the seven-course tasting menu in order to sample Corrigan's finest creations. **Expensive**

Patisserie Valerie *café for cakes* 9 F3

44 Old Compton Street, W1 • 020 7437 3466
>> www.patisserie-valerie.co.uk
Open 7:30am–8:30pm Mon–Fri, 9am–9pm Sat, 9am–7pm Sun

A Soho legend, the original Patisserie Valerie opened in neighbouring Frith Street in 1926 and moved to Old Compton Street after World War II. The cramped interior is a 1950s Parisian time warp, with a cake-stuffed glass counter at the front, a high ceiling, Formica tables and Toulouse-Lautrec cartoons on the walls; there's also a brighter, airier 50-seat first-floor café.

Snacks, light meals and a fine breakfast are served, but it's the sweet stuff that's the main draw. Resistance is useless against the likes of pear william franzipan tart, mixed berry mousse, fresh fruit flan, and chocolate, strawberry and banana gateaux – not to mention the handmade truffles. Such indulgences and Valerie's unique atmosphere draw in a mixed crowd of local office workers, students, tourists and the few remaining louche Soho habitués. **Cheap**

Red Fort *noble Indian* `9 F3`

77 Dean Street, W1 • 020 7437 2115
»www.redfort.co.uk Open lunch & dinner Mon–Fri, dinner Sat

For top-notch traditional northern Indian cooking in central London, you can't beat the Red Fort. The opulent setting (including a water feature) helps prepare you for the richness and depth of Mughal court cuisine. Chef Mohammed Rais' lamb biriani follows a 300-year-old family recipe. **Expensive**

Eagle Bar Diner *North American* `9 F2`

3–5 Rathbone Place, W1 • 020 7637 1418
»www.eaglebardiner.com Open noon–11pm Mon–Sat (to 1am Thu–Sat), 11am–6pm Sun

A hip, all-day haven from the chaos of Oxford Street. The Eagle's remit stretches from breakfast to late-night cocktails, taking in first-rate burgers and grills, salads and sandwiches along the way. The look is New York chic, but the service is friendly. **Cheap**

Hakkasan *Chinese of the highest order* `9 F2`

8 Hanway Place, W1 • 020 7907 1888
Open lunch & dinner daily; bar noon–12:30am daily (to 1:30 Sat)

It's no exaggeration to say that Hakkasan has redefined Chinese dining in London – combining stunning design with exceptional high-quality Chinese cuisine. This airy basement restaurant and bar is the creation of Alan Yau, the man behind Wagamama *(see p43)*, but couldn't be more different from the noodle bar chain in terms of atmosphere (and prices).

The seductive interior is a cunning contemporary take on chinoiserie – all dark wood, lattice work and candle light. The Michelin-star-winning food shows off the full range and depth of China's varied cuisines. Savour beautifully balanced dishes such as roast pork with red rice, ginger and Shao Hsing wine, or roasted silver cod with champagne and Chinese honey. Even clichéd standards such as sesame prawn toast are exemplary. Prices are high, but for a splurge you can't beat Hakkasan. **Expensive**

Centre

Rasa Samudra *Keralan home cooking*

9 E1

5 Charlotte Street, W1 • 020 7637 0222
>> www.rasarestaurants.com
Open lunch & dinner Mon–Sat, dinner only Sun

Das Sreedharan has firmly placed the delicate cuisine of Kerala in southwest India on the London restaurant map. The first Rasa (55 Stoke Newington Church Street, N16) opened in 1994, specializes in Keralan vegetarian cooking. Rasa W1 (6 Dering Street) offers a range of dishes, including meat, from northern Kerala; and the speciality at this branch is seafood.

In a maze of smart, pink-clad little rooms, you can experience such little-seen delights as *murukku* (crunchy rice-flour sticks) with home-made pickles and chutneys, Keralan shellfish soup, crab *thoran* (the chef's grandmother's recipe for crab stir-fried with coconut, mustard seeds and ginger) and *kappayum meenum* (spicy king fish and steamed cassava). If you can't make up your mind, order a set feast, either seafood or vegetarian. **Moderate**

Fino *modern tapas*

9 E2

33 Charlotte St, W1 (entrance: Rathbone St) • 020 7813 8010
>> www.finorestaurant.com
Open lunch & dinner Mon–Fri, dinner only Sat

Sleek, sassy and contemporary, Fino is a light, airy tapas restaurant and cocktail bar in which tortilla, Galician-style octopus and other classics are cooked with conviction and presented with flair. It has fine sherries and a globe-trotting wine list. **Moderate**

Navarro's *traditional Spanish*

9 E1

67 Charlotte Street, W1 • 020 7637 7713
>> www.navarros.co.uk Open lunch & dinner Mon–Fri, dinner Sat

The interior is a riot of Andalucian tiling and painted furniture, while the menu features some of the capital's most unusual Spanish dishes. Savour, for example, the velvety, piquant grilled chicken with prawns in an oloroso sherry and paprika sauce. This gem of a place is favoured by many hispanophile Londoners. **Cheap**

Sardo *pasta & other Italian classics* `9 E1`
45 Grafton Way, W1 • 020 7387 2521
>> www.sardo-restaurant.com
Open lunch & dinner Mon–Fri, dinner only Sat

No-nonsense, squeaky-fresh Sardinian specialities are presented in a bright, simply decorated space. Try the likes of *spaghetti bottariga* (with dried mullet roe) or grilled steak topped with Sardinian blue cheese, served by delightful, knowledgeable staff. **Moderate**

Matsuri *Japanese fun* `9 H2`
71 High Holborn, WC1 • 020 7430 1970
>> www.matsuri-restaurant.com Open lunch & dinner Mon–Sat

The team behind the acclaimed Matsuri in St James's opened this more modern sister restaurant in 2002. The *sashimi* (raw fish) and *teppanyaki* (grills) are as authentically Japanese as you'll find in London. If you're on a budget, try a lunchtime *bento* box; otherwise, the set menus are excellent. **Expensive**

Rock and Sole Plaice *fish & chips* `9 G3`
47 Endell Street, WC2 • 020 7836 3785
Open 11am–11:30pm Mon–Sat, noon–11pm Sun

Founded in 1871, this Covent Garden fish and chip shop has been run for the past 25 years by a Turkish Cypriot, though the menu is traditional British. Expect crisp, golden slabs of fish accompanied by mounds of chunky chips and mugs of steaming tea. You can eat in, sit at pavement tables in summer or take away. **Cheap**

Paul *French-style café* `9 G3`
20 Bedford Street, WC2 • 020 7836 3304
>> www.paul.fr Open 7:30am–9pm Mon–Fri, 9–9 Sat & Sun

You'll find no more agreeable lunch stop around Covent Garden than this exemplary Gallic patisserie/café. Exquisite breads, cakes, tarts and flans are sold in the shop, or you can enjoy big salads, omelettes or *tartines* (toasted bread with toppings) from the elegant café at the rear. **Cheap**

>> *A great place to enjoy a snack from Paul's café is St Paul's Churchyard, just off Bedford Street*

Rules *British through & through*

9 G3

35 Maiden Lane, WC2 • 020 7836 5314
>> www.rules.co.uk
Open noon–11:30pm daily (to 10:30pm Sun)

Open continuously since 1798, and owned by just three families since then, Rules in Covent Garden is the capital's oldest restaurant and it positively drips with history. Venerable diners have included William Makepeace Thackeray, Evelyn Waugh, Graham Greene, Charlie Chaplin and Clark Gable.

The interior is a Victorian fantasy, with chandeliers and spectacular coloured-glass skylights illuminating walls lined with dark wood and crimson banquettes. Everywhere you look are portraits, pastoral scenes and animal trophies characteristic of the style of grand English country houses. The restaurant is particularly beautiful over Christmas, decked out in traditional ornaments. Altogether, there are three floors and several private dining rooms. One of the rooms is named after the best-known author of the

Victorian era, Charles Dickens, who was himself a regular at this restaurant. However, what prevents Rules being a mere Dickensian pastiche are the slickness of its service and the supreme standard of its food. The menu is carnivore heaven, and one of the few places in London where you can sample superb game – especially wild duck and pheasant – much of which comes from Rules' own estate, Lartington Hall Park, in the High Pennines. (You can sign up for a shooting party or fishing at the estate, if you already have experience.)

Don't believe there's such a thing as high-quality traditional British cuisine? An indulgent meal here of, say, hare soup with armagnac, or Morecambe Bay potted shrimps, or roast young grouse with celeriac and damson sauce, or fillet of Highland venison with wild mushrooms and Chartreuse sauce is guaranteed to change your mind. Round off the experience with sticky toffee pudding oozing butterscotch and vanilla custard, or apple and blackberry crumble. **Expensive**

Hazuki *mid-range Japanese* `9 G4`

43 Chandos Place, WC2 • 020 7240 2530
» www.sushihazuki.co.uk
Open lunch & dinner Mon–Fri, dinner only Sat & Sun

Hazuki nimbly bridges the gap between pricey, formal
Japanese restaurants and casual sushi bars. Its look
is contemporary, its staff efficient, its food exemplary.
Lunch dishes – such as grilled belly pork with rice
and soup – are particularly good value. **Moderate**

J Sheekey *fish, pure & simple* `9 F3`

28–32 St Martin's Court, WC2 • 020 7240 2565
Open lunch & dinner daily (to midnight)

If you despair of ever getting a table at The Ivy
(see p34), fear not: this effortlessly classy sister
restaurant offers just as seductive a setting, sublime
food and lovely service. The emphasis is on fish, and
the ethos is to keep it simple. You won't find a finer
fish pie in London. **Expensive**

Cecconi's *established Italian venue* `9 E4`

5A Burlington Gardens, W1 • 020 7434 1500
Open 8am–11pm Mon–Fri, 9am–11pm Sat, 9am–10pm Sun

A sleek thoroughbred of a restaurant, Cecconi's man-
ages to be both serious and fun, stylish yet relaxed.
Though it's been around for decades, thoughtful
renovation has breathed new life into an old favourite.
The great cocktail menu survives, as does classic
Italian food using the freshest ingredients. **Expensive**

Le Caprice *classy comfort food* `9 E4`

Arlington House, Arlington Street, SW1 • 020 7629 2239
Open lunch & dinner daily

Le Caprice has been a famous name on the London
dining scene for decades. There's a disconcerting
1980s monochrome bistro look to the décor, but the
slick service and modern European dishes never
disappoint. Their fish and chips with mushy peas is
heavenly. **Expensive**

The Wolseley *fashionable all-day haunt*   `9 E4`

160 Piccadilly, W1 • 020 7499 6996
Open 7am–midnight Mon–Fri, 9am–midnight Sat & Sun
(breakfast to 11:30am)

Chris Corbin and Jeremy King are the talented double act behind the sustained success of the exclusive Ivy *(see p34)* and Le Caprice *(see p31)* over the past decade or so. Their involvement with these twin pillars of the fashionable London preening-and-dining scene may now be over, but their newest venture has become just as essential a stop on the celebrity circuit.

The Wolseley occupies the opulent 1920s former showroom of the eponymous car manufacturer. It has been made over to resemble a grand Mittel-European café, with a high vaulted ceiling, black-and-white tiled floor and lashings of gilt and black coating the walls. Highly professional staff serve up the type of reliable mix-and-match international dishes that will be familiar to anyone who's managed to bag a table at Le Caprice or The Ivy in the past, though there's an additional hearty Central European slant here to match the surroundings.

You could go for a spicy steak tartare, earthy cassoulet (meaty bean stew) or a superior hamburger, or head east for a wiener schnitzel, a Hungarian goulash or a German pancake-based dish called *Kaiserschmarren*. Perhaps the Wolseley's greatest strength, however, is that it's open all day, offering everything from breakfast through lunch and afternoon tea to dinner. **Expensive**

Kiku *exceptionally good Japanese* `8 D4`
17 Half Moon Street, W1 • 020 7499 4208
Open lunch & dinner Mon–Sat, dinner only Sun

Decked out in light wood and with artful flower arrangements, this smart restaurant is a utilitarian stage for virtuoso Japanese cuisine. The sushi is exemplary, as are less commonly encountered dishes, such as *agedashi-dofu* (deep-fried tofu and dried fish in a broth with grated ginger and Japanese radish). **Expensive**

Tamarind *tandoori as it should be* `8 D4`
20 Queen Street, W1 • 020 7629 3561
>> www.tamarindrestaurant.com
Open lunch & dinner Mon–Fri, dinner only Sat & Sun

This Michelin-starred restaurant shows just how varied and refined good Indian food can be. The menu's heart is the tandoor oven, stalwart of northwest India, from which emerge stunning meats, game, fish and breads. Service is impeccable. **Expensive**

Kaya *rare Korean* `8 D4`
42 Albemarle Street, W1 • 020 7499 0622
Open lunch & dinner Mon–Sat

The classiest of London's Korean restaurants is a serene spot in which to experience the subtleties of this under-appreciated cuisine. Grilling your own food on a tabletop griddle is fun, or you can rely on the traditionally dressed staff to recommend piquant dishes seldom encountered outside Korea. **Moderate**

Patara *taste of Thailand* `8 D3`
3 & 7 Maddox Street, W1 • 020 7499 6008
Open lunch & dinner daily

The handful of London branches of this upmarket Thai restaurant group offer an impressively authentic overview of one of Asia's most versatile cuisines. Enjoy dishes such as black cod broth with ginger, or chicken and pork dumplings, against a restful backdrop of greenery and Thai antiques. **Moderate**

Restaurants

Al Sultan _Middle Eastern delicacies_ `8 C5`
51–52 Hertford Street, W1 • 020 7408 1155
>> www.alsultan.co.uk Open noon–midnight daily

For a taste of just how good high-class Lebanese cuisine can be, head for this discreet Mayfair restaurant near Hyde Park Corner. The chargrilled meats are superb, while the magnificent meze is thoroughly authentic, right down to the range of offal offered. _Beid ghanam_ – lamb's testicles – anyone? **Moderate**

Mômo/Mô _Moroccan restaurant/tearoom_ `9 E3`
23 Heddon Street, W1 • 020 7434 4040
>> www.momoresto.com Restaurant open lunch & dinner Mon–Sat, dinner only Sun; tearoom open all day Mon–Sat

Mourad Mazouz's fabulously theatrical restaurant, Mômo, is an expensive treat, but you can also enjoy a similar ambience next door in a tearoom-cum-bazaar. Sip a mint tea or a fresh fruit juice while nibbling on excellent sandwiches and meze. **Expensive/Cheap**

Golden Hind _perfect fish & chips_ `8 C2`
73 Marylebone Lane, W1 • 020 7486 3644
Open lunch & dinner Mon–Fri, dinner only Sat

The finest chippie in W1 has been serving up prime fish and chips since 1914. Bring your own booze (no corkage charge) and make an evening of it, with a big portion of moist, flaky haddock or cod, thinly coated in crisp batter, alongside perfect chips, mushy peas and home-made tartare sauce. Bliss. **Cheap**

The Hottest Tables in Town
London's premier restaurants are world-class. The problem for ordinary mortals is securing a table. It's just possible that if you call on the day you might strike lucky; otherwise, you'll need to book months in advance. Among these hallowed temples of gastronomy are: **Locanda Locatelli**, the superlative Italian run by the ebullient Giorgio Locatelli; Jamie Oliver's much-publicised **Fifteen**; **The Ivy**, still the posh bistro of choice for most celebrities; even more fashionable **Nobu**, with its superb Japanese fusion menu; quite possibly London's finest restaurant, **Gordon Ramsay**; and certainly the capital's most expensive dining spot, gloriously over-the-top **Sketch**. For all restaurant contact details, _see pp220–1._

Providores/Tapa Room *international* `8 C1`
109 Marylebone High Street, W1 • 020 7935 6175
>> www.theprovidores.co.uk Open lunch & dinner daily (brunch Sat & Sun); Tapa Room 9am–10:30pm daily (from 10am Sat & Sun)

New Zealander Peter Gordon helped introduce the concept of "fusion" food to London when he opened the much-lauded Sugar Club *(see p25)* in 1995. He remains one of the few chefs capable of consistently marrying diverse, pan-global ingredients harmoniously.

The good work continues at the Providores, a tiny, simple dining space with an agreeably relaxed vibe, and a regularly changing menu that might include pork cheek braised with five spice, cardamom and Turkish chilli on chorizo mash with pickled okra, or roast New Zealand venison on black bean and chocolate stew with roast celeriac, green beans and quince aïoli. The ground-floor Tapa Room is a combination of wine bar, breakfast bar and tapas bar. The "Tapa" in question, though, is a ceremonial cloth used for celebratory feasts throughout the Pacific. **Expensive**

The Orrery *modern European/French* `8 C1`
55 Marylebone High Street, W1 • 020 7616 8000
>> www.orrery.co.uk Open lunch & dinner daily

Of all Sir Terence Conran's London restaurants, the Orrery is probably the classiest act (it is also very expensive). This is a long, light, elegant dining space with arched windows overlooking Marylebone Parish Church gardens. The largely Gallic waiting staff are extremely attentive and happy to talk you through the French-leaning menu.

An indulgent evening here might commence with seared sea scallops, pork belly and cauliflower, moving on to fillet of Scottish beef with slow-cooked oxtail, salsify (oyster plant) and red wine *jus*, before ending with a fondant of Amedei chocolate with milk ice cream. If you fancy something less than a full meal, head for the Orrery Epicerie (on the corner of Marylebone High Street and Beaumont Street), to find tasty breakfasts, light lunches and snacks, plus delicatessen products to take away. **Expensive**

Restaurants

Phoenix Palace *a Chinese treat* `8 B1`
3–5 Glentworth Street, NW1 • 020 7486 3515
Open noon–11:30pm Mon–Sat, 11am–10:30pm Sun

You need to venture beyond Chinatown to find London's best Chinese food. This smart Marylebone restaurant is one of the finest – as the number of Cantonese clients here testifies. If you're feeling adventurous, try the monthly specials menu. The soup of the day is reliably tasty. **Cheap**

Original Tagines *North African* `8 B2`
7A Dorset Street, W1 • 020 7935 1545
≫ www.originaltagines.com
Open lunch & dinner Mon–Fri, all day Sat & Sun

If the scented, sweet-savoury allure of North African cuisine has passed you by, visit this restaurant. The eponymous tagines are excellent (and come in 11 versions – try the chicken with preserved lemon), as are the couscous dishes and grills. **Moderate**

La Galette *French crêpes* `8 C1`
56 Paddington Street, W1 • 020 7935 1554
≫ www.lagalette.com
Open 9am–11pm Mon–Fri, 10am–11pm Sat & Sun

An authentic Breton crêperie brings the thrifty delights of crêpes and *galettes* to a pricey part of town. Fill your cup with strong cider and dig in to a *galette complète* (ham, cheese, egg), followed by an indulgent crêpe with chestnut cream and crème Chantilly. **Cheap**

Maroush Gardens *Middle Eastern* `8 A3`
1–3 Connaught Street, W2 • 020 7262 0222
Branch: 21 Edgware Road • 020 7723 0773
≫ www.maroush.com Open all day (noon–midnight) daily

This classy, sober spot is one of Marouf Abouzaki's newer additions to the Maroush chain, and specializes in fish, though the classic Lebanese meze and grills are equally fine. The atmosphere is a little more refined than at livelier sibling Maroush I. **Moderate**

Cinnamon Club *creative Indian* 15 F1
Old Westminster Library, Great Smith St, SW1 • 020 7222 2555
>> www.cinnamonclub.com
Open breakfast, lunch & dinner Mon–Fri, dinner only Sat

A spacious library has been sensitively transformed into one of London's finest Indian restaurants. The original parquet flooring remains, as do some of the bookshelves, but they've been augmented by marble and stone imported from Rajasthan to create a light-filled, spacious dining room. Vivek Singh's menu combines Indian flavours with European culinary techniques, as, for instance, in the French-inspired use of sauce reductions. This results in exquisite dishes such as clove-smoked tartare of Charolais beef with pickled beetroot, tandoori breast of pheasant with spiced mushroom sauce, and saffron-poached pear with cinnamon ice cream. The restaurant's proximity to the Houses of Parliament means that most of its clientele is curry-loving politicos and civil servants – but don't let that put you off. **Expensive**

Foliage *exquisite modern European* 8 B5
Mandarin Oriental Hyde Park Hotel,
66 Knightsbridge, SW1 • 020 7201 3723
>> www.mandarinoriental.com Open lunch & dinner daily

Some tables enjoy wonderful views out over Hyde Park, and the food is beyond reproach. Dishes such as roast saddle of rabbit, pithivier of wild mushrooms, asparagus, Alsace bacon and vanilla cream will leave you stumbling for superlatives. **Expensive**

Patogh *superior kebabs* 8 A2
8 Crawford Place, W1 • 020 7262 4015
Open noon–midnight daily

It's little more than a hole in the wall, but Patogh offers the most richly satisfying chargrilled meats in London. Choose from one of seven types of kebab, squeeze around one of the handful of tables and feast on a massive round of fresh flat bread, squeaky-fresh salads and your meat of choice. **Cheap**

Restaurants

14 D1

Noura *meze to astonish*
16 Hobart Place, SW1 • 020 7235 9444
>> www.noura-brasseries.co.uk Open noon–11pm daily

The glamorous atmosphere at this Lebanese restaurant reflects its posh Belgravia location, but it's far from stuffy, and the quality of the food is superb. Grilled meats don't come any finer, while the range of hot and cold meze cannot help but impress, with around 50 choices on offer. **Moderate**

Hunan *specialist Chinese* 14 C3
51 Pimlico Road, SW1 • 020 7730 5712
Open lunch & dinner Mon–Sat

London's only restaurant specializing in the spicy cuisine of China's westernmost province is a pint-size treat. Leave your preconceptions about Chinese set meals at the door and let the staff put together a feast for you that you'll long remember. The stuffed baby squid with bitter melon is supreme. **Moderate**

Zuma *high-class sushi & more* 14 A1
5 Raphael Street, SW7 • 020 7584 1010
>> www.zumarestaurant.com Open lunch & dinner daily

Zuma aims to provide a sophisticated metropolitan take on traditional Japanese *izakaya*-style (informal pub) dining. This being Knightsbridge, the result is resolutely upmarket, though far from snobby. The large dining room is clad in soothing earth tones, with wood-slat screens dividing up the space. If you're popping in on a whim, you can sit at the sushi counter and watch expert chefs whip up a California *maki* roll or some choice sashimi for you. Or pick something like salt-grilled sea bass with burnt tomato ginger relish from the *robata* grill.

The full menu includes Zuma specials like baby chicken marinated in barley *miso* and oven-roasted in cedar wood. The freshness and quality of ingredients are exemplary. If you merely fancy a drink, there's a lounge and sake bar, which offers more than 20 types of sake as well as cocktails. **Expensive**

Zafferano *Italian greats* `14 B1`
15 Lowndes Street, SW1 • 020 7235 5800
Open lunch & dinner daily

Zafferano has long been recognized as one of the capital's premier Italian restaurants. It's a discreet place, where the emphasis is firmly on the food. Dishes such as risotto with white truffle and char-grilled lamb with aubergine allow the quality of the ingredients to shine through. **Expensive**

Racine *traditional French* `14 A2`
239 Brompton Road, SW3 • 020 7584 4477
Open lunch & dinner daily

This hugely popular French restaurant has made a virtue out of simplicity. The décor is ascetically plain and the food is a glorious throwback to the days of classic Gallic cuisine. Expect succulent *daubes* (braised meat stews) and *marmites* (pot soups). For the quality of the food, prices are a steal. **Moderate**

Tom Aikens *modern European creativity* `14 A3`
43 Elystan Street, SW3 • 020 7584 2003
Open lunch & dinner Mon–Fri

Michelin-starred Tom Aikens made his name in the 1990s and is now undoubtedly one of the most gifted chefs working in London. The sober, masculine tones of the almost brutally plain décor of his eponymous restaurant leave diners in no doubt that this is a serious restaurant for serious foodies. Even if you balk at over-complex food, it's hard not to admire the attention to detail and careful balancing of colour, texture and taste that distinguish his menu.

A typical meal might start with basil-marinated scallops, courgettes and almond mousse, followed by pigeon steamed with thyme, chestnut velouté, cannelloni and soft lettuce, and crowned with pineapple roasted with vanilla and rum. If you can stretch to a blow-out, you won't regret going for the tasting menu; those with smaller budgets can still eat like royalty with the set lunch. **Expensive**

Restaurants

Tendido Cero *well-chosen tapas* `13 G3`
174 Old Brompton Road, SW5 • 020 7370 3685
>> www.cambiodetercio.com Open 11:30am–11pm daily

Much of the tapas in London tend to be lacklustre, but not so at Tendido Cero. This smart, sleek sibling of upmarket Iberian stalwart Cambio de Tercio across the road serves up the choicest Spanish cheeses, hams and charcuterie. There's no drinks licence, so you have to bring your own alcohol. **Moderate**

The Painted Heron *Indian* `13 H5`
112 Cheyne Walk, SW10 • 020 7351 5232
>> www.thepaintedheron.com
Open lunch & dinner Mon–Fri, dinner only Sat

Yogesh Datta's innovative, refined yet unfussy take on traditional Subcontinental cuisine is evident in dishes such as duck livers in tandoori spices, and spinach and partridge curry. The restaurant is as elegant and understated as the food. **Moderate**

Lots Road Pub *gastropub* `13 G5`
114 Lots Road, SW10 • 020 7352 6645
Open 11am–11pm daily (to 10:30pm Sun)

There may be a gastropub with airy, stripped-down décor on almost every corner these days, but this place remains one of the best. It's the friendliness of the staff and the quality of the food that mark it out; the ingredients are supremely fresh. You won't find a better burger in London. **Moderate**

Chutney Mary *intimate Indian* `13 G5`
535 King's Road, SW10 • 020 7351 3113
>> www.realindianfood.com
Open lunch & dinner Sat & Sun, dinner only Mon–Fri

A stylish makeover of restaurant and menu confirmed Chutney Mary as both a beacon of Indian culinary excellence and a chic, romantic spot. The pan-Indian menu exploits the depth and range of the country's cuisine, and service is impeccable. **Expensive**

To pick restaurants with good disabled access, use >> www.elondon.dk.com

The River Café *inspirational Italian*   `12 A5`
Thames Wharf, Rainville Road, W6 • 020 7386 4200
➤➤ www.rivercafe.co.uk
Open lunch & dinner Mon–Sat, lunch only Sun

No London restaurant has had more influence on both restaurant food and (with the spawning of five books) home cooking than the River Café. When Rose Gray and Ruth Rogers opened up in 1987, most Italian eateries were stuck in a 1970s candle-in-a-chianti-bottle time warp. Their versions of simple Italian regional dishes, carefully sourced and immaculately prepared, were revelatory, and inspired a string of talented chefs who worked in their kitchen   Jamie Oliver among them

(see Fifteen on p34). The restaurant's appeal remains undimmed today. You do, though, pay heavily for the privilege, with few main courses under £25.The prices and ambience are not café-style.

A typical spring menu might include char-grilled marinated leg of lamb with fresh borlotti beans, Swiss and rainbow chard, and anchovy and rosemary sauce. The relatively stark, utilitarian dining space was designed by architect Richard Rogers (Ruth's husband) within converted 19th-century warehouses. Its floor-to-ceiling windows give access to a garden and the river beyond. To enjoy the restaurant to the full, try to book a table here in fine weather. **Expensive**

The Gate *vegetarian*   `12 A3`
51 Queen Caroline Street, W6 • 020 8748 6932
➤➤ www.gateveg.co.uk   Open lunch & dinner Mon–Fri, dinner Sat

For more than a decade, brothers Adrian and Michael Daniels have been running this classy, relaxed Hammersmith restaurant. The food they serve (aubergine schnitzel, Thai red curry) is so good that even devoted meat-eaters won't feel hard done by. Ask for a table in the leafy courtyard. **Moderate**

Restaurants

Lisboa Patisserie *Portuguese café*   `6 C2`

57 Golborne Road, W10 • 020 8968 5242
Open 8am–8pm Mon–Sat, 8am–7pm Sun

Today the heart of London's sizeable Portuguese community may be south of the river around Stockwell and Vauxhall, but Notting Hill's Golborne Road is home to one of the oldest and best-loved *pastelarias* in town. Such has been the success of Lisboa Patisserie that it has spawned a mini chain (currently numbering four branches) across the capital, but the original site is certainly the most fun to visit when the Portobello Road market *(see p159)* is in full swing.

Portuguese cakes and tarts are the speciality, and come in an impressive range and at low prices; you won't find better or more authentic cinnamon-topped *pasteis de nata* (custard tarts) in the city. Equally fabled are the *bolos de arroz* (rice cakes) and the *castanhas de ovo* (literally, "egg chestnut", a sweet, eggy nugget). Savouries are sold too – try the *pasteis de bacalhau* (salt cod and potato cakes). **Cheap**

S&M Café *bangers 'n' mash*   `6 D3`

268 Portobello Road, W10 • 020 8968 8898
Open 11am–11pm Mon–Thu, 9am–11pm Fri–Sun

Less is more at the Sausage & Mash Café, in terms of décor and menu. Choose your type of sausage (including veggie options), mash and gravy, and feast on the likes of wild boar sausages with calvados and apples, or pork sausages with bubble and squeak, mash and red onion gravy. **Cheap**

E&O *Oriental in style*   `6 C3`

14 Blenheim Crescent, W11 • 020 7229 5454
Open lunch & dinner daily

This western sister to the Great Eastern Dining Room *(see p48)* is every bit as chic as its counterpart. It draws in the beautiful people of Notting Hill to preen, pout and gaze about while nibbling on the seriously tasty mix-and-match Oriental dishes. A great choice for vegetarians. **Moderate**

Al Waha *Middle Eastern* `7 E3`
75 Westbourne Grove, W2 • 020 7229 0806
>> www.waha-uk.com Open noon–midnight daily

This gracious restaurant offers some of the best Lebanese food around town in modest, tranquil surroundings (the name means "the oasis"). Vegetarians are well catered for in the list of almost 50 hot and cold meze, and it's always worth trying the daily specials. The set meals are particularly good value. **Moderate**

Magic Wok *cheap & cheerful Chinese* `7 F3`
100 Queensway, W2 • 020 7792 9767
Open noon–10:30pm daily

Queensway has long been a centre for Chinese culinary excellence, and Magic Wok has been in its vanguard for many years. The décor is thoroughly undistinguished, but the food shines out. Stick to the specials menu and you can't go wrong; the rich, flavourful hot pot dishes are especially good. **Cheap**

Satay House *traditional Malaysian* `7 H2`
13 Sale Place, W2 • 020 7723 6763
>> www.satayhouse.com Open lunch & dinner daily

For toothsome, freshly cooked Malaysian food you can't beat this modest little Paddington restaurant. A lively, multinational crowd head here for classic rice and noodle dishes, and such delicacies as deep-fried sea bass cooked in salted beans, and fermented durian fruit with anchovies and turmeric leaves. **Cheap**

Chain Restaurants
For conveyor-belt sushi head for **Yo! Sushi** or venture a little further upmarket at **Itsu**, where the belt delivers up dishes from all over Southeast Asia. Groundbreaking noodle bar group **Wagamama** is still the business for huge bowls of *ramen* (noodle soup) in a canteen atmosphere, while there's a more intimate vibe at pan-Oriental mini-chain **Busaba Eathai**. Venturing further west across the globe, **Masala Zone** has done for Indian food what Wagamama did for Japanese. Reaching Europe, you can't beat **Strada** for wood-fired pizza, pasta and Italian staples. More unusual is idiosyncratic Belgian *moules-frites* specialist **Belgo**, while the dishes served at **Giraffe** span the world. For all restaurant details, *see pp220–1*.

Moro *Spanish & North African* `4 A5`

34–36 Exmouth Market, EC1 • 020 7833 8336
» www.moro.co.uk
Open lunch & dinner Mon–Fri, dinner Sat
(private functions only for Sat lunch & all day Sun)

Few restaurants have attracted plaudits as unanimous and enthusiastic as those applied to Moro since it opened in 1997. Confusingly named husband-and-wife team Sam and Sam Clark shared their culinary schooling at the pioneering Eagle gastropub *(see below)* just down the road, and also at the celebrated River Café *(see p41)* in Hammersmith. From these two gastronomic beacons they've adopted the sensible policy of letting the quality of fine ingredients shine through in simple dishes. Their unique contribution to both the concept and the London food scene comes from applying these principles to an inspired crossover of Spanish and North African cuisine (as the name Moro, meaning "Moor" in Spanish, implies). The results can be sampled in, say, a meal of *ajo blanco* (Spanish garlic and almond soup), followed by quail baked in flatbread, with rosewater and cardamom ice cream to finish. If you only want to snack, tapas are available from the long zinc bar that runs along one side of the casual though often frenetically noisy dining room. **Moderate**

The Eagle *the original gastropub* `10 A1`

159 Farringdon Road, EC1 • 020 7837 1353
Open all day from noon Mon–Sat, lunch only Sun

Credited with starting the gastropub revolution that has now swept the country, The Eagle is still up there with the best of its progeny more than a decade later. Garrulous media folk pack out the tightly packed tables and feast on perfectly cooked rustic stomach-fillers and grilled meats. **Moderate**

Fish Central *fish & chips in style* `4 C5`
149–51 Central Street, EC1 • 020 7253 4970
>> www.fishcentral.co.uk Open lunch & dinner Mon–Sat

An oasis of value and charm in the overpriced and often unfriendly City, Fish Central was converted in 2003 from a takeaway with attached dining room into a swish, minimalist restaurant. Yet the prices are still low, the welcome cheery and the food superb – haddock in matzo is a slice of piscine heaven. **Cheap**

Flâneur Food Hall *modern European* `10 A1`
41 Farringdon Road, EC1 • 020 7404 4422
Open 9am–10pm Mon–Sat, 9am–6pm Sun

Eating a meal in a grocery shop might not seem appealing, but high-ceilinged Flâneur is a superior seller of choice comestibles, and its restaurant offers a similarly elevated menu of contemporary dishes. The emphasis is on fresh ingredients. Rich cakes dominate the desserts selection. **Moderate**

Smiths of Smithfield *modern European* `10 B2`
67–77 Charterhouse Street, EC1 • 020 7251 7950
>> www.smithsofsmithfield.co.uk Café open breakfast & lunch daily; dining room open lunch & dinner Sun–Fri

Revelling in the industrial chic of bare brick and raw concrete, Smiths is a multi-floor venue successfully combining a buzzing bar-café (brunch is a must), a lively dining room, and a polished restaurant catering to City high-flyers. **Moderate/Expensive**

The Sutton Arms *proper gastropub* `10 B1`
6 Carthusian Street, EC1 • 020 7253 0723
Open lunch & dinner Mon–Fri

This reconstructed pub on the fringes of the City is everything a good gastropub should be: solid, stripped back, unselfconscious. Within the small, dark, wood-clad upstairs dining room you can enjoy robust dishes, such as smoked haddock chowder and roast chicken with fennel. **Moderate**

Restaurants

St John *iconic British restaurant* `4 B5`
26 St John Street, EC1 • 020 7251 0848
>> www.stjohnrestaurant.com
Open lunch & dinner Mon–Fri, dinner only Sat

Chef Fergus Henderson has been in the vanguard of modern British cooking since this unique restaurant opened in 1994. His philosophy of "nose to tail eating" – no part of an animal is off limits – has led to the creation of classic, no-compromise dishes such as roast bone marrow and parsley salad, and veal tongue, beetroot and pickled walnut. But faint hearts need not fear: less offbeat gems include boiled ham, carrots and parsley sauce, and veal chop with chicory and anchovy. Desserts are straight from the nursery: apple crumble and custard, and hot chocolate pudding. There are no decorative frills to detract from the supreme quality of the food in this eccentric building that is part Georgian townhouse, part former smokehouse. An on-site bakery and bar offer snacks such as welsh rarebit, and tripe and chips. **Expensive**

Café Spice Namaste *Indian* `11 F3`
16 Prescot Street, E1 • 020 7488 9242
>> www.cafespice.co.uk Open lunch & dinner Mon–Sat

No-one has done more than Bombay-born chef Cyrus Todiwala to revitalize British Indian restaurants for the 21st century. He opened Café Spice Namaste in Whitechapel in 1995, and it remains one of the capital's premier Subcontinental dining destinations a decade later. A central bar separates the two dining rooms, which are decorated in fiery colours to reflect the zip of a menu that marries traditional Indian culinary techniques with unusual ingredients. Sample the delights of venison tikka flavoured with roasted fennel, star anise and cinnamon, and fresh buffalo mozzarella served with Parsee-style pickle and *sarias* (crackers). Or experience the depth of flavour in a classic lamb dansak. Even the home-made pickles and chutneys that accompany the pre-meal pappadoms are exceptional. You can enjoy Indian nibbles and bottles of icy Cobra lager in the beer garden, too. **Moderate**

For food deliveries from pizza to gourmet delicacies, go to >> www.elondon.dk.com

Club Gascon *hearty French* `10 B2`
57 West Smithfield EC1 • 020 7796 0600
Open lunch & dinner Mon–Fri, dinner only Sat

The earthy flavours of Southwest France are Club Gascon's speciality, with foie gras prominent on a menu that features a range of small courses rather than the traditional starter-main-dessert. Some of the dishes raise a smile: wild sea bass might come with a "surprised" turnip (a tiny root veg topped with foam), or your apple pie could arrive seemingly empty, only for you to realize that the filling is within the accompanying ice cream. The presentation is as imaginative as the food, with courses appearing on slate, glass and ceramic tiles as well as china. If your budget will stretch to it, order the five-course degustation menu; each dish is paired with a different glass of wine. A couple of doors away, Cellar Gascon serves up cheaper, but equally fine, bistro food to accompany a superb selection of Gallic wines. Staff are cheery, confident and utterly professional. **Expensive**

Les Trois Garçons *characterful French* `5 F5`
1 Club Row, E1• 020 7613 1924
>> www.lestroisgarcons.com Open dinner daily

A welcome antidote to minimalism, this joyously over-the-top Gallic eaterie heaves with stuffed animals, Murano glass chandeliers and baroque bric-a-brac (all for sale). Yet, the food is straight-down-the-line classic French of a high order. Not cheap, but worth it for a unique dining experience. **Expensive**

Cantaloupe *trend-setting Mediterranean* `5 E5`
35 Charlotte Road, EC2 • 020 7613 4411
>> www.cantaloupegroup.co.uk
Open lunch & dinner Mon–Fri, dinner only Sat & Sun

This versatile bar-restaurant is still a trailblazer of the trendy Hoxton/Shoreditch scene, but doesn't sacrifice substance for appearance. The setting is revamped industrial, and there's plenty of fire and imagination on the short, Mediterranean-slanted menu. **Moderate**

Restaurants

Great Eastern Dining Room *Oriental* `5 E5`
54–6 Great Eastern Street, EC2 • 020 7613 4545
» www.greateasterndining.co.uk Open noon–midnight
Mon–Thu, noon–1am Fri, 6pm–1am Sat

The lively, noisy GEDR draws in a young, fashionable crowd for artfully conceived oriental treats like pork and prawn dumplings, rare beef salad with red chilli dressing, and lemongrass and ginger pannacotta. *(See also E&O, p42.)* **Moderate**

Real Greek *real Greek* `5 E5`
14–15 Hoxton Market, N1 • 020 7739 8212
Branch: 140–42 St John St, EC1 • 020 7253 7234
» www.therealgreek.co.uk Open lunch & dinner Mon–Sat

The moribund London Greek restaurant scene was given a life-saving shot in the arm when Theodore Kyriakou opened this stylish place in 1999. Dishes rarely encountered outside Greece are cooked with conviction and served with a smile. **Moderate**

Viet Hoa *the original Vietnamese* `5 E4`
70–72 Kingsland Road, E2 • 020 7729 8293
Open lunch & dinner daily

Hoxton has a sizeable and vibrant Vietnamese community, and this airy, one-time local canteen was the first place in London to bring the sharp, clean flavours of their cuisine to a non-native audience. It's still packing the crowds in, and you won't find a better bowl of *pho* (meat and noodle soup) in town. **Cheap**

Green Papaya *neighbourhood Vietnamese* `5 H1`
191 Mare Street, E8 • 020 8985 5486
Open dinner Tue–Sun

Hackney is home to a great mix of ethnicities, a fact reflected in its diverse community cafés. Green Papaya is a step up in terms of décor (stripped floorboards, crimson walls, candlelight and a lovely garden) and cooking. Try a classic noodle soup or go for something more unusual from the daily specials menu. **Cheap**

Gallipoli *day-long meze* `4 B2`

102 Upper Street, N1 • 020 7359 0630
Open 10am–11pm Mon–Thu, 10am–midnight Fri & Sat

Islington's Upper Street is lined with restaurants, and
one of the most popular is this cracking Turkish bistro.
The atmosphere is lively, and the food fresh, gener-
ously proportioned and cheap. As well as a fine all-day
breakfast, there's a long menu of authentic Turkish
dishes, especially meze and grilled meats. **Cheap**

The Drapers Arms *great gastropub* `4 A2`

44 Barnsbury Street, N1 • 020 7619 0348
Open lunch & dinner Mon–Sat, lunch only Sun

Of all the Islington gastropubs, none provides a
better all-round package of great food, convivial
ambience and willing service than the Drapers. You'll
pay West End prices for food in the airy first-floor
restaurant, but you can expect top-quality delivery
from the globe-trotting menu. **Moderate**

The House *prize-winning gastropub* `4 B1`

63–9 Canonbury Road, N1 • 020 7704 7410
➤➤ www.inthehouse.biz
Open lunch & dinner Tue–Sun, dinner only Mon

North London is awash with gastropubs, but few
come close to matching the award-winning House for
quality of food. The setting is relaxed and friendly,
with a modern, stripped-down bar area, an open fire
in winter and a decked terrace and beer garden for
when the sun shines. It's only when you start
exploring the menu, though, that you understand why
this place has become many Islingtonians' favourite
spot to eat. There's a French emphasis to the dishes,
such as roast sea bass with *piperade* (sauté
peppers), olive tapenade and langoustine oil, and
terrine of chicken, sweetbreads, Grelot onions and
foie gras wrapped in Parma ham. There's also a
superb, varied brunch menu at weekends and
good-value lunch and pre-theatre set meals.
Not cheap, but absolutely worth it. **Moderate**

Odette's *romantic modern European* `2 B2`

130 Regent's Park Road, NW1 • 020 7586 5486

Open lunch & dinner Mon–Fri, dinner only Sat, lunch only Sun

One of North London's best-loved restaurants, Odette's is a prime spot for a romantic dinner *à deux*. Though it was given a sensitive renovation in 2003, it retains all the old-fashioned idiosyncrasy that has long endeared it to the moneyed media folk of Primrose Hill. Scores of gilded mirrors reflect candlelight around the intimate dining rooms, providing a seductive setting for adventurous but not over-fussy contemporary cooking.

Pithivier of rabbit with white bean cream would be a typical starter; for mains, chargrilled leg of lamb with Italian seasoning, roasted artichokes and fondant potatoes, or loin of veal with herb gnocchi and fresh peas. The wine list is also notable, and features an impressively international spread of vintages. Service can be a touch uneven, but overall Odette's is a North London jewel. **Expensive**

El Parador *superior tapas* `3 E4`

245 Eversholt Street, NW1 • 020 7387 2789

Open lunch & dinner Mon–Fri, dinner only Sat & Sun

An oasis of Iberia in the unpromising area between Euston station and Camden Town, El Parador is at its best in the summer, when the dining room and basement are augmented by a small garden. The tapas are better than the London norm, with fresh, high-quality ingredients to the fore. **Cheap**

Café Corfu *Greek delights* `3 E2`

7 Pratt Street, NW1 • 020 7267 8088

>> www.cafecorfu.com Open all day from noon Tue–Sun

Many Greek restaurants in London are lacklustre. Not so Café Corfu, which offers an excitingly varied menu of rarely encountered specialities from the Greek mainland and islands, as well as classic roast lamb dishes. The setting is lively, stylish and thoroughly contemporary, and service spot-on. **Moderate**

Manna *vegetable dishes from heaven*   `2 B2`
4 Erskine Road, NW3 • 020 7722 8028
>> www.manna-veg.com
Open dinner only Mon–Sat, lunch & dinner Sun

Serving well-crafted dishes for more than 40 years, Manna is still noteworthy among vegetarian restaurants. Tuck in to a meal of, say, soba noodle salad, organic fennel schnitzel, and star anise brûlée accompanied by a fine organic beer or wine. **Moderate**

The Lansdowne *reliable gastropub*   `2 C2`
90 Gloucester Avenue, NW1 • 020 7483 0409
Open dinner only Tue–Sat, lunch & dinner Sun

The Lansdowne has long been one of the capital's premier gastropubs, and its standards remain as high as ever. Snacks can be ordered from the chalkboard in the lively downstairs bar, or go for something more substantial on the short, reliable menu in the posher red-and-black-clad first-floor restaurant. **Moderate**

Mango Room *the best Caribbean in town*   `2 D1`
10 Kentish Town Road, NW1 • 020 7482 5065
Open dinner only Mon, lunch & dinner Tue–Sat, lunch only Sun

First-class Caribbean food is surprisingly scarce in London and almost never found in a restaurant as friendly, stylish and buzzy as the Mango Room. Jerk chicken and curried goat are the classics. Creole snapper with mango and green peppercorn sauce is an unusual alternative. **Moderate**

The Wells *gastropub with a view*   `1 B4`
30 Well Walk, NW3 • 020 7794 3785
>> www.thewellshampstead.co.uk Open lunch & dinner daily

Enjoy the views of leafy Hampstead from the spacious, streamlined first-floor restaurant of this pub, while you savour the menu of well-honed comfort food – rich, calorie-packed and utterly irresistible. For a blow-out, try the classic Chateaubriand with thrice-cooked chips, followed by custard tart. **Moderate**

>> *For an index of restaurants by cuisine,* see pp220–22

Base *light Mediterranean cuisine* `2 C4`
71 Hampstead High Street, NW3 • 020 7431 2224
>> www.basefoods.com Bistro open 8am–6pm daily;
restaurant open dinner Tue–Sat

By day, a local clientele packs out the bistro, chatting animatedly over light, bright Mediterranean food (grilled vegetable salads, seared tuna, risotto). By night, the upstairs dining room takes centre stage for similar fare in marginally more formal surrounds. **Moderate**

Kovalam *great-value, high-quality Indian*
12 Willesden Lane, NW6 • 020 7625 4761 • ⊖ Kilburn
Open lunch & dinner daily

Willesden Lane in Kilburn is something of a mecca for fans of good, cheap South Indian food, and Kovalam is probably the pick of the bunch. The décor may be humble, but the depth of flavour in its superb Keralan dishes is regal – try the breadfruit curry. Many dishes are suitable for vegetarians. **Cheap**

Blueprint Café *European by the river* `11 F5`
Design Museum, Shad Thames, SE1 • 020 7378 7031
>> www.conran.com Open lunch & dinner Mon–Sat, lunch Sun

The twin attractions of this classy restaurant – it's certainly no café – within the Design Museum are expansive views of the Thames and a daily-changing, Italian-leaning menu. The room is a no-nonsense setting for superior peasant food, such as roast partridge with cabbage and bacon. **Expensive**

Champor-Champor *Malaysian fusion* `10 D5`
62 Weston Street, SE1 • 020 7403 4600
>> www.champor-champor.com Open dinner Mon–Sat

Primary colours burst from the walls of this lively little restaurant, reflecting the zesty flavours on the inventive menu. The essence is Malaysian, but with pan-Asian influences. Typical dishes include steamed tilapia with turmeric leaf, crab and coconut bisque, and masala lamb fillet with aubergine mousse. **Moderate**

Tas *uncommonly good Turkish* `10 A5`
33 The Cut, SE1 • 020 7928 1444
>> www.tasrestaurant.com Open all day from noon daily

Named after a traditional Anatolian cooking pot, Tas has proved that high-quality Turkish cooking and a contemporary setting can harmonize. The menu is strong on grilled meats and perkily fresh meze, with a huge choice for vegetarians. Add in friendly staff and fair prices, and you have a winner. **Moderate**

Livebait *fish in myriad forms* `10 A5`
41–5 The Cut, SE1 • 020 7928 7211
>> www.santeonline.co.uk/livebait
Open all day from noon Mon–Sat

With its cheery tiled interior and booth seating, Livebait looks like a classy fish and chip shop. But this won't prepare you for the wonderful menu roving from the simple pleasures of a bowl of cockles to the epicurean heights of oven-roast halibut. **Moderate**

Mesón Don Felipe *authentic Spanish* `10 A5`
53 The Cut, SE1 • 020 7928 3237
Open all day from noon Mon–Sat

For many hispanophiles this perennially packed little tapas bar is as close as you can get in London to the real thing. Regulars perch at the huge bar in the middle of the room, while friendly staff distribute melting *bacalao* (deep-fried salt cod), broad beans with ham, and perfect tortilla. **Cheap**

Masters Super Fish *fish & chips* `10 A5`
191 Waterloo Road, SE1 • 020 7928 6924
Open dinner Mon, lunch & dinner Tue–Sat

Clad in dark wood and exposed brick, this is much better than the average "chippie". True, you can get a classic cod'n'chips with mushy peas, but there's also fresh Cromer crab and crisp, mustard-coated haddock for the more adventurous. A favoured haunt of London cab drivers – who know a thing or two. **Cheap**

Oxo Tower *fine food and fabulous views*   `10 A4`
Top floor, Oxo Tower Wharf, Barge House St, SE1
020 7803 3888
>> www.harveynichols.com Open lunch & dinner daily

There are few locations in London as spectacular as the top floor of the Oxo Tower. Floor-to-ceiling glass walls and a 250-ft (90-m) long terrace allow uninterrupted views over the Thames. It's stunning, and yours to admire for the price of a drink at the sleek bar.

Eating here will make a greater dent in your wallet, though the cost is justified by the consistently high standard of the creative modern European food served at the relaxed Brasserie and more formal Restaurant. Lunch at the Brasserie might consist of chilli crab with egg linguine, followed by sea bass and warm halloumi, and finishing with coconut parfait with passion fruit. The refinement of the menu (and prices) rise in the Restaurant, with such delicacies as warm salad of quail with foie gras and truffle, monkfish with oxtail or pink grapefruit with Campari sorbet. Both venues serve more affordable set lunches. **Expensive**

Tsunami *way-out Japanese*
5–7 Voltaire Road, SW4 • 020 7978 1610 • ⊖ Clapham North
Open dinner Mon–Fri, all day (12:30–11:30pm) Sat

Tsunami is one of that rare breed of restaurants that thrill and satisfy in equal proportions. The first surprise is finding such a smart, stylish space just off Clapham's workaday high street. With its ascetically plain décor and nattily attired staff, it has an air of both simplicity and sophistication. A similar balance is found on the menu, which combines classic Japanese cooking – excellent, biting-fresh sashimi, sushi and tempura – with originality and imagination. Witness the mingling of sautéed foie gras with Asian pear and truffle, quail with ginger honey soy, and the green tea tiramisu.

There are parallels between Tsunami and ultra-chic Nobu *(see p34)*, where some of the staff trained, but Tsunami is free of "attitude", and there's no need to book months in advance. **Expensive**

Thyme *well-executed modern European*

14 Clapham Park Rd, SW4 • 020 7627 2468 • ☺ Clapham Common
≫ www.thymeandspace.com Open lunch & dinner Tue–Sat

The cooking at Thyme is some of the most assured and imaginative that you'll find in South London, with the added quirk of dishes coming only in starter-sized portions. If you can't make up your mind, choose one of the two tasting menus; each course is paired with a different wine. Note: at the time of going to press, Thyme was considering a move to Soho. **Moderate**

Le Petit Max *Battersea bistro*

Riverside Plaza, Chatfield Road, SW11 • 020 7223 0999
☺ Wandsworth or Clapham Junction
Open 10am–10:30pm Mon–Sat, 10am–2:30 Sun

Over the last decade Max Renzland has been behind some of London's most inventive and consistently excellent French restaurants. Most have been located in obscure parts of southwest London; this one is sited in an unprepossessing riverside development in Battersea. The dominant feature of the interior is a handsome 1930s mahogany bar imported from Lille.

Le Petit Max is essentially a reasonably priced bistro. The *menu du jour* is particularly good value, but the *carte* is also within the reach of most budgets. A typically earthy meal could start with *boudin noir* (blood sausage) with potato salad, then braised shoulder of milk-fed Pyrenean lamb with haricot beans and garlic, finishing with rum baba, red fruits and Chantilly. **Moderate**

Chez Bruce *Battersea bistro*

2 Bellevue Road, SW17 • 020 8672 0114
☺ Wandsworth Common Open lunch & dinner daily

Few establishments are as universally admired (and enjoyed) as Bruce Poole's longstanding Wandsworth restaurant. The traditions of French cuisine provide the framework, but expect inspired borrowings from elsewhere in Europe and a focus on seasonal ingredients. Relaxed, knowledgeable staff add to a sophisticated yet easygoing atmosphere. **Moderate**

Putney Bridge Restaurant *French*

2 Lower Richmond Road, The Embankment, SW15
020 8780 1811 • ☺ Putney Bridge
Open lunch & dinner Mon–Sat, lunch only Sun

The award-winning glass-and-steel building does impress, but the restaurant's lovely river views and impeccable food are the main attractions. The airy first-floor dining room, set above a buzzing bar, provides a serene setting for French *haute cuisine*. **Expensive**

≫ *In pubs or restaurants away from the centre of town, Sunday lunch can be great value*

shopping

London's retail landscape is as diverse as the city itself, yielding up traditional tailors and radical fashion designers, antiquarian booksellers and alternative record shops, luxury department stores and gritty markets. Of course, it has its fair share of international chains, but you don't have to travel far off the beaten track to find quirky contemporary boutiques and time-honoured delicatessens.

FLAGSHIP STORES	OBJETS D'ART	SHOES & ACCESSORIES
Paul Smith 120 Kensington Park Rd, W11 The interior of this fabulous Regency house is casually strewn with Paul Smith's refined yet cheeky tailoring. *(See p84)*	**Mint** 70 Wigmore St, W1 A miscellany of antique and modern homewares, furniture and lighting. Pieces by recent design graduates add to the mix. *(See p73)*	**Jimmy Choo** 169 Draycott Ave, SW3 Jimmy Choo's is a treasure trove of glamorous and decadent shoes, from diamanté sandals to sleek, knee-high boots. *(See p77)*
Joseph 77 Fulham Rd, SW3 Contemporary tailoring for men and women. The Essentials shop, Gigi boutique and café are across the street. *(See p77)*	**Graham & Green** 4 & 10 Elgin Crescent, W11 Stocking everything from Mongolian cushions to cool Modernist lamps, at equally wide-ranging prices, this is a great place to browse. *(See p85)*	**Lulu Guinness** 3 Ellis St, SW1 Guinness's apparently endless variations on the humble bag transform it into an object of veneration. Witty, fun and expensive. *(See p77)*
Stella McCartney 30 Bruton St, W1 McCartney's Mayfair townhouse is a glamorous setting for slinky dresses and beautifully cut suits. *(See p70)*	**Aram** 110 Drury Lane, WC1 Classic Gropius and Aalto furniture, and pieces by young British designers are displayed in a slick showroom. *(See p60)*	**>>** *For a fantastic range of cheap and fashionable accessories, check out TopShop (see p68) or the revamped New Look chain.*
>> *More dash than cash? Visit Designer Bargains at 29 Kensington Church Street for a good selection of barely second-hand attire.*	**Camden Passage** Off Upper St, N1 This pedestrian street behind the modish shops of Upper Street is lined with antique shops of all kinds. *(See p90)*	
The Conran Shop Michelin House, 81 Fulham Rd, SW3 Occupying the former headquarters of Michelin, Conran's elegant homewares share house room with a couple of great eateries. *(See p78)*		**Philip Treacy** 69 Elizabeth St, SW1 On swanky Elizabeth Street, Philip Treacy produces dashing hats, as well as offering a bespoke service. *(See p76)*

BEST OF BRITISH

Neal's Yard Dairy
17 Shorts Gardens, WC2
This outstanding cheesemonger's produce is sourced mostly from independent UK producers. Also at Borough Market. *(See pp62 & 163)*

James Smith & Sons
53 New Oxford St, WC1
Stalwarts of urbanity since 1830, the Smiths make canes and umbrellas so dapper that rain is almost welcome. *(See p63)*

>> *Classic clothes emporia Burberry and Pringle have recently metamorphosed from bastions of tradition into cool brands (see p69).*

A. Gold
42 Brushfield St, E1
This little deli sells mainly British produce, such as Cumberland sausages and cider brandy from the West Country. *(See p87)*

Smythson
40 New Bond St, W1
Top-quality stationer Smythson offers elegant leather-bound diaries and notebooks, and watermarked correspondence sets. *(See p69)*

VINTAGE & RETRO

Rokit
Brick Lane, E1
This spacious, two-shop outlet is packed with 60s and 70s vintage wear, notably well-worn leather jackets and 70s T-shirts. *(See p88)*

Persiflage
Alfie's Antiques Market, Church St, NW8
Persiflage is a tiny shop with modest prices, some 19th-century clothes and great 1920s pieces.

Portobello Green
Portobello Rd at Cambridge Gdns, W11
On Fridays and Saturdays, this market sells new designs and an excellent mix of second-hand and vintage clothing. *(See p83)*

DESIGNER COUTURE

Oki-ni
25 Saville Row, W1
The gallery-style shop of this British-Japanese group displays pieces designed in collaboration with labels such as Levi's and Evisu. *(See p68)*

b Store
6 Conduit St, W1
This funky boutique showcasing hot talent such as Boudicca and Peter Jensen reputedly attracts fashionista Kate Moss. *(See p67)*

>> *On Thursdays, London's hottest young designers display their latest creations at Spitalfields Market (see p161). Sniff out some beautifully crafted garments at preview prices.*

aQuaint
38 Monmouth St, WC2
The ready-to-wear range in this young London designer's store makes good use of luxurious materials. *(See p61)*

Browns
23–27 South Molton St, W1
Five interlinked boutiques sell top designer labels. Across the street, Browns Focus features hip young designs. *(See p70)*

Floral Street   *big names & small boutiques*   `9 G3`
Cobbled pedestrian street in Covent Garden, WC2
For individual shop details, see pp210–11

This winding lane tucked behind Covent Garden Market is packed with well-known fashion stores ranging from young, trendy labels, for example **Diesel StyleLab**, to established designer names such as **Paul Smith**, **Ted Baker**, **Agnès B**, **Nicole Farhi** and **Camper**. Dotted among these are some unusual shops, such as **Kirk Originals**, which sells colourful, retro-inspired eyewear (at No. 29); **Burro** for clothing with logos and patterns (also at No. 29); and **Jones**, which displays supercool designer menswear (Raf Simons, Jo Casely-Hayford, et al) in an extraordinary industrial setting at Nos. 13–15. Posh combatwear is the theme at **Maharishi**, where a jungle-like interior comes complete with palm trees and mini military helicopters (No. 19a). **The Tintin Shop** (No. 34) is devoted to the famous Belgian comic strip, selling books in several languages, posters, T-shirts and other themed items.

Vertigo   *original film posters*   `9 G3`
22 Wellington Street, WC2 • 020 7836 9252
»» www.vertigogalleries.com Open 11–6:30 Mon–Fri, 11–5:30 Sat

This light-filled little gallery showcases original movie posters and "lobby cards" (small posters displayed in American cinemas). The selection and prices range from affordable modern items to rarities going for thousands. For an original gift idea, choose a film from someone's birth year, or one with a British theme.

Aram   *iconic modern furniture*   `9 G3`
110 Drury Lane, WC2 • 020 7557 7557
»» www.aram.co.uk Open 10–6 Mon–Sat (10–7 Thu)

A champion of contemporary design since the 1960s, Aram now has a vast converted warehouse to show off its modern-classic furniture to stunning effect. Wandering around its five floors, admiring iconic pieces by Le Corbusier and Eileen Gray, is like visiting a museum. Indeed, the shop hosts regular exhibitions.

Monmouth Street *girls' pampering zone* `9 F3`
Covent Garden, WC2
For individual shop details, *see pp210–11*

Monmouth Street is rapidly turning into Boutique
Central, with a line-up of classy shops. At No. 23 is
London's chicest sex shop, **Coco de Mer**, selling
beautiful lingerie (some emblazoned with discreet
pornographic prints), a range of tasteful sex toys such
as arty, coloured-glass dildos, and erotic books. The
décor is neo-Victorian with crimson floral wallpaper,
and the dressing rooms have a peephole concealed
behind a picture through which your partner can spy
on you from a hidden chamber next door – very kinky.

American skincare supremo **Kiehl's** is at No. 29.
The company's excellent products, based on natural
ingredients, are instantly recognizable in their
no-frills packaging. Be warned, however – they're far
more expensive here than in the US. **Poste Mistress**
at Nos. 61–3 has the feel of a 1970s boudoir, with
designer shoes from the likes of Angelo Figus and
Pucci perched amid kitsch, framed photos and
burgundy velvet pouffes.

The talented buyer at **Koh Samui** (Nos. 65–7)
always selects exciting pieces from well-known
designers (Dries Van Noten, Miu Miu, Clements
Ribeiro), plus cutting-edge offerings by up-and-
coming talent. The jewellery and accessories are
especially creative. Across the street at **aQuaint** (No.
38), Ashley Isham's grown-up, tailored-yet-feminine
womenswear hangs side by side with neat modern
clothing by British designers Emma Cook and Boyd,
and exquisite, expensive frocks by Lanvin.

Earlham Street *bustling street market* 9 F3
At the Seven Dials intersection, Covent Garden, WC2
For individual shop details, *see pp210–11*

The west end of Earlham Street is packed with market stalls hawking cheap T-shirts and casual clothes. Sprawling over several stalls is **The Wild Bunch** florist, which offers a wide array of good-quality blooms. The shops lining the street are mainly funky fashion chains, including global surf-skate-style brand **Stüssy** at No. 19, futuristic club label **Cyberdog** at No. 9 and expanding British chain **All Saints** at No. 5, which sells cool clothes and jeanswear for men and women.

Adding to the mix is traditional ironmonger **F W Collins & Son** at No. 14, which opened in 1835 when the area still had a reputation as a meeting-place of criminals. A branch of design bookshop **Magma** is at No. 8 *(see also p86)*. At the east end of Earlham Street are the surf/skatewear shops of the **Thomas Neal Centre** and hip young American clothing/home emporium **Urban Outfitters**, at Nos. 42–56.

Neal's Yard Dairy *British cheeses* 9 G3
17 Shorts Gardens, WC2 • 020 7240 5700
➤➤ www.nealsyarddairy.co.uk
Open 11–6:30 Mon–Thu, 10–6:30 Fri & Sat

The very smell of this tiny shop will have cheese-lovers swooning. The counter and shelves groan under the weight of massive whole cheeses. Regional gems by independent producers include Colston Bassett Stilton, Lincolnshire Poacher and Montgomery's Cheddar.

Size? *trendy trainer store* 9 G3
17–19 Neal Street, WC2 • 020 7240 1736
Open 9:30–7:30 (to 8pm Thu), noon–6 Sun

Sneaker freaks will be in their natural habitat at this always-busy shop, which sells big names such as Converse, Nike and Lacoste – including limited-edition styles – alongside elusive cult brands. Adidas fans should head for the basement and one of the UK's few official shops dedicated to the label.

Forbidden Planet *sci-fi/fantasy megastore* `9 F2`
179 Shaftesbury Avenue, WC2 • 020 7420 3666
➤➤ www.forbiddenplanet.com Open 10–7 (to 8 Thu), noon–6 Sun

For shoppers with an unhealthy obsession with *Lord of the Rings* or *Star Trek*, this is the place to come for the full range of action figures and videos. Forbidden Planet is the world's largest sci-fi and fantasy retailer, and the London megastore is packed with books and comics. There is even an "adults only" section.

Falkiner Fine Papers *paper supplies* `9 G1`
76 Southampton Row, WC1 • 020 7831 1151
Open 9:30–5:30 Mon–Fri, 10:30–5:30 Sat

Located near St Martins College of Art, Falkiner sells all manner of products relating to paper. There's equipment for making it, quill pens, sketchbooks and shelf upon shelf of individual sheets, from marbled patterns to parquet and bricks for dolls' houses. Japanese silkscreen prints are another line.

James Smith & Sons *umbrellas* `9 G2`
53 New Oxford Street, WC1 • 020 7836 4731
➤➤ www.james-smith.co.uk Open 9:30–5:25 Mon–Fri, 10–5:25 Sat

This family business has been making umbrellas and canes for over 170 years. The Victorian shop, still with its original signs and fittings, is an attraction in itself. Inside are racks crammed with umbrellas in every pattern – stripes, checks, paisley, frilled parasols – and walking sticks with curious carved handles.

Contemporary Wardrobe *vintage wear* `9 G1`
The Horse Hospital, Colonnade, WC1 • 020 7713 7370
➤➤ www.thehorsehospital.com Open noon–6 Mon–Sat

Over 15,000 items of vintage street fashions can be found at this hire shop, which shares its site – formerly a hospital for sick horses – with a venue for avant garde art and film. Rooting around here could turn up a piece used in the film *Quadrophenia* or a video shoot with Kylie or David Bowie. Some garments are for sale.

Gay's The Word *specialist bookshop* `3 G5`
66 Marchmont Street, WC1 • 020 7278 7654
➤➤ www.gaystheword.co.uk Open 10–6:30 Mon–Sat, 2–6 Sun

The UK's largest gay bookshop has been in business since the late 1970s. Titles cover fiction, philosophy, history, politics, erotica, relationships and emotional issues. Gay detective novels have a section to themselves. Videos and second-hand books are also on sale in this friendly shop.

Rennies *modern British collectibles* `9 H1`
At French's Dairy, 13 Rugby Street, WC1 • 020 7405 0220
➤➤ www.rennart.co.uk Open noon–6:30 Tue–Sat

Hidden in a residential street is this delightful shop in the premises of an old dairy, with its original blue-tiled shopfront. Paul and Karen Rennie specialize in practical British 20th-century art and design: club badges, transport and events posters, paperbacks, patterned scarves and commemorative china.

Cecil Court *antiquarian books & prints* `9 F3`
Pedestrian lane off Charing Cross Road, WC2
For individual shop details, *see p211*

This narrow street, lined with quirky little shops, is a collector's paradise. **Nigel Williams** at No. 25 specializes in first editions, with lots of Enid Blyton and P G Wodehouse, while, across the street, **Marchpane** also deals in antique children's titles, especially sumptuously illustrated fairy stories. **P J Hilton** has a good selection of beautifully bound 19th-century literature, and **David Drummond** sells books and ephemera relating to the performing arts.

Continuing the dramatic theme **Stage Door Prints** (No. 9) has signed photos of stars such as Laurence Olivier, Vivien Leigh, Edith Piaf and Anna Pavlova, plus theatre-related prints. You'll find a wider selection of antiquarian prints – encompassing fish, fashion, maps, the military and much more – at **Storey's** (No. 3). Opposite, **Tindley & Chapman** deals in immaculate first editions of 20th-century fiction.

Charing Cross Road *bookshops* `9 F3`
Road bordering Covent Garden & Soho, WC2
For individual shop details, *see p211*

The name "Charing Cross Road" gets bibliophiles' pulses racing. Together with offshoot Cecil Court *(see left)*, it is London's main centre of new, second-hand, specialist and antiquarian bookshops. Check out the commemorative plaque on the site of the defunct Marks & Co, whose address gave its name to the book and film *84 Charing Cross Road*.

Recently refurbished, the famous **Foyles** stocks everything from popular fiction to academic texts on its five floors. It now also houses London institution **Ray's Jazz** – a music shop, with a café attached where you can dig the tunes – and renowned women's bookshop **Silver Moon**. There's also an art gallery on the premises. Even if you're not buying for children, go and have a look at the live piranhas in the children's department. Across the street is a massive branch of **Borders** with the chain's usual all-embracing selection of magazines, books and CDs. It has a café and comfy chairs for lounging in, too. A large branch of **Blackwell's** bookshop is at No. 100.

Of the second-hand bookshops on Charing Cross Road, many are appealingly ramshackle emporiums, where the pleasure comes from rooting out treasures from the packed, dusty shelves. **Quinto** at No. 48A and **Henry Pordes** at Nos. 58–60 are well reputed. For coffee-table art tomes and scholarly subjects, visit **Shipley** at No. 70. Its sister shop, **Shipley Media**, at No. 80 specializes in photography, film and fashion.

Helter Skelter *music bookshop* `9 F2`
4 Denmark Street, WC2 • 020 7836 1151
» www.helterskelterbooks.com Open 10–7 Mon–Fri, 10–6 Sat

On a road lined with music shops, Helter Skelter occupies the former Regent Sound Studios, where the Rolling Stones recorded their first single. The shelves are stuffed with biographies and reference books covering every style of popular music – rock, jazz, country, soul and more.

Kokon To-Zai *sounds & style* `9 F3`
57 Greek Street, W1 • 020 7434 1316
Open 11–7:30 Mon–Sat, noon–6 Sun

Revamp your record collection and your wardrobe at this compact one-stop shop selling cutting-edge clothes and music. Staff man the decks so you can browse to the electro beat. On the rails are street designs for both sexes by local and global talent, as well as the store's own sportswear-influenced line.

Gerry's *wines & spirits* `9 F3`
74 Old Compton Street, W1 • 020 7734 4215/2053
Open 9–6:15 Mon–Fri, 9–5:30 Sat

This is the place to come if you're looking for an obscure liqueur or spirit – there are over 100 varieties of vodka alone. The shop is crammed with a huge variety of booze from all over Europe, South America and elsewhere, from strawberry-flavoured tequila to absinthe in a bottle shaped like the Eiffel Tower.

Shop *trendy designer boutique* `9 E3`
4 Brewer Street, W1 • 020 7437 1259
Open 10:30–6:30 Mon–Fri, 11–6:30 Sat

Blink and you'll miss this tiny basement shop in the heart of the red-light district. The names inside couldn't be further from the scene on the street, with Marc by Marc Jacobs, Cacharel and Sonia Rykiel's diffusion line rubbing shoulders with the boutique's own Shopgirl range and hip new London labels.

Vintage *entertainment memorabilia & mags* `9 E3`
39–43 Brewer Street, W1 • 020 7439 8525
>> www.vinmag.com Open 10–8 (to 10pm Fri–Sat), noon–8 Sun

The ground floor is devoted to entertainment memorabilia (Charlie's Angels T-shirts, Bond mousepads). The basement holds 75,000 vintage magazines, organized by decade and theme. In addition to *Picture Post* and *Vogue*, you'll find such obscurities as *The Naturist* and a *Dr Kildare Annual*.

Agent Provocateur *kitsch-sexy lingerie* `9 E3`
6 Broadwick Street, W1 • 020 7439 0229
>> www.agentprovocateur.com Open 11–7 Mon–Sat

Branches of this lingerie company, run by designer Vivienne Westwood's son, have popped up all over town, but only the original Soho shop maintains the slightly seedy air befitting its porn-chic image. Staff in pink uniforms sell 1950s pin-up-style underwear, and accessories such as diamanté-handled riding crops.

Phonica *vinyl-lovers' paradise* `9 E3`
51 Poland Street, W1 • 020 7025 6070
Open 11:30–7:30 Mon–Sat

Primarily a haunt of DJs, this shop has a counter lined with record decks and 70s lounge chairs on which customers can relax and leaf through back copies of *Jockey Slut*. Among the vinyl, you'll find Afrobeat, electronica, hip hop, nu jazz from the Jazzanova-Compost label and Donna Summer disco heaven.

Anything Left-Handed *specialist tools* `9 E3`
57 Brewer Street, W1 • 020 7437 3910
>> www.anythingleft-handed.co.uk
Open 10–6 Mon–Fri, 10–5:30 Sat

In business since 1968, the shop delivers what it says above the door – everyday items specially made for lefty adults and children, from kitchen implements and manicure sets to educational games and books. The helpful staff are left-handed as well.

b Store *radical designer fashion* `8 D3`
6 Conduit Street, W1 • 020 7499 6628
>> www.buddhahood.co.uk Open 10:30–6:30 Mon–Fri, 10–6 Sat

This small boutique for men and women sells its own range of funky footwear – Buddhahood – alongside cutting-edge designs from Peter Jensen, Boudicca and Michelle Lowe-Holder. Although the shop attracts such lofty clientele as model Kate Moss and pop princess Kylie, the mood is pleasantly down to earth.

Shopping

Newburgh Street *Carnaby's cooler cousin* `9 E3`
Cobbled pedestrian street, W1
For individual shop details, *see p212*

Running parallel behind brash, touristy Carnaby Street, this little strip couldn't be further away in spirit. Among the line-up of small street-fashion outlets, **RedDot** stands out for its amusing T-shirts and sweatshirts emblazoned with anarchic slogans and images such as Princess Diana playing happy families with Darth Vader. **Jess James** offers modern jewellery from up-and-coming and well-known designers – displayed in innovative ways, such as in a long leather case with portholes which light up as you approach. **The Dispensary** sells laid-back clothes on the wearable side of fashionable for both sexes, from designers local and far-flung. Tiny perfumery **Scent Systems** stocks unusual fragrances and skincare, many of them not available elsewhere in the UK. These include the German products Just Pure, meant to be used according to the cycles of the moon.

Oki-ni *limited-edition designs* `9 E3`
25 Savile Row, W1 • 020 7494 1716
≫ www.oki-ni.com Open 10–6 Mon–Sat (to 7 Thu)

A totally original concept, Oki-ni is a British-Japanese design group that collaborates with such diverse labels as Adidas, Paul Smith, Levi's, Evisu and Zakee Shariff to create exclusive garments. The shop is more a showroom than a retail site, as most items have to be ordered from the website.

Liberty *English-eccentric department store* `8 D3`
210–20 Regent Street, W1 • 020 7734 1234
≫ www.liberty.co.uk
Open 10–7 Mon–Sat (to 8pm Thu), noon–6 Sun

London's quirkiest department store maintains its rich history while embracing the 21st century. Tudor House contains the global furniture, Oriental rugs and printed fabrics that made Liberty's name, while Regent House has extravagant lingerie and ultra-fashionable shoes.

Topshop *fashion superstore* `9 E2`
36–38 Great Castle Street, W1 • 020 7636 7700
≫ www.topshop.co.uk
Open 9–8 Mon–Sat (to 9pm Thu), noon–6 Sun

"The world's largest fashion store" attracts 180,000 shoppers a week. Blaring music and video screens may be for kids, but stylists trawl it for cheap garments. The basement Boutique has affordable pieces by Preen, Maria Chen-Pascual and others.

Georgina Goodman *unique shoes*   `8 D5`
12–14 Shepherd Street, W1 • 020 7499 8599
≫ www.georginagoodman.com Open 10–6 Mon–Fri, 11–4 Sat

Goodman's sculptural, hand-painted shoes (created to
individual specifications in the workshop downstairs)
are wearable works of art with pricetags to match, but
there is a more affordable, ready-to-wear line, too.
Also on sale in the airy, gallery-style space are baby
bootees, bags and other leather goods.

Smythson *impeccable stationery*   `8 D3`
40 New Bond Street, W1 • 020 7629 8558
≫ www.smythson.com
Open 9:30–6 (from 10am Thu & Sat)

This posh stationer is great for gifts, especially leather-bound
notebooks in a range of classic colours, some embossed with witty
titles such as *Blondes Brunettes Redheads*, as well as the more
practical *Travel Notes*. Other wonderfully traditional accessories
include visitors' books and travel wallets.

REN *British natural body products*   `8 D4`
19 Shepherd Market, W1 • 020 7495 5960
≫ www.ren.ltd.uk Open 11–6:30 Mon–Sat (to 7:30 Tue & Thu);
often closed 3–4:30, sometimes closes 5:30 on Mon & Wed

Ren means "clean" in Swedish, reflecting the philosophy behind this British hair- and skincare brand.
Products such as the Moroccan rose otto shower wash
and the grapefruit and jojoba cream are made without
pore-blocking additives and have a lovely scent.

Traditional British Brands
Some bastions of British conservatism have recently
been given the kiss of life. **Burberry** has been
transformed from staid raincoat manufacturer to
"it" label. And, although the hallowed check has
gained popularity among football fans, the macs
are still top-quality, and the more exclusive catwalk
line, available at the New Bond Street flagship,
exudes urban chic. The traditional knitwear brand
Pringle now has cool variations on its famous
argyle sweaters and neat, classic separates.
Mulberry has shaken off its former frumpiness with
contemporary takes on English country style: the
renowned bags in mock-croc leather and durable,
synthetic Scotchgrain are now streamlined with modern shapes. All outlets on New Bond St; *see p223.*

Poste *trendy men's shoes* `8 D3`
10 South Molton Street, W1 • 020 7499 8002
Open 10–7 Mon–Sat, noon–6 Sun

With its Chesterfield sofa and framed pictures of sporting heroes, this small shop teasingly has the air of a gentlemen's club. Most of the shoes are updates of classics by designers such as Jeffery-West, Paul Smith and Dries Van Noten, with a selection of fashionable trainers by the likes of Adidas and Puma.

Browns *international designer boutique* `8 D3`
23–7 South Molton Street, W1 • 020 7514 0000
>> www.brownsfashion.com Open 10–6:30 Mon–Sat (to 7pm Thu)

The mother of all London boutiques has been in business for over 30 years, occupying five interconnecting shops. The mood is decidedly grown-up, with Dries Van Noten, Lanvin, Alaia and an entire floor devoted to Jil Sander. Across the street, black-mirrored Browns Focus showcases young hip labels.

Spymaster *espionage emporium* `8 C2`
3 Portman Square, W1 • 020 7486 3885
>> www.spymaster.co.uk Open 9:30–6 Mon–Fri, 10–5 Sat

Aspiring James Bonds will love this store, which caters to amateur sleuths, government departments and law-enforcement agencies. All your espionage needs are catered for, from trained sniffer dogs and armoured cars to shark repellent and a nifty bug detector disguised as a pen. Eat your heart out, Q.

N Peal *indulgent cashmere* `9 E4`
37 & 71–2 Burlington Arcade, W1 • 020 7493 5378
>> www.npeal.com Open 9:30–6 Mon–Sat

A resident of London's famous Burlington Arcade since 1936, N Peal has managed to move with the times. The range of cashmere in its two tiny shops (women's at No. 37, men's at 71–2) is impressive, from classic rollnecks and cardies to younger, street-inspired styles in the more affordable npealworks collection.

Stella McCartney *cool designerwear* `8 D4`
30 Bruton Street, W1 • 020 7518 3100
>> www.stellamccartney.co.uk Open 10–6 Mon–Sat (to 7pm Thu)

A spacious Mayfair townhouse is a suitably glamorous setting for McCartney's figure-skimming dresses, slim-fitting suits and separates in seductive fabrics. The non-leather shoes are displayed in a parlour decorated with wallpaper created by the designer herself. Vegetarian footwear has never been so sexy.

Selfridges *department store heaven* 8 C3
400 Oxford Street, W1 • 0870 837 7377
>> www.selfridges.com
Open 10–8 Mon–Fri, 9:30–8 Sat, 12–6 Sun

Look out, Harrods; watch your back, Harvey Nicks, because Selfridges is a serious contender for London's best department store. Constantly introducing new labels and innovations, the Oxford Street giant can truly be said to have all the bases covered. Whether you're looking for the latest bestseller, a new iBook or a vintage frock, you're likely to find it in this retail universe.

The fashion department embraces almost every high street brand as well as emerging design talent. The cosmetics hall on the ground floor takes in the big names and cult imports from Europe and the US,

while a branch of modern holistic chemist **Farmacia** offers organic options on the fifth. The food hall features cuisine from around the globe; the shoe department has been revamped with glamorous mini salons of exclusive labels **Jimmy Choo** *(see also p77)* and **YSL**; there's an **Agent Provocateur** outpost *(see also p67)* in the massive lingerie section; and the expanded sports department includes must-have surfing and skateboard labels.

The slick Superbrands section has also created a buzz. Accessed through a red resin tunnel, it consists of eight hot designers, including **Stella McCartney**, **Alexander McQueen** and **Balenciaga**, grouped around a branch of sumptuous, souk-style Moroccan restaurant **Mômo** *(see also p34)*, which provides respite from traipsing round the store's six massive floors.

St Christopher's Place *shopping oasis* `8 C3`
Pedestrian square, W1
For individual shop details, *see pp222–5*

Opposite Bond Street Tube station, a narrow alleyway leading off Oxford Street (Gees Court) widens into a hidden square with shops and eateries. This appealing enclave features a modern fountain and is dominated by a large branch of Italian gourmet café chain **Carluccio's**. Drinkers from the pub opposite spill out onto the pavement, and you can often catch live jazz on summer nights. Shopping highlights include a branch of **Mulberry** (11–12 Gees Court; *see also p69*) and the spacious flagship of women's chain **Whistles**

(12 St Christopher's Place), which stocks hot designers alongside the shop's own-label – signature styles include bias-cut dresses and modern tailoring.

Next door, **Osprey** is the place for mid-priced, classic British-designed handbags (structured shapes in mock croc are a key look), while across the way at Nos. 20–21, former theatrical "shodders" **Anello & Davide**, who made Dorothy's ruby slippers for *The Wizard of Oz*, sells a range of men's and women's shoes, hand-crafted in Italy. There's also a branch of Scandinavian fabric company **Marimekko** (Nos. 16–17), which is known for its bright abstract patterns, featuring on everything from bags to bedding.

Margaret Howell *updated British classics* `8 C2`
34 Wigmore Street, W1 • 020 7009 9009
≫ www.margarethowell.co.uk Open 10–6 Mon–Sat (to 7pm Thu)

This vast, gallery-style space showcases the designer's collections for men and women, and a selection of simple tableware and vintage and reissued post-War furniture. The clothes are best described as relaxed modern classics, made of quality British fabrics suited to the national climate, such as tweed and cashmere.

Mint *unusual designer homewares* `8 C2`
70 Wigmore Street, W1 • 020 7224 4406
Open 10:30–6:30 Mon–Sat (to 7:30pm Thu)

Mint brings together an international collection of furniture and homewares, a mix of the ultra-modern and the antique, made by both established designers and recent graduates. Pottery and glassware are hand-made and appealingly asymmetrical. Even tea towels are elevated from the ordinary by lovely prints.

Paul Rothe *traditional delicatessen* `8 C2`
35 Marylebone Lane, W1 • 020 7935 6783
Open 8–6 Mon–Fri, 11:30–approx 5:30 Sat

Established in 1900, this old-fashioned deli is run by the original Rothe's grandson and great-grandson, who wear dapper white coats. Chunky soup and neatly cut sandwiches are served on proper china, while the "English and foreign provisions" include preserves, traditional sweets and Scottish biscuits.

Calmia *yoga emporium & spa retreat* `8 C1`
52–4 Marylebone High St, W1 • 020 7224 3585
» www.calmia.com
Open 9–9 Mon–Sat, 10–7 Sun

Yoga has never been so chic. While achieving inner peace, you can look fabulous in expensive gear from supermodel Christy Turlington's Nuala range or DKNY Pure. Everything related to yoga is here, from mats and relaxation tapes to candles and organic skincare. Luxurious spa treatments are available downstairs.

Sixty 6 *creative mix 'n' match for women* `8 C1`
66 Marylebone High Street, W1 • 020 7224 6066
Open 10:30–6:30 Mon–Sat, 1–5 Sun

Embroidery and beading abound at this shop celebrating eclectic, feminine style. Separates are often paired up in unusual combinations, providing plenty of inspiration. Designs by the likes of Temperley, Megan Park and Roland Mouret are supplemented by pretty scarves and bags.

» *Newly fashionable Marylebone High Street also has a branch of the Conran Shop (see p78)*

Shopping

Daunt Books *elegant shop for travellers* 8 C1
83 Marylebone High Street, W1 • 020 7224 2295
Open 9–7:30 Mon–Sat, 11–6 Sun

Arguably London's most beautiful bookshop, Daunt
retains its original Edwardian character, with oak
shelves and green-shaded lamps. General titles are in
the front; the galleried rear conservatory is devoted to
travel and related fiction organized by country. It's a
great place to browse even if you're not planning a trip.

Skandium *nordic interiors* 8 C1
86–7 Marylebone High Street, W1 • 020 7935 2077
» www.skandium.com Open 10–6:30 Mon–Sat, noon–5 Sun

The design chain's flagship shop brings together the
best of Scandinavia's characteristically clean,
contemporary design under one roof. Compare the
modern-classic furniture by Alvar Aalto and Arne
Jacobsen with the functional yet fashionable tableware, accessories, books and jewellery.

Madeleine Press *understated urban styles* 8 C1
90 Marylebone High Street, W1 • 020 7935 9301
» www.mpress.com
Open 10:30–6:30 Mon–Sat (to 7pm Thu); 11:30–4:30 Sun

The designer behind the late, lamented label Press &
Bastyan has gone solo with an exquisitely simple
womenswear collection that exudes effortless chic.
Neat jackets, body-draping cotton tops, slip dresses
and slim jeans are characteristic pieces.

La Fromagerie *divine deli* 8 C2
2–4 Moxon Street, W1 • 020 7935 0341
» www.lafromagerie.co.uk Open 10:30–7:30 Mon,
8–7:30 Tue–Fri, 9–7 Sat, 10–6 Sun

Known for its "cave" packed with cheeses from
independent producers across Europe, this rustic-
modern shop also sells condiments, bread, coffee,
wines and charcuterie. Sample these at the in-store
café, or ask for a picnic box to take to Regent's Park.

Prestat *high-class chocolatier* 9 E4
14 Princes Arcade, SW1 • 020 7629 4838
>> www.prestat.co.uk Open 9:30–6 Mon–Fri, 10–5 Sat

This tiny shop looks like a chocolate box itself, its shelves covered in fabulously packaged, handmade confectionery. Choose from traditional mint wafers, rose and violet creams and fondants, or such new-fangled sweet treats as banoffee truffles, presented in old-fashioned boxes with flamboyant hues.

Patrick Cox *slick designer shoes* 14 B2
129 Sloane Street, SW1 • 020 7730 8886
>> www.patrickcox.co.uk Open 10–6 (to 7pm Wed), noon–6 Sun

The Canadian designer launched his label in London in the 1980s and has recently revitalized the French brand Charles Jourdan. Shoes for men and women are on the flashy side, with mod and punk influences, bright colours and glitzy trims. The diffusion range, Wannabe, offers basics with a designer edge.

Jo Malone *luxury skincare & fragrances* 14 B2
150 Sloane Street, SW1 • 020 7730 2100
>> www.jomalone.co.uk
Open 10–6 (to 7pm Wed & Thu), 11–5 Sun

Gorgeous scents greet you upon entering this classy store. The skincare range is simple yet effective, while fragrances are based on delectable ingredients such as orange blossom, nutmeg, ginger – even coffee. Enjoy a sample with a complimentary hand massage.

Maria Grachvogel *glamorous dresses* 14 B2
162 Sloane Street, SW1 • 020 7245 9331
>> www.mariagrachvogel.com Open 10–6 Mon–Sat (to 7pm Wed)

Popular with the crème of Hollywood, Grachvogel's sophisticated evening dresses celebrate the female form with simple, body-skimming lines, sensuous fabrics and subtle detailing of feathers or sequins. In this glamorous, pink-walled shop, you'll also find the designer's collection of understated yet sexy daywear.

Shopping »»»»»

Elizabeth Street *sophisticated shopping* `14 C2`
Off Eaton Square, SW1
For individual shop details, *see pp223–5*

A short stroll from Knightsbridge is this attractive street with a diverse selection of appealing shops. The friendly perfumery **Les Senteurs** at No. 71 sells unusual European fragrances, such as Annick Goutal and Parfums Caron. If you've bagged a ticket to Ascot or just want to turn heads with an exquisite trilby or extravagant, feathered creation, visit celebrated hatter **Philip Treacy** at No. 69. Across the street at No. 46 is wonderful French bakery **Poilâne**, where you can buy authentic croissants, fruit tarts and rustic loaves

– at a price. At No. 42 is the bright, cheerful shop of British designer **Tracey Boyd**, where girlish strappy dresses, cute short-sleeved blouses and flared skirts in fun patterns are strengths. Jeweller **Erickson Beamon** at No. 38 is a long-standing favourite never long out of the fashion press. Dramatically cascading gold chains and beads make for a strong signature look.

If you're flagging, have a cup of the best hot chocolate you've ever tasted at **The Chocolate Society** shop and café at No. 36 – the society is dedicated to promoting high-quality chocolate. Opposite, at No. 45, is gorgeous modern florist **Woodhams**, which is worth visiting just to breathe the scented air.

Anya Hindmarch *personalized bags* `14 B2`
15–17 Pont Street, SW1 • 020 7838 9177
» www.anyahindmarch.com Open 10–6 Mon–Sat (to 7pm Wed)

Hindmarch is known for classic bags printed with striking images. You can have one made up with your own photo. She also makes impeccable leather bags, including the popular double-handled Ebury, which you can have embossed inside with a personal message. Dainty shoes are also on offer.

Lulu Guinness *head-turning bags & more* `14 B2`
3 Ellis Street, SW1 • 020 7823 4828
>> www.luluguinness.com Open 10–6 Mon–Fri, 11–6 Sat

With its nostalgic illustrations and vintage fashion ads, this shop's décor is as striking as the witty handbags on display. Guinness's creations include a flower pot bursting with fabric roses and an embroidered circus tent complete with performing seal. Her retro-look cosmetics range is also sold.

Neisha Crosland *contemporary fabrics* `14 A3`
137 Fulham Rd, SW3 • 020 7589 4866 Open 10–6, noon–5 Sun
8 Elystan Street, SW3 • 020 7584 7988 Open 10–5:30 Mon–Sat
>> www.neishacrosland.com

Neisha Crosland started out designing scarves and has branched out into clothes, accessories and home furnishings, all in her striking abstract prints. The tiny Fulham Road shop sells her Ginka fashion label; go round the corner for cushions and wallpaper.

Joseph *high-class urban separates* `13 H3`
77 Fulham Road, SW3 • 020 7823 9500
Open 10–6:30 Mon–Sat (to 7 Wed), 12–5 Sun

Joseph's de luxe basics, especially his well-cut trousers, have devoted fans. This minimalist flagship sells his collection alongside pieces from Prada, YSL and Marni; the basement is devoted to designer shoes. Across Draycott Street, Joseph Essentials, Gigi boutique and Joe's Cafe complete the colony.

Jimmy Choo *celebrated designer heels* `14 A3`
169 Draycott Avenue, SW3 • 020 7584 6111
>> www.jimmychoo.com Open 10–6 (to 7pm Wed), 1–6 Sun

This plush Chelsea townhouse, with velvet couches for luxurious lounging, is devoted to Jimmy Choo's fabulous footwear and handbags. The sleek styles are subtle enough not to date next season – essential when you're splashing out hundreds. The bridal range caters for those who demand the best on their big day.

>> *Harvey Nichols' top floor restaurant and bar is an ideal stop-off during Knightsbridge shopping* (see p79)

The Conran Shop *Sir Terence's place*

14 A2

Michelin House, 81 Fulham Rd, SW3 • 020 7589 7401
» www.conran.com Shop open 10–6 Mon, Tue, Fri, 10–7 Wed,
Thu, 10–6:30 Sat, 12–6 Sun. Bibendum restaurant lunch &
dinner daily; Oyster Bar all day from noon daily

Iconic designer and entrepreneur Terence Conran has
housed his London flagship in the magnificent former
HQ of Michelin Tyres. This curious Art Deco building,
which features stained-glass panels depicting the
Michelin Man and is crowned with lights in the form
of stacked tyres, is also home to Conran's acclaimed
Bibendum restaurant on the first floor (expensive
modern European cuisine). For the best views of the
architectural curiosity, enter via the front portico with
its picturesque flower stall and cart selling crustacea
and fresh fish. This entrance is also the setting for the
tiled Oyster Bar (less formal, but no cheaper, than the
main restaurant).

In the shop, a more affordable line of contemporary
furniture, Content by Conran, is now sold alongside
the main collection of classic modernist designs. In
fact, there are many reasonably priced items for
home, garden and office. There's also a selection of
high-tech gadgets, including the latest cameras, and
a good range of bath products, coffee-table books
and high-quality children's toys.

Kate Kuba *high-fashion footwear* `14 B3`
22 Duke of York Sq, King's Road, SW3 • 020 7259 0011
» www.katekuba.com Open 10–6:30 (to 7pm Wed), noon–6 Sun

This North London shoe shop has recently expanded into the city centre, and divas Mary J Blige and Beyoncé are already fans of its flamboyant footwear. Stock in this spacious, contemporary branch runs from basic loafers to jewelled killer heels. Flashy variations on the cowboy boot are a perennial favourite.

Oliver Sweeney *men's shoes* `14 B3`
29 King's Road, SW3 • 020 7730 3666
» www.oliversweeney.com Open 10–7 (to 8 Wed), 12–6 Sun

A combination of comfort, craftsmanship and cool has made the shoes of choice for David Beckham, Brad Pitt and Noel Gallagher. A wide range of traditional and more cutting-edge styles is available (including smart leather trainers), all made on Sweeney's supportive Anatomical Last.

Korres *natural Greek skincare* `14 A3`
124 King's Road, SW3 • 020 7581 6455
» www.korres.com Open 10–7 Mon–Sat, noon–6 Sun

This long, narrow shop is stocked with the Athenian company's products for skin and hair, all in vivid packaging. Tantalizing aromas emanate from lotions based on olives, rosemary and other natural plant extracts characteristic of Greece. Anti-cellulite creams and sun milks are part of the range.

Department Stores

London has excellent department stores. In Knightsbridge, you really can buy anything in **Harrods**, where even the chandeliers are dripping with grapes. Nearby at sophisticated **Harvey Nichols** the focus is on designer fashion; ladies who lunch love the Fifth Floor restaurant at "Harvey Nicks". On Piccadilly, elegant **Fortnum & Mason** is famous for its food hall, staffed by frock-coated assistants and selling such oddities as dried edible insects among the quaintly packaged teas and jams. A short stroll up Bond Street leads to **Fenwick**, which has the feel of a boutique and is renowned for accessories. On Oxford Street, **John Lewis** has affordable basics, while **Selfridges** *(see p71)* steals the show. For all shop details, *see p222*.

Shopping

Designers Guild *modern homewares* `14 A4`

267 & 277 King's Road, SW3 • 020 7351 5775
» www.designersguild.com Open 10 6 Mon Sat,
noon–5 Sun (fabric shop closed on Sun)

Who says modern design has to be muted and mini-
mal? Tricia Guild's contemporary emporium explodes
with colour and pattern. There are cushions, bedding,
funky fashion accessories, furniture, a children's
range, stationery, bath products and design books.

Antiquarius *antiques emporium* `14 A4`

131–41 King's Road, SW3 • 020 7351 5353
Open 10–6 Mon–Sat

Many of the stalls behind the green awnings of
Antiquarius sell antique furniture, but there are other
smaller treasures to be found, too. A few antique
jewellery stalls at the front are worth a browse;
otherwise go to the back room for rare finds such as vintage Louis Vuitton luggage and original movie posters.

Space.NK *cult cosmetics and a spa* `7 F3`

127–31 Westbourne Grove, W2 • 020 7727 8063
» www.spacenk.com Open 11–7 Mon, 10–7 Tue, Fri, Sat,
10–8 Wed, noon–6 Sun

This capacious branch of the beauty-products empire
has a spa on the ground floor, offering luxurious
treatments. Upstairs there is a vast array of cosmetics
from around the world, as well as Space.NK's own
range, which includes grooming for the boys.

202 *lifestyle shop and café* `7 F3`

202 Westbourne Grove, W11 • 020 7792 6888
» www.nicolefarhi.com Open 8:30–6 (from 10am Mon), 10–5 Sun

Nicole Farhi's "lifestyle" store brings together an airy,
French-style café buzzing with beautiful people, selected pieces from Farhi's collections for both men and
women (trademarks are relaxed separates in natural
fabrics, chunky sweaters and sheepskin coats), home
accessories and a smattering of antique furniture.

Bill Amberg *leather goods* `7 E2`
10 Chepstow Road, W2 • 020 7727 3560
»www.billamberg.com Open 10–6 Mon–Sat (to 7pm Thu)

Long-established leather designer Bill Amberg produces unfussy, high-quality bags and accessories in calfskin, suede and bridle leather. There are also sheepskin-lined baby slings, and, for hunters, gun cases and a cartridge belt. The Library Tote features limited-edition prints on undyed leather.

Miller Harris *exquisite London perfumery* `7 E3`
14 Needham Road, W11 • 020 7221 1545
»www.millerharris.com Open 10–6 Mon–Sat

Lyn Harris trained in Grasse – the perfume capital on the French Riviera – before opening this London shop. Her gorgeous scents have a complexity that transcends most department store fragrances, yet the prices are comparable. You may even have your own bespoke perfume created if you can wait several weeks.

Rough Trade *legendary indie record shop* `6 D3`
130 Talbot Road, W11 • 020 7229 8541
»www.roughtrade.com Open 10–6:30 Mon–Sat, 1–5 Sun

Established more than 25 years ago, Rough Trade was an essential outpost of the London punk scene. It's still flying the indie flag, offering everything from electro-pop to alternative country. Every inch of wall space is covered with gig fliers; selected records are displayed with hand-written staff recommendations.

J&M Davidson *neo-classic bags & clothes* `6 D3`
42 Ledbury Road, W11 • 020 7313 9532
»www.jandmdavidson.com Open 10–6 Mon–Sat, noon–5 Sun

John and Monique are best known for their beautifully crafted bags. Based on classic shapes such as the bowling bag, and executed in offbeat colours and animal skins, they have an air of nostalgia. The Anglo-French duo also design tasteful, retro-influenced clothes and home accessories.

J W Beeton *eye-catching apparel* `6 D3`
48–50 Ledbury Rd, W11 • 020 7229 8874
Open 10:30–6 Mon–Fri, 10–6 Sat, noon–5 Sun

The look is fashionable yet individual at this small boutique, where you'll find Fake London's quirky takes on British classics rubbing shoulders on the rails with unusual patterned pieces from Panepinto, a label by an ex-Marni designer. Accessories from emerging home-grown talent add to the mix.

Simon Finch Rare Books *first editions* `6 D3`
61A Ledbury Rd, W11 • 020 7792 3303
≫ www.simonfinch.com Open 10–6 Mon–Fri, 11–6 Sat

This groovy, white, pod-like branch of the antiquarian booksellers (the main store is in Maddox Street, W1) specializes in modern first editions of literature, art books and prints. Where else will you find a signed photo of the Sex Pistols and firsts of *Lady Chatterley's Lover* and *The Day of the Triffids* under one roof?

Nick Ashley *biker-inspired menswear* `6 D3`
57 Ledbury Road, W11 • 020 7221 1221
≫ www.nickashley.com Open 10–6 Mon–Fri, 11–6 Sat

Son of the late queen of English country style Laura Ashley, motorbike enthusiast Nick has designed a range of classic British gear with more than a hint of 1960s mod styling. Everything from cool helmets and boots to weather-resistant coats and leather jackets is on display amid biker memorabilia.

Duchamp *flamboyant men's accessories* `6 D3`
75 Ledbury Rd, W11 • 020 7243 3970
≫ www.duchamp.co.uk Open 10–6 Tue–Sat

Modern dandies will delight in Duchamp's flashy wares. The range of cufflinks is huge, from mini abstract artworks in painted enamel to extravagant creations studded with jewel-bright Swarovski crystals. Ties in contemporary patterns and shirts with flamboyant prints will have peacocks strutting with pride.

Intoxica! *rare vinyl in kitsch setting* `6 D3`
231 Portobello Road, W11 • 020 7229 8010
» www.intoxica.co.uk Open 10:30–6:30 Mon–Sat, noon–5 Sun

A Polynesian *tiki*-hut interior complete with bamboo walls, indigenous gods and a model hula-dancer provides a bizarre backdrop to rare vinyl pop, jazz, ska, reggae and soul from the 50s to the 90s. Amid the surf, funk and punk are oddities such as *We're the Banana Splits* and the soundtrack to *Vixen*.

Honest Jon's *black music specialist* `6 D3`
278 Portobello Road, W10 • 020 8969 9822
» www.honestjons.com Open 10–6 Mon–Sat, 11–5 Sun

This shop has been a fixture of the Portobello scene since 1974, selling a combination of vinyl and CDs. On the ground floor you'll find reggae, funk, soul, hip-hop and R&B; head downstairs for jazz embracing "outernational" sounds, plus blues, Portuguese fado, African pop and Indian classical.

Portobello Green *designer enclave* `6 C2`
Arcade at Ladbroke Grove end of Portobello Road, W10
For individual shop details, *see p222–5; see also* Streetlife *p159*

Nestling under the Westway overpass, this arcade looks rather uninspiring but is home to some very interesting shops. There is also a buzzing market in the courtyard on Fridays and Saturdays, with stalls selling new and vintage clothes. The arcade's most celebrated resident is avant-garde design duo **Preen** at Unit 5 (open Thu–Sat only), whose deconstructed, punky clothes often feature asymmetric details, dangling straps and buckles. At **Suite 20** (Unit 20, closed Wed), you'll find retro-inspired separates and bags, some made in original 60s and 70s fabrics.

The floaty, patterned chiffon and embroidered silk tops and dresses at **Red Hot** (Unit 9, closed Mon) have been seen on numerous celebrities. **Bedstock** (Unit 26) sells bedlinen and a range of camp cushions decorated with everything from cute kittens to Carmen Miranda and Mao.

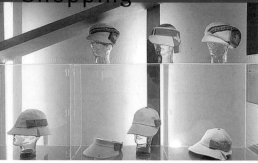

Willma *hats, hairclips & a whole lot more* `6 C2`
339 Portobello Road, W10 • 020 8960 7296
>> www.willma.co.uk Open 11–6 Tue–Sat

If you're after something different to liven up an outfit, this little shop specializes in fun accessories by up-and-coming designers in the UK and abroad. Displayed on colourful perspex units is every kind of thing from cute knitted hats to quirky socks – with striking jewellery, bags and belts in between.

Coco Ribbon *girly emporium* `6 C3`
21 Kensington Park Road, W11 • 020 7229 4904
>> www.cocoribbon.com
Open 10–6:30 (to 6pm Sat), 12:30–5:30 Sun

Half the stock is Australian, and much is embroidered, frilled or adorned with feathers. You'll find sequined cushions, glam costume jewellery, designer dresses and books such as *The Lazy Girl's Guide to a Fabulous Body* displayed on antique boudoir furniture.

Paul Smith *all the designer's collections* `6 D4`
120 & 122 Kensington Park Road, W11 • 020 7727 3553
>> www.paulsmith.co.uk
Open 10:30–6:30 Mon–Thu, 10–6:30 Fri & Sat

In this rambling stucco house, Smith's exquisite classic-with-a-twist men's and women's collections are draped artlessly over antique tables or hung in oversized wardrobes. The Playroom displays children's clothes alongside toys.

Marilyn Moore *funky, feminine knitwear* `6 C3`
7 Elgin Crescent, W11 • 020 7727 5577
Open 10–6 Mon–Sat

Marilyn Moore worked for Jaeger before launching her own label, so it's not surprising her collection includes modern interpretations of British classics. While the main focus in-store is on luxurious knitwear – ribbon-trimmed cashmere, or vintage-look argyle – there's also a range of updated traditional separates.

Graham & Green *eclectic home stores* `6 C3`
4 & 10 Elgin Crescent, W11 • 020 7727 4594
» www.grahamandgreen.co.uk
Open 10–6 Mon–Sat, 11:30–5:30 Sun

A popular source of inspiration for magazine interior stylists, these two family-run shops are a browsable, global jumble of furniture and oddments. Mongolian lambswool cushions, silk kimonos, Venetian mirrors and vintage-style radios are among the offerings.

The Cross *chic lifestyle boutique* `6 C4`
141 Portland Road, W11 • 020 7727 6760
Open 11–5:30 Mon–Sat

This unassuming, white-painted boutique attracts devoted fashion folk. The ground floor is packed with pretty home accessories, cult-brand toiletries, children's clothes and toys, while downstairs there are feminine separates from European and US designers such as Ann-Louise Roswald, Anna Sui and Rozae Nichols.

Rellik *vintage designer gear* `6 C1`
8 Golborne Road, W10 • 020 8962 0089
Open 10–6 Tue–Sat

This is an outpost of fabulous vintage in a wasteland of housing estates (the name plays on the monstrous Trellick Tower opposite, and spells "killer" backwards). London fashion celebrities are often spotted scanning the 1970s Liberty-print frocks and accessories by Zandra Rhodes, Vivienne Westwood and others.

Chain Stores

Global fashion chains rub shoulders on every major shopping street in the capital, but there are some British labels that stand out from the crowd. Popular **Jigsaw** bridges the gap between budget and designer, with well-made, feminine womenswear. Younger, hipper and cultivating an irreverent image with its double-entendre name is **FCUK**, which offers high-quality casual clothes for both sexes. The **Karen Millen** empire has built on the enduring success of her sharp, sexy suits and figure-flattering dresses. And let's not forget good old **Marks & Spencer**: as well as its excellent lingerie ranges, it has harnessed designer talent to great effect in its Autograph and Per Una collections. For individual shop details, *see pp222–5*.

Saloon *style shop* `4 A4`

23 Arlington Way, EC1 • 020 7278 4497
» www.saloonshop.co.uk
Open 11–7 Mon, Wed–Fri, 11–6 Tue, noon–6 Sat

Unusual patterns and colours are the unifying factors in the medley of stock at this boutique. There are clothes by independent designers, handmade jewellery, Marimekko homewares, unusual stationery and one-off pieces by product designers.

Lara Bohinc 107 *super-chic jewellery* `5 E5`

51 Hoxton Square, N1 • 020 7684 1465
» www.larabohinc107.co.uk Open 10–6:30 Mon–Fri only

Slovenian-born designer Bohinc creates unusual jewellery in precious metals ranging from delicate, finely detailed pieces to dramatic geometric styles. Her store is the epitome of arty chic, set in ground-breaking designer Alexander McQueen's former studio next to the cool White Cube Gallery.

Inflate *inflatables & more for the home* `4 A5`

28 Exmouth Market, EC1 • 020 7713 9096
» www.inflate.co.uk Open 10–6 Mon–Fri only

A nifty line in blow-up goods – ranging from egg cups to light shades – is presented alongside innovative items in other media, such as a squidgy, drip-moulded plastic toast rack. The shop also sells a perfectly round beanbag that you can shape to your body using a vacuum cleaner.

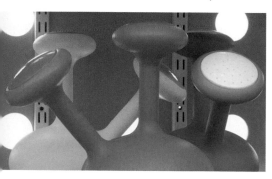

Hoxton Boutique *edgy urban chic* `5 E5`

2 Hoxton Street, N1 • 020 7684 2083
» www.hoxtonboutique.co.uk
Open 10–6 Mon–Fri, 11–5 Sat, noon–5 Sun

This boutique fits in well with Hoxton's painfully hip bars. As well as urbanwear by cutting-edge designers such as Peter Jensen and House of Jazz, there's the shop's own label, characterized by stretchy black and printed pieces with a punky feel.

Magma *modern design bookshop* `10 A1`

117–19 Clerkenwell Road, EC1 • 020 7242 9503
» www.magmabooks.com Open 10–7 Mon–Sat

Colourful covers line the walls of this art and design bookshop, which has a leather sofa for relaxed browsing. As well as works on graphic design, advertising and photography, there are avant-garde illustrated books that are definitely not for kids, hip stationery and many obscure magazines. *(See also p62.)*

Wink *young hipsters' essentials* `11 F1`
20 Hanbury Street, E1 • 020 7655 4820
» www.winkclothes.co.uk Open noon–7 daily

Tucked away on a Brick Lane side street is this trendy
boutique selling laid-back, club-friendly fashion for
both sexes – perfect for nearby Hoxton's hip nightspots.
Typical stock includes the Maggie line by Zakee
Shariff and witty, hand-printed Ts, sweatshirts and
underwear by many other young designers.

Story *unique shop-cum-gallery* `11 F1`
4 Wilkes Street, E1 • 020 7377 0313
Open 1–7 daily

In a lovely period street, this extraordinary retail space
looks like a contemporary gallery and sells an
interesting mix of items. Immaculate vintage frocks,
antique furniture, reclaimed hotel and airline linen,
and simply packaged natural toiletries are set among
beautiful dried leaves and shells.

Artcadia *printed wall hangings* `11 F1`
108 Commercial St, E1 • 020 7426 0733
» www.artcadia.co.uk
Open 10–5:30 Mon–Fri, 10:30–6 Sun, closed Sat

Artcadia's digital prints are an easy way to give a
room instant contemporary cred. Buy "off the peg" in
the gallery or choose from a wide range of up-to-date
patterns and images, from groovy abstracts to
flowers, printed up on any size of canvas.

A Gold *British foodstuffs* `11 E1`
42 Brushfield Street, E1 • 020 7247 2487
Open 11–8 Mon–Fri, 11–6 Sun, closed Sat

This wonderful old shop near Spitalfields Market sells
traditional British foods, many in attractive old-
fashioned packaging. Wild boar pancetta from Cumbria,
Stinking Bishop cheese from Gloucestershire, Yorkshire
Brack (fruitbread), English wine and honey made from
hives kept on a rooftop in London all make great gifts.

Cheshire Street *unusual homewares* `5 F5`
Off Brick Lane, E1 Market open Sun; shops Sat & Sun
For individual shop details, *see pp222–5*

A cluster of interesting home accessory shops has appeared on this Brick Lane sidestreet, which on Sundays is lined with market stalls selling everything from bedlinen to hardware. Most shops are only open at weekends – it's best to ring first. **Inexterior** (No. 14) sells an enticing mix of furry cushions, handmade crockery and pretty clothes. At No. 16, **Mar Mar Co** deals predominantly in colourful Scandinavian tableware and interior accessories. **Labour and Wait** (No. 18) is a wonderful source of old-fashioned British household items, from vintage watering cans, earthenware jars and clothespegs to hand-knitted Guernsey sweaters and Welsh blankets. For unique gifts, **Shelf** (No. 40) showcases modern decorative items by British and European artists, such as jokey, illustrated mugs, notebooks and tiles. Next door at **Mimi** there are handmade leather bags.

Tatty Devine *witty trinkets* `11 F1`
236 Brick Lane, E2 • 020 7739 9009
⟫⟫ www.tattydevine.com Open 10–6 Mon–Fri, 11–5 Sat & Sun

Bracelets made of colourful guitar picks, earrings that dangle tiny LPs, and tape-measure belts... Tatty Devine's ironic trashy trinkets have attained cult status. Also for sale at the design duo's shop/studio are fun, punky, printed T-shirts and arty postcards, while the walls are given over to temporary exhibitions.

Rokit *all sorts of second-hand clothes* `11 F1`
101 & 107 Brick Lane, E1 • 020 7375 3864
⟫⟫ www.rokit.co.uk Open 11–7 Mon–Fri, 10–7 Sat & Sun

From a small second-hand shop in Camden in the 80s, Rokit has expanded, with a store in Covent Garden, as well as these premises sprawling over two storefronts. The diverse stock is in great condition, encompassing jeans, leather jackets, army gear, vintage dresses, quirky accessories and customized items.

Comfort & Joy *chic & cheap boutique* `4 B3`
109 Essex Road, N1 • 020 7359 3898
Open 10:30–6 Mon–Sat

Fed up with chain-store fashion? Try this unpretentious boutique; it sells reasonably priced womenswear designed and made on the premises. Stylish without slavishly following catwalk trends, the simple clothes often sport interesting prints or subtle details such as piping or a crossover neckline.

To find out about antiques sales in London, check ⟫⟫ www.elondon.dk.com

Upper Street *furnishings & fashion*

4 B2

Islington, N1

For individual shop details, *see pp222–5*

As befits one of London's centres of affluent living, Islington has no shortage of stylish interior shops on its main street. Contemporary emporium **Aria** at Nos. 295–6 has wares for every room of the house by the likes of Philippe Starck and Alessi, while its satellite shop across the street at No. 133 stocks cards, leather notebooks, frames and understated designer bags. Heading north, **twentytwentyone** at No. 274 combines immaculate modern-classic and new pieces of furniture. **After Noah** (No. 121) stocks an irresistible jumble of vintage and vintage-style items in a barn-

like space – old-fashioned dial phones, antique metal tins, toys and retro toiletries. The empire of **Gill Wing** spans several diverse, high-quality shops: No. 182 showcases modern jewellery; the cookshop at No. 190 sells all the kitchen paraphernalia you could need, with kitschy touches such as feather-trimmed washing-up gloves; and there are Gill Wing shoe and gift shops nearby, too.

Bringing a high-fashion touch to the strip is **Scorah Pattullo** (No. 137), with footwear by big names like Miu Miu and Gucci, and intriguing boutique **Labour of Love** (No. 193), selling an assortment of items such as handmade knickers, and clothes by Visconti's grand-daughter that are inspired by classic cinema.

For more on Brick Lane and the Spitalfields area see pp160–1

Shopping ≫ ≫≫≫≫

Camden Passage *antiques & curios* **4 B3**

Cobbled lane in Islington, N1 Antiques market Wed & Sat; book market Thu. For individual shop details, *see pp224–5*

This narrow, meandering continuation of Islington High Street is jammed with antiques shops and market stalls, which are busiest on Saturdays, Wednesdays and Thursdays. En route, check out the **Rock Archive** gallery at No. 110 Islington High Street for limited-edition prints of British greats such as Paul Weller and Pete Townshend. Tiny, atmospheric shops are hidden away in the poky Pierrepont Arcade: **Caroline Carrier's** nook is piled high with 18th- and 19th-century porcelain. **Judith Lassalle** sells antique puzzles and games, and **Jubilee Photographica** deals in photographs from the 19th century onwards.

Near the junction of Charlton Place is **Origin**, for 1930s–50s furniture by the likes of Eames, and **Annie's Vintage Clothes**, which has well-preserved flapper dresses. The Victorian **Camden Head** pub is conveniently placed for mid-rummage refreshment.

Primrose Hill Nexus *village shops* **2 B2**

Regent's Park Road, NW1 For individual shop details, *see pp222–5*

An array of inviting shops nestles between the cosy cafés of Regent's Park Road, Primrose Hill's villagey main street. **Anna** at No. 126 serves the area's affluent residents a mix of fashion from designers as diverse as Betty Jackson, Orla Kiely and Maharishi, plus pieces from newly graduated talent and unusual British-made cashmere sweaters. A few doors along, compact **Primrose Hill Books** has many signed copies from local authors. There's a branch of interiors shop **Graham & Green** *(see also p85)* at No. 164, while at No. 170 **Studio Perfumery** offers seductive European scents from Acqua di Parma, L'Artisan Perfumeur, Serge Lutens and others. Around the corner at No. 13 Princess Road, **Rachel Skinner** sells exquisite hats, ranging from trimmed, updated trilbies and cloches for everyday wear to fabulous one-off feathered or floral creations for Ascot and weddings.

Oxo Tower Wharf *craft studios*

`10 A4`

Bargehouse Street, SE1 • 020 7401 2255
>> www.oxotower.co.uk Open 11–6 Tue–Sat
For individual shop details, *see p224*

This London landmark on the South Bank is a hotbed of creativity, housing over 30 designers' studios. The stylish **Oxo Tower Restaurant, Brasserie and Bar** *(see p54)* commands great river views at the top.

There's a diverse assortment of interesting goods, including jewellery, fashion, accessories and textiles. Don't miss funky handmade children's clothes by **Bunny London** (worn by Madonna's little material girl Lourdes). **Black+Blum** offers quirky, affordable designs, such as a lamp in the shape of a figure (the lightbulb) reading a book (the shade), and a rubber doorstop in the shape of a man pushing the door open. **Bodo Sperlein** specializes in elegant bone china and sculptural lighting. Hip duo **Odie & Amanda** design bold hand-printed dresses, slinky tops and tailored tweeds.

Lower Marsh/The Cut *hidden gems*

`10 A5`

Roads behind Waterloo Station, SE1
For individual shop details, *see pp219–25*

There's still something of old-fashioned London in Lower Marsh, a slender side road that feels a world away from all the pomp and ceremony by the Thames on the other side of Waterloo. The nostalgia is especially strong in shops such as **Radio Days** (a real joy to browse at No. 87) and **What the Butler Wore** (No. 131), both of which sell a well-selected range of vintage clothing of the mid- to late 20th century.

The small daily market deals mostly in cheap fashions and CDs. In contrast, **Grammex** at No. 25, is a refined shop for classical records and CDs. Cafés around here offer fry-ups, sushi and Cuban food. Over on The Cut is the excellent **Calder Bookshop** (No. 51). This publisher has an impressive list of 20th-century literary heavyweights, including all the main works of Samuel Beckett, and the shop is a venue for talks and poetry readings.

art &
architecture

Some of the world's most treasured cultural artifacts and paintings are gathered in London's blockbuster museums and grand mansions. The city's architecture is a thrilling ad hoc mix of medievalism, stately classicism and dynamic bursts of modernism. And counterbalancing the historical heavyweights is a thriving contemporary art scene, centred on East London.

Somerset House *a treasury of culture* `9 H3`

Strand, WC2 • 020 7845 4600
>> www.somerset-house.org.uk
Galleries open 10–6 daily (last entry 5:15)

A stately building set around a grand courtyard, Somerset House contains three galleries. Gloriously free of crowds, the **Courtauld Institute of Art Gallery** numbers some formidable Impressionist and Post-Impressionist paintings among its superb collection: Gauguin's *Nevermore*, Manet's *Bar at the Folies-Bergère* and Van Gogh's *Self Portrait with Bandaged Ear*, to name a few. It also has some splendid early Flemish and Italian paintings, including Fra Angelico's *Man of Sorrows* and Quentin Metsys's sublime *Virgin and Child with Angels*.

The **Hermitage Rooms** echo the style of the famous namesake museum in St Petersburg and are used to exhibit changing displays on loan from the enormous Hermitage collection. The **Gilbert Collection** was opened in 2000. It focuses on the decorative arts,

with a glittering array of gilt snuff boxes, European silverware and jewel-encrusted objets d'art.

Reminiscent of a European piazza, the courtyard at the centre of Somerset House sparkles with illuminated fountains on summer evenings. In mid-July it is used as the venue for a series of outdoor gigs, with artists such as Goldfrapp, Röyksopp and Calexico performing. Most spectacularly, an outdoor ice rink is installed in the courtyard in winter (late Nov to late Jan), offering skating sessions to the public.

The south wing of the building is home to a plush French restaurant **The Admiralty** (020 7845 4646), which also runs a year-round deli/café and the Summer Café on the River Terrace. The terrace runs the length of the building on the Thames side; you can walk along it whether you've come here for a meal, a coffee or simply for the views. In summer the river is largely obscured by plane trees, but to the east you can glimpse St Paul's, and to the west are the Gothic towers of Westminster. **Adm to galleries**

Theatre Museum *behind the scenes* `9 G3`
Russell Street, WC2 • 020 7943 4700
» www.theatremuseum.org Open 10–6 Tue–Sun

A rambling foray into the past and future of theatre in London. The work of theatrical pioneers such as Edward Gordon Craig and Peter Brook is brought to the fore through archive film, set designs and models. Enthusiastic guides tell stories about famous performers, and there are make-up demonstrations.

Photographers' Gallery *pics & books* `9 F3`
5 & 8 Great Newport Street, WC2 • 020 7831 1772
» www.photonet.org.uk Open 11–6 Mon–Sat, noon–6 Sun

Occupying two sites on a short road – one with a vegetarian café, the other with an excellent bookshop – the gallery presents London's most concentrated programme of photography exhibitions. Some shows are devoted to emerging talent, others to high-profile names such as Robert Capa and André Kertesz.

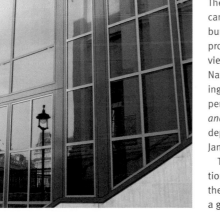

Sainsbury Wing of the National Gallery *the oldest Masters* `9 F4`
Trafalgar Square, SW1 • 020 7747 2885
Crivelli's Garden (restaurant) 020 7747 2869
» www.nationalgallery.org.uk Open 10–6 daily (to 9pm Wed)

The East Wing and main rooms of the National Gallery can be horribly crowded. By comparison, the Sainsbury Wing is relatively quiet, and its modern design provides the perfect lighting conditions for close viewing of the oldest and most precious works in the National's collection – the Early Renaissance paintings. Among the greats on display are Leonardo's pensive drawing of *The Virgin and Child with St Anne and St John the Baptist* (c. 1500), Botticelli's mighty depiction of post-coitus *Venus and Mars* (c. 1485) and Jan van Eyck's vivid *Arnolfini Portrait* (1434).

The basement is the setting for temporary exhibitions. The first floor has a micro-gallery for referencing the entire collection via computer terminals, and also a good restaurant with views across Trafalgar Square.

» *Admission to the Tate and National galleries, V&A and British Museum is free (but donations are welcome)*

National Portrait Gallery

St Martin's Place, WC2 • 020 7306 0055

»» www.npg.org.uk Open 10–6 daily (to 9pm Thu & Fri)

A large assembly of images of prominent Britons, the collection includes the only known contemporaneous portrait of Shakespeare, fantastic miniatures by John Hilliard, and photographs by Cecil Beaton and David Bailey. For a chronological tour, start at the top and work down. The rooftop restaurant has great views.

ICA *institute of contemporary art*

The Mall, SW1 • 020 7930 3647

»» www.ica.org.uk Galleries open noon–7:30 daily

Once the rebellious upstart to the Royal Academy's stuffy old order, the ICA is an institution itself these days. It retains a sense of adventure, however, mixing well-known artists with group shows of the young pretenders. It also has a small cinema, a funky café-bar (open to 1am Tue–Sat) and a great bookshop. **Adm**

Royal Sights

Historic residences and other places connected with the British monarchy are magnets for visitors. Unfortunately, this means that many royal sights are over-crowded and overtly touristy.

Of the palaces, **Hampton Court** in southwest London is the most satisfying: a vast Tudor estate set off by 60 acres of beautiful gardens banking the Thames. By contrast **Buckingham Palace** offers merely a perfunctory excursion around a handful of State Rooms. The neighbouring **Queens Gallery** is well worth a visit though; it was revamped in 2002 and displays selections from one of the world's greatest collections of paintings. At the western edge of Kensington Gardens, **Kensington Palace** is an attractive building and has the wonderful **Orangery** (*see p170*), but contains only a collection of ceremonial dresses. (Some belonged to the late Princess Diana, which brings in a bit of a crowd.)

The **Tower of London** is awash with the trappings of tourism (ice-cream vans, toy Beefeaters). It contains the glitzy Crown Jewels, which, in a measure designed to control the crowds, you are obliged to view from a slow-moving travelator. Nevertheless, the buildings and attendant history are deserving of their World Heritage Site status.

Westminster Abbey offers a fascinating insight into British architecture and sovereignty, but in summer the queues stretch out into Parliament Square from early morning. There are free organ recitals in the abbey at 5:45pm on Sundays (the day when it is otherwise closed to visitors).

Nearby **St Margaret's Church** (*see p99*) provides a good alternative to the abbey. Other less crowded sights with a regal air include the **Banqueting House** (*see p99*) and, in southeast London, **Eltham Palace** (*see p113*) and the **Queen's House** (*see p112*). For location details of all these sights, *see p226*.

Sir John Soane's Museum   `9 H2`

13 Lincoln's Inn Fields, WC2 • 020 7405 2107
>> www.soane.org Open 10–5 Tue–Sat (to 9pm first Tue of the
month); tours at 2pm (first come, first served)

Sir John Soane (1753–1837) was a renowned architect
in his day, and the interior of this unique, labyrinthine
house is a testament to his passion for the Classical
world. On the face of it, you are entering a Georgian
terraced house, but Soane's rebuilding throws into
disarray the usual neatness of a Georgian interior. A
dark, warm corridor gives way to a staircase spiralling
up three floors. A succession of skylights – often
glazed in yellow to bathe sculptures in what Soane
perceived as a Mediterranean light – illuminates the
jumbled rooms. At every turn you come across
fragments of ancient sculptures and architectural
mouldings. Among these are glimpses of an alternative London – beautifully drafted, but unfulfilled
plans for betempled bridges, a royal palace for Green
Park and a Neo-Classical Houses of Parliament.

The ingenious design of the house reaches its high
point in the Picture Room, formerly the stableyard of
the house next door. As Soane's painting collection
grew, space became a problem, and so he installed
hinged screens in the place of solid walls. An attendant will open up panels to reveal works by Turner and
Piranesi, and the complete set of original paintings
by Hogarth which make up *The Rake's Progress*. In
the New Picture Room (added after Soane's death) is
one of Canaletto's finest works, *View towards Santa
Maria della Salute, Venice*.

RIBA   *architectural resource*   `8 D1`

66 Portland Place, W1 • 020 7580 5533
>> www.riba.org Open 9–6:30 Mon–Fri, 9–5 Sat

The Royal Institute of British Architects puts on a
range of shows, including homages to architectural
greats. The RIBA building itself is a rather lovely
1930s Deco-Classical hybrid, with a café-restaurant
and an excellent bookshop, where you can buy all
manner of books on architecture and design.

>> *RIBA sells a cheap fold-out map by Architectural Dialogue, which pinpoints modern architecture in London*

Art & Architecture »»»»

9 F2

Great Court & Reading Room, British Museum *entrance to the treasure house*

Great Russell St, WC1 • 020 7323 8000
»» www.thebritishmuseum.ac.uk Museum open 10–5:30 daily (to 8:30 Thu & Fri); Great Court open to 11pm Thu–Sat

Architect Norman Foster's reworking of the British Museum's central courtyard has created a vast foyer beneath a curving glass roof at the heart of the building. Like a new city square, this is a great meeting area, with cafés surrounding the gleaming rotunda of the famous Reading Room. This is now a reference library for the BM's collection, and also offers the best free Internet access in London. A staircase winds around the rotunda, leading up to the Court Restaurant, magnificently set at the level of the building's pediments and architrave. From the courtyard, signs point off north, south, east and west to the various departments of the British Museum's massive collection of artifacts – from Africa, Asia, Egypt, the Americas, Europe, Greece and Rome.

Dr Johnson's House *literary pad*

10 A2

17 Gough Square, EC4 • 020 7353 3745
»» www.drjh.dircon.co.uk Open 11–5 Mon–Sat (to 5:30 summer)

The house where the doctor compiled the world's first proper English dictionary in the mid-18th century was dutifully restored in the 20th. After a look around one of the few buildings of its kind to survive, head round the corner to one of Johnson's favoured watering holes: Ye Olde Cheshire Cheese on Fleet Street. **Adm**

Temple Church *secret history*

10 A3

Inner Temple, off Fleet St, EC4 • 020 7353 3470
»» www.templechurch.com Open Wed–Sun (usually)

This honey-stoned pot of a building dates from the 12th century when it was the church of the Knights Templar *(see p168)*. Restored after World War II bomb damage, it has a round form (unusual in Britain) that echoes the Church of the Holy Sepulchre in Jerusalem. There are free organ recitals at 1:15pm on Wednesdays.

St Margaret's Church *stained glass* `15 G1`
Sanctuary, SW1
>> www.westminster-abbey.org/stmargarets
Open 9:30–3:45 Mon–Fri, 9:30–1:45 Sat, 2–5 Sun

Though often overlooked, St Margaret's Church contains an amazing variety of stained glass. Especially notable are John Piper's abstract designs of 1966, and fragments of the 19th-century Caxton Window (honouring the pioneer of printing) on the north aisle.

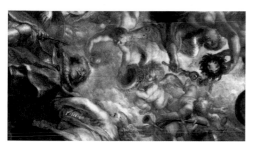

Banqueting House *grandiose building* `9 G5`
Whitehall, SW1 • 0870 751 5178
>> www.hrp.org.uk Open 10–5 Mon–Sat

An epic, heavenly Rubens ceiling and the architecture of Inigo Jones (the artist who brought Renaissance classicism to Britain) lure visitors. The video and audio tour are overly pompous, so it's better to visit the place as part of the lively Old Westminster tour offered by Original London Walks *(see p231)*. **Adm**

Tate Britain *more space for British art* `15 G3`
Millbank, SW1 • 020 7887 8000
>> www.tate.org.uk Open 10–5:50 daily

Ever since more than half of the Tate's collection sailed off down the Thames to set up home in Tate Modern, the original gallery has had to work hard to retain its audience. This it has done with aplomb – sprucing up the interior, creating more viewing space and focusing on British art. There is now more room to wander an excellent, wide-ranging collection, taking in the homely landscapes of Constable, the world's largest assemblage of Turners (grouped in the Clore Gallery), the landscape-influenced modernism of Hepworth and Moore, and the savage, existential paintings of Francis Bacon.

More up-to-date works can be seen in the Art Now spaces, one of which is used especially for video work. There's a good (and pricey) restaurant in the basement, where the dining area is surrounded by a fantastical mural depicting the "pursuit of rare foods".

>> *Tate Britain hosts the annual Turner Prize for contemporary art, from October to December*

Art & Architecture

The Art Boat *a waterborne Hirst* `15 G3`
Millbank Pier to Bankside Pier Operates 10am–5pm;
15-minute journey every 40 mins in each direction

Sporting Damien Hirst's trademark coloured dots, the
Art Boat zips between Tates Britain and Modern. The
cost includes as many trips as you like in a day, and
the pier at Tate Modern is useful for other sights – the
Globe *(see p130)*, St Paul's (via the Millennium Bridge),
Borough Market *(see p163)* and Southwark Cathedral.

Sackler Wing, RA *high-tech gallery space* `9 E4`
Burlington House, Piccadilly, W1 • 020 7300 8000
>> www.royalacademy.org.uk Open 10–6 daily (to 10pm Fri)

While the main gallery of the Royal Academy puts on
blockbuster shows (Monet, the Summer Exhibition),
the Norman Foster-designed Sackler Wing offers greater
variety and more surprises. Recent exhibitions include
Flemish manuscripts, Tamara de Lempicka, and the
minimalist landscapes of William Nicholson. **Adm**

St James's Piccadilly *Wren's joy* `9 E4`
197 Piccadilly, W1 • 020 7734 4511
>> www.st-james-piccadilly.org Open 8–7 daily

This Wren church of 1684 is said to have been the
architect's favourite. It's a little haven from the busy
street outside, with a beautifully structured interior
and astounding 1680s wood carvings by Grinling
Gibbons. There's also an energetic programme of
events, including recitals most afternoons at 1:10pm.

Wren's London

Christopher Wren's influence on London stems from
the Great Fire of 1666, after which he was put in
charge of creating 51 new City churches and a new
cathedral, **St Paul's**. The ceiling and crypts of the
cathedral are well worth viewing (8:30–4 Mon–Sat;
adm). A beautiful wooden model in the crypt reveals
Wren's original, more Classical design for St Paul's.

St Stephen Walbrook provided a prototype for
St Paul's dome, and the steeple of **St Mary-le-Bow**
shows Wren's appreciation for the Classical architectural orders. **St Bride's** on Fleet Street, meanwhile,
provided inspiration, it is said, for the familiar
tiered wedding cake. For location details, *see p226*.

Original London Walks *(see p231)* do a Wren tour
on Tuesday afternoons.

The Wallace Collection *Old Masters* `8 C2`

Hertford House, Manchester Square, W1 • 020 7563 9500
➤➤ www.the-wallace-collection.org.uk
Open 10–5 Mon–Sat, noon–5 Sun

A stately Georgian house is the setting for this outstanding collection, left to the nation in 1897. Highlights include Frans Hals's hugely famous, flamboyantly moustached *Laughing Cavalier*, and a touching painting by Rembrandt of his son Titus. Two brilliant portraits by Van Dyck hang close by. There are also several lively painted sketches by Rubens, including an *Adoration of the Magi* and the celebrated *Rainbow Landscape*.

The Wallace Collection also celebrates the artistry found in the weaponry of Europe and the Middle East in past centuries, and includes a pair of pistols with stocks intricately carved with images of Samson and Hercules. The glass-roofed central courtyard is where you'll find Café Bagatelle, a very civilized and relaxing spot for afternoon tea.

Serpentine Gallery *contemporary art & architecture* `7 H5`

Kensington Gardens, W2 • 020 7402 6075
➤➤ www.serpentinegallery.org Open 10–6 daily

Located in a former tea house in Kensington Gardens, the Serpentine has built a reputation for putting on solo shows by some of the big guns of contemporary art. Each year, moreover, a different architect is invited to create a one-off summer pavilion in the grounds just outside the gallery – Zaha Hadid, Daniel Libeskind and Oscar Niemeyer have created brilliant structures in previous years.

Brompton Oratory *Catholic encounter* `14 A2`

Brompton Rd, SW7 • 020 7808 0900
➤➤ www.brompton-oratory.org.uk

Built in the 1880s but looking like a product of 17th-century Italy, the Oratory's façade gives way to a full-on Baroque interior, with no surface escaping ornamentation. An arched and many-domed roof provides a canvas for heavenly images. At ground level, dark confessionals occupy every corner.

Art & Architecture

Exhibition Road *museum row*   `13 H2`

Science Museum • 020 7942 4454
>> www.sciencemuseum.org.uk Open 10–6 daily
Natural History Museum • 020 7942 5000
>> www.nhm.ac.uk Open 10–5:50 Mon–Sat, 11–5:50 Sun
V&A • 020 7942 2000
>> www.vam.ac.uk Open 10–5.45 daily (to 10pm Wed)

Three very different museums, each of world renown, lie at the Cromwell Road end of Exhibition Road.

Animatronic dinosaurs and interactive exhibits in the Earth Galleries draw hordes of families to the **Natural History Museum**. Visitors of a more artistic leaning may appreciate more the building itself, a wonderful creation by Alfred Waterhouse, with carvings of living species on the west side, extinct species on the east. Meanwhile, anyone interested in technology will enjoy the neighbouring **Science Museum**, not least for Charles Babbage's Difference Engine of 1832, a vastly complicated automatic calculator that's often been described as the world's first computer.

With fewer child-pleasing features, the **Victoria and Albert Museum** (V&A) is less crowded than its neighbours and all the more enjoyable for this. In particular, the Pirelli Garden courtyard and the beautiful Morris and Gamble Rooms (where there's a small café) are delightfully restful places. Elsewhere in the museum are a series of monumental cartoons by Raphael; medieval religious art; the 20th Century Galleries, which focus on product design; a brilliant Photography Gallery; and the British Galleries, which feature fashion, furniture and interiors from 1500 to 1900.

Linley Sambourne House   `13 E1`

18 Stafford Terrace, W8 • 020 7602 3316
>> www.rbkc.gov.uk/linleysambournehouse Tours Sat & Sun

Home makeovers are nothing new, as proved by this beautifully preserved 1870s townhouse, former home of the noted *Punch* cartoonist. Glazed window boxes reflect the Victorian passion for conservatories, while bare patches behind paintings cruelly reveal the Sambournes' frugal use of wallpaper. **Adm**

Leighton House Museum `12 D1`

12 Holland Park Rd, W14 • 020 7602 3316
>> www.rbkc.gov.uk/LeightonHouseMuseum
Open 11–5:30 Wed–Mon

This wonderfully idiosyncratic studio-house was built for the fashionable Victorian painter Frederick, Lord Leighton. Mirroring the success of his career, the house was aggrandized in the late 19th century, when its defining feature, the Arab Hall, was added. This lovely space has a pool with a tiny tinkling fountain, and walls decorated with deep turquoise tiles from Damascus.

The back rooms, overlooking a pleasant garden (open Apr–Sep), are hung with paintings by the main Pre-Raphaelite players – Millais, Burne-Jones, Waterhouse – as well as Leighton's exotic and incredibly detailed Oriental and Classical scenes. Upstairs, light pours into the studio and salon. Here, among paintings of varied success, are small landscape studies and preparatory sketches, which are some of Leighton's most enduring works. **Adm**

St Bartholomew the Great `10 B2`

West Smithfield, EC1 • 020 7606 5171
>> www.greatstbarts.com Open Tue–Sun exc during services

Your imaginative powers are called upon to fully appreciate this 12th-century Norman priory, London's oldest parish church. Much of the nave is now an open churchyard, and the former entrance door is now a gateway leading on to Smithfield Market. But it still has a lot of atmosphere.

19 Princelet Street *a house of refuge* `11 F1`

Spitalfields, E1 • 020 7247 5352
>> www.19princeletstreet.org.uk Open occasional Sun afternoons & Refugee Week (mid-Jun); check website

Now set up as a small museum about immigration in Spitalfields, this terraced house was home to French Huguenots and, later, Jewish émigrés. Beyond the small front rooms is No. 19's most startling secret: a creaking three-storey synagogue of 1869.

Dennis Severs' House *time capsule* `11 E1`
18 Folgate Street, E1 • 020 7247 4013
» www.dennissevershouse.co.uk Open Mon evenings by candlelight (booking required) & occasional afternoons

The modern world closes behind you as you enter this terraced house in Spitalfields. The late artist Dennis Severs interpreted the history of his home by furnishing its ten rooms in ways that evoke moments (more than just periods) in its past. Each room is a still life: in the front parlour, time seems to have stopped in the 1700s, with rich pies, half-eaten fruit and glasses of wine abandoned on the table. The cold and dusty attic rooms leap straight out of the early 1900s, with silk-weaving apparatus and crumbling damp ceilings. The level of detail is extraordinary. Cracked oyster shells indicate a snack just eaten; the pungent scent of oranges, cloves and lavender fills the nostrils. Clocks chime the hour, while a sly black cat ghosts about. Only by the sight of other visitors are you reminded of the present. **Adm**

Whitechapel Gallery *contemporary art* `11 F2`
80–82 Whitechapel High Street, E1
• 020 7522 7878 (recorded info) • 020 7522 7888 (enquiries)
» www.whitechapel.org Open 11–6 Tue–Sun (to 9 Thu)

One of London's largest galleries, the Whitechapel puts on attention-grabbing exhibitions of modern and contemporary art. The history of performance art and Gerhard Richter were among recent subjects. The slick café was designed by artist Liam Gillick.

Museum of the Order of St John `10 B1`
St John's Gate, EC1 • 020 7253 6644
Tours Tue, Fri & Sat

Be sure to catch the hour-long tour that takes you down into a hidden 12th-century crypt, then up into a Tudor gatehouse. The history of the Knights of St John is fascinating and far-reaching – the Crusades, 14th-century Poll Tax Riots, Shakespeare, *The Gentleman's Magazine* and modern first-aid volunteers all appear.

Geffrye Museum *homes in history* `5 E4`
136 Kingsland Rd, E2 • 020 7739 9893
>> **www.geffrye-museum.org.uk** Open 10–5 Tue–Sat, 12–5 Sun

A row of neat little almshouses has been converted into a charming museum on the theme of English domestic interiors and gardens of the last 400 years. The Victorian rooms reach a zenith of clutter before the modern world storms in with the 1930s house. An open loft apartment represents the 1990s.

Wapping Project Space *art, industry, food*
Wapping Wall, E1 • 020 7680 2080
⊖ **Wapping**
Open noon–6 Thu–Sat (usually)

At the same time that Tate Modern was reshaping Bankside Power Station, the smaller-scale Wapping Project Space was emerging from the defunct industrial space of Wapping Hydraulic Power Station.

Brainchild of theatre director Jules Wright, WPS puts on lively shows of contemporary art, dance and music in a space that seems to have remained largely untouched since the time of its industrial death throes in the late 1970s. Bits of machinery stand idle, and sounds echo off concrete and metal surfaces.

The space works particularly well for video projections and installations: Richard Wilson (*Butterfly*, 2003), Jane Prophet (*Conductor*, 2000) and Finnish artist Elina Brotherus (*Baigneurs*, 2004) have created brilliant works here. There's an excellent restaurant too, called Wapping Food.

Victorian Cemeteries

London's great old cemeteries have a poetic equilibrium, the artistry of stonemasons jostling for space with the natural world of brambles and trees. **Highgate Cemetery** is where you'll find the lumpish bust of Karl Marx. **Kensal Green Cemetery** is home to some fanciful Egyptian-style tombs and a chapel built to look like a Greek temple.

Brompton Cemetery is a more civilized affair, with sharp paths and avenues. Like Kensal Green, it has a Neo-Classical temple; its silhouette and golden sandstone are especially striking in the evening light. The wildest cemeteries are **Abney Park** *(see p173)* and the gothic forest of **Nunhead**, where angels and crucifixes seem to sprout from ivy-clad trees. For location details, *see p226*.

>> *Highgate Cemetery can be visited with a guided tour; for details, check www.highgate-cemetery.org*

Art & Architecture

Docklands *industrial past, commercial future*
Isle of Dogs, E14 • ⊖ Canary Wharf
Museum in Docklands: West India Quay • 0870 444 3857
» www.museumindocklands.org.uk Open 10–6 daily (to 8 Wed)

From the driverless trains of the DLR to the pumped-up steel and glass commercial buildings mushrooming all around, there is something exhilarating (albeit not pretty) about Docklands. A shiny new city has all but replaced the wharfs and warehouses of the old port.

The **Museum in Docklands**, set in a beautiful brick warehouse, which once held spices, rum and cotton, tells the 2,000-year tale of London as a place of trade.

That trade continues in the multinational offices at **Canary Wharf**, served by three interconnected shopping malls (Cabot Place, Canada Place and Jubilee Place). There are many pubs and restaurants, most of them chains. Two worth seeking out are **1802**, a smart restaurant and bar next to the museum, overlooking Future Systems' lime-green footbridge; and Conran's stylish **Plateau**, on the fourth floor of Canada Place.

Estorick Collection *Futurism* `4 B1`
39 Canonbury Sq, N1 • 020 7704 9522
» www.estorickcollection.com Open 11–6 Wed–Sat, 12–5 Sun

Tucked away on a leafy backroad, this gallery is dedicated to the Italian Futurist Movement of the early 20th century. It's the perfect antidote to London's gargantuan museums, a place to quietly peruse Severinis, Boccionis and also works by Modigliani and de Chirico. The House *(see p49)* is nearby for refreshment. **Adm**

Camden Arts Centre *contemporary art*
Arkwright Road, NW3 • 020 7472 5500 • ⊖ Finchley Road
» www.camdenartscentre.org Open 10–6 Tue–Sun (to 9 Wed)

Newly refurbished, the arts centre continues to showcase influential artists and Britain's best up-and-coming talent. Art/architectural group MUF created the garden, which features a terrace that traces the "footprint" of two houses destroyed by a bomb during World War II.

Lord's *sporting traditions, modern architecture*
Wellington Road, NW8 • ◉ St John's Wood
》 www.lords.org Tours daily (020 7616 8595 to book)

Lord's is more than just a cricket ground: it is the home of the game, the keeper of its beguiling rules and the custodian of its traditions. You may be surprised, then, to discover that it also sports some leading-edge architecture. The stands surrounding the pitch are by Nicholas Grimshaw and Michael Hopkins – pioneers of High-Tech building design. In playful fashion, the Hopkins Stand has been designed to look rather like a temporary summer marquee.

The Media Centre was built in 2000 by Future Systems. This sensuous white cocoon, created with the aid of boat manufacturers, rises dramatically from the Mound end, in contrast to the stately Victoriana of Thomas Verity's Pavilion (1890) at the opposite end.

Tours of Lord's are conducted by cricket enthusiasts, and take in the ground's architecture and the MCC Museum, which charts the history of cricket.

Fenton House *17th-century traditions* `1 A4`
Windmill Hill, NW3 • 020 7435 3471
Open Apr–Oct: Sat & Sun 11–5, Wed–Fri 2–5

Set in formal gardens, this handsome 17th-century house has displays of early keyboard instruments, fine Chinese porcelain and some precious, if florid, English and Continental figurines. The Dining Room provides a splendid venue for a summer concert series of early music (eight Thursdays May–Oct). **Adm**

2 Willow Road *modern living perfected* `1 C4`
2 Willow Road, NW3 • 020 7435 6166
Apr–Oct: noon–5 Thu–Sat; Mar & Nov: noon–5 Sat

The former home of architect Ernö Goldfinger looks unprepossessing from outside, but the Modernist interior is superb. Flexible living areas, picture windows and sophisticated colour schemes are defining features. Dotted about are paintings by Henry Moore, Max Ernst and Bridget Riley. **Adm**

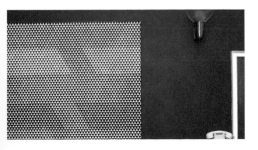

Freud Museum *the doctor's final home*
20 Maresfield Gardens, NW3 • 020 7435 2002 • ⊖ Finchley Road
» www.freud.org.uk Open noon–5 Wed–Sun

Preserved as the "Father of Psychoanalysis" left them, the library and study in Sigmund Freud's house contain a great collection of Greek, Roman, Egyptian and Oriental antiquities. But pride of place goes to the original psychoanalytical couch, with its plumped-up cushions and richly patterned Persian rug. **Adm**

Kenwood House *Masters on the Heath* `1 C1`
Hampstead Heath, NW3 • 020 8348 1286
Open Apr–Oct 10–6 daily; Nov–Mar 10–4 daily

Architect Robert Adam's cream Neo-Classical house at the top of Hampstead Heath provides a stately home for the Iveagh Bequest. The often-overlooked collection includes fine paintings by Turner, Reynolds and Gainsborough, as well as a masterful late Rembrandt *Self-Portrait* and Vermeer's *Guitar Player*.

Keats House *home of the young Romantic* `1 C5`
Keats Grove, NW3 • 020 7435 2062
» www.keatshouse.org.uk
Open mid-Apr–Oct: 12–5 Tue–Sun; Nov–Mar: 12–4 Tue–Sun

Romantic poet John Keats lived in this genteel house in 1818–20, hoping that the good air and waters of Hampstead would alleviate his tuberculosis. Letters, possessions and manuscripts tell the tale of a sensitive writer who died young. **Adm**

London's Georgian Squares
The most elegant chapter of London's expansion happened during the Georgian era (1714–1830), when homogeneous Neo-Classical streetscapes were created, often set around garden squares. Many of these squares are open to the public. Among the best are the quietish **Golden Square** (Map 9 E3) and thronged **Soho Square** (9 F2); **Berkeley Square** (8 D4) for its magnificent plane trees; **St James's Square** (9 E4) for its exceptional Georgian townhouse surrounds; **Bloomsbury Square** (9 G2) for its jollity; and **Queen's Square** (9 G1) for its tucked-away charm and enticing pubs and cafés on Cosmos Place. Many other squares to which access is normally restricted are open to all on the annual **London Garden Squares Day** *(see p10)*.

Saatchi Gallery *home of 1990s Brit art* `9 H5`
County Hall, SE1 • Info 020 7823 2363 • Tickets 020 7928 8195
>> www.saatchi-gallery.co.uk Open 10–8 daily (to 10 Fri & Sat)

Saatchi's move to County Hall has brought the gallery
closer to the cultural life of the South Bank, albeit in
a spot that's surrounded by games arcades and fast-
food outlets. However, the collection is impressive,
focusing on contemporary British artists, such as the
Chapman brothers and Tracey Emin. **Adm**

Jerwood Space *hot competition* `10 B5`
171 Union Street, SE1 • 020 7654 0171
>> www.jerwoodspace.co.uk Open Tue–Sun afternoons

The programming at this contemporary art gallery
is based on three annual prizes for painting,
drawing and sculpture. Such divisions may seem
traditional, but the work is cutting edge, and The
Jerwood Artists Platform always seeks to promote
less-established British artists.

Hayward Gallery *avant-garde shows* `9 H4`
South Bank Centre, SE1 • 020 7960 4242
>> www.hayward.org.uk Open 10–6 daily (to 8 Tue & Wed)

Arguably London's premier gallery for temporary exhibitions, particularly of contemporary art, the Hayward
is a versatile space. It was built in the late 1960s in a
Brutalist style, and in recent years the occupiers have
been learning to love it again. The interior has been
stripped back to the original rough concrete surface
that, when empty, gives it the appearance of a multi-
storey car park. Brutal it may be, but it is a provoking
alternative to the white-box look of many galleries.

Paintings don't necessarily look their best here, but
the Hayward is an exceptional space for modern
sculpture and multimedia installations. Video works
such as Douglas Gordon's *24-Hour Psycho* and Bruce
Nauman's *Anthro/Socio* have been highly acclaimed.
The new foyer, incorporating a glass pavilion by Dan
Graham, houses touch-sensitive screens playing a
mix of cartoons and art videos. **Adm**

Art & Architecture

Old Operating Theatre *scary surgery* `10 D5`
9a St Thomas's Street, SE1 • 020 7955 4791
>> www.thegarret.org.uk Open 10:30–5 daily

Accessed via a Herb Garret that lulls you with the idea of quaint botanical potions, the operating theatre of 1822 comes as a shock. An oversize chopping board is set on a stage surrounded by tiered seats for students and onlookers, while in an adjacent room is a vast array of knives and amputation saws. **Adm**

Design Museum *modern design institute* `11 F5`
28 Shad Thames, SE1 • 020 7403 6933
>> www.designmuseum.org Open 10–5:45 daily (to 9 Fri)

Temporary exhibitions take in the breadth of modern designers, from 19th-century engineer Isambard Kingdom Brunel to music-industry graphic artist Peter Saville. On the top floor there is a permanent collection of mass-produced design classics – check out how many you have owned. **Adm**

South London Gallery *big players/new blood*
65 Peckham Road, SE5 • 020 7703 6120
☺ Elephant & Castle, then bus 171
>> www.southlondongallery.org
Open 11–6 Tue, Wed & Fri, 11–7 Thu, 2–6 Sat & Sun

This one-hall gallery stages exhibitions of contemporary artists. International names have included Sherrie Levine and Christian Boltanski; home-grown talents have included Tracey Emin and Sarah Lucas.

Independent & Commercial Galleries
The most exciting galleries for up-and-coming artists are mainly in East London. There are clusters in Hoxton *(see p162)*, including **White Cube** and **The Agency,** and near Victoria Park (**Matt's Gallery, Chisenhale, The Showroom** and **Wilkinson Gallery**). There's also a small gallery, **The Approach,** above a friendly pub of the same name. In Central London, on Heddon Street, are **Sadie Coles HQ** and **Gagosian.** Gagosian has also opened a space on Britannia Street at King's Cross. There are many galleries around Cork Street, but don't miss **Stephen Friedman** on neighbouring Old Burlington Street. One of the best is out on its own: the **Lisson** near Marylebone Station. Try **www.newexhibitions.com** for information. For location details, *see p225.*

Tate Modern *power plant of modern art*
Bankside, SE1 • 020 7887 8000
» www.tate.org.uk Open 10–6 Sun–Thu, 10–10 Fri & Sat

Since it opened in 2000, Tate Modern has been spectacularly popular. A large part of this success is due to the building itself: a monolithic, brown-brick power station transformed into an elegant Modernist gallery by architects Herzog & de Meuron.

The vast Turbine Hall is the dramatic focus of the building, installations (each in situ for six months) have been created by artists such as Louise Bourgeois, Juan Muñoz and Olafur Eliasson. The dimensions of the hall are so great – it's 155 m (500 ft) long by 35 m (115 ft) – that works have been increasingly theatrical in an attempt to fill the void. In *Weather Project* (2004), for example, Olafur Eliasson filled the hall with orange light from a giant "sun", covered the entire ceiling with mirrors and pumped in steamy clouds.

The permanent collection is relatively modest for the size of building, occupying just two of the floors. Controversially, it is arranged thematically, with titles such as Nude/Action/Body to throw together the work of Matisse, Rodin, Bruce Nauman and other giants of modern art. This approach may have its drawbacks, but it's a refreshing way to view the works of art, giving the exhibition the feel of a contemporary group show rather than a place of academia.

Tate Modern has an increasingly strong quota of video work, including Bill Viola's monumental *Five Angels for the Millennium* and Paul McCarthy's seminal *Rocky* (1976), in which the artist beats himself up and collapses into a naked heap. Amid this vastness and energy, it is good to know that small paintings can still hold their own, as exemplified by Picasso's exquisite *Girl in a Chemise* (1905).

The Level 4 galleries are given over to invariably brilliant temporary exhibitions, for which an entrance fee is charged. There is a moderately priced café on Level 2, offering good food and efficient, friendly service. The café on Level 7 gets extremely busy – if you want the views, visit before or after the lunchtime rush (12:30–2:30pm) and be prepared to wait.

» *As well as offering free guided tours daily, the Tate Modern has also introduced Palm Pilot tours*

Art & Architecture »»

Dulwich Picture Gallery *fine paintings*
Gallery Road, Dulwich Village, SE21 • 020 8693 5254
🚇 West Dulwich
»» www.dulwichpicturegallery.org.uk
Open 10–5 Tue–Fri, 11–5 Sat & Sun

Leafy Dulwich is home to a small and perfectly formed collection of European Old Master paintings from the 17th and 18th centuries. The gallery was purpose-built in 1811 by Sir John Soane *(see p97)* and is illuminated mainly by natural light entering through lantern windows – a Soane innovation that has been much copied. This creates a perfect, even light in which to compare the artistic forces of Italy, France, the Netherlands and England.

The quality of the work is extremely high, as exemplified by Guido Reni's *St Sebastian*: two other versions of the composition exist, one in the Prado, the other in the Louvre. There's also a delicate little Rembrandt (*Portrait of Jacob III de Gheyn*), and works by Raphael, Poussin, Rubens, Hogarth and Gainsborough, including the instantly recognisable *Unknown Couple in a Landscape*. There are many wonderful smaller discoveries too, such as a recently restored *River Landscape* by Aelbert Cuyp, perfectly described as a "tiny limpid masterpiece" in the wall text. Restoration included removing a herd of cows that had been added in the 1800s.

A recent overhaul of the gallery by architect Rick Mather has added a glazed cloister and a moderately priced café-restaurant. Dulwich itself centres around a pleasant park and the Crown & Greyhound pub. **Adm**

Queen's House *architectural delight* `16 C2`
Greenwich Park, SE10 • 020 8853 0035
»» www.nmm.ac.uk Open 10–5 daily

Besides some fine furniture and a few paintings of note, the triumph of Queen's House is its architecture. This is the work of Inigo Jones (1573–1652), and in details such as the Tulip spiral staircase you can see not only the Classicism that this building precipitated in Britain, but also a foreshadowing of Modernism.

To find the lesser-known sights of London, check »» **www.elondon.dk.com**

Eltham Palace *medieval meets Art Deco*
Court Yard, SE9 • 020 8294 2548 • 🚇 Eltham
➤➤ www.elthampalace.org.uk
Open 10–6 Wed, Thu, Fri & Sun (10–4 in winter)

Having fallen ungracefully from its status as one of Henry VIII's hunting residences to become a humble barn in the 18th century, salvation finally came for Eltham Palace in the 1930s. By then, all that remained were the Banqueting Hall and parts of the garden, including the moat bridge. Arts patron Stephen Courtauld decided to restore the Hall and build a new, and very modern, country house around it.

Designed by Seely and Paget, the 1930s house is a seductive piece of Art Deco styling, with sweeping, light-filled rooms; curving walls lined with maple, aspen and sycamore panelling; and ocean-liner style furnishings. It's easy to envisage the sophisticated, Martini-sipping party set who would have weekended with the gregarious Courtaulds. Stories abound about Jonggy, the pet ring-tailed lemur who favoured the Flower Room when he wasn't up in his bunk. **Adm**

Along the River

It's taken a while, but the Thames shows clear signs of having undergone a renaissance. Its waters are cleaner than they've been for several centuries, the riverbank is alive with culture *(see p164)* and increasing numbers of boats now ply up and down the river. The waterway is a brilliant means of traversing the city along its east-west axis: the Houses of Parliament show their most elegant side, the views of the bridges are unparalleled, and the many stop-off points are situated right outside some of London's most attractive sights.

The **Art Boat** *(see p100)* ferries up and down the river between **Tate Britain** *(see p99)* and **Tate Modern** *(see p111)* – a 15-minute trip every 40 minutes in each direction. The boat stops off at the **London Eye** (www.londoneye.com), too. The views from this oversize fairground wheel can be amazing, especially at sunset *(see p18)*. The London Eye pier is also handy for the **Saatchi Gallery** *(see p109)*, **London Aquarium** (www.londonaquarium.co.uk) and, across Westminster Bridge, the **Houses of Parliament**, **Westminster Abbey** and **St Margaret's Church** *(see p99)*.

Boats run over longer distances: Westminster Pier or Embankment Pier to **Greenwich** *(see p174)* is a favourite (every 40–45 minutes from 10am–3:45pm; returning until 5:20pm); and Westminster Pier to **Kew** *(see p175)* and **Hampton Court** (11am and noon; one-and-a-half hours to Kew, three-and-a-half hours to Hampton Court, *see p12*).

Of the river websites, **www.transportforlondon. gov.uk/river** gives the best information for river travel; **www.riverthames.co.uk** has a lively overview of the entire river and associated events, including boat races; while **www.citycruisers.com** is a company offering historical tours.

performance

London's theatres in the West End and on the South Bank are world famous, but cutting-edge drama is increasingly found further afield, in places such as the Tricycle in Kilburn and the Almeida, Islington. The city's musical stage stretches from the cupboard-sized 12 Bar Club to the majestic Royal Opera House. A lively comedy circuit is found in a host of pubs and clubs, while cinemas dotted around the city compete for coolness.

CLASSICAL VENUES	DANCE	CUTTING-EDGE THEATRE
Wigmore Hall 36 Wigmore Street, W1 The fine acoustics of the Wigmore Hall's beautiful auditorium make it an outstanding venue for classical music. *(See p122)*	**Sadler's Wells** Rosebery Avenue, EC1 The Wells is an attractive venue for performances by the big names of modern dance, such as Michael Clark and Ballet Rambert. *(See p126)*	**Tricycle** 269 Kilburn High Road, NW6 Political and satirical plays are given an airing at the Tricycle, a theatre that dares to experiment with our expectations of drama. *(See p129)*
St John's Smith Square Smith Square, SW1 An 18th-century church arena is the pre-eminent venue for performances of Early Music. The lunchtime concerts are a bargain. *(See p122)*	**The Place** 17 Duke's Road, WC1 Experimental dance is showcased at the Robin Howard Dance Theatre, which is part of this centre for dance education. *(See p122)*	**>>** *The Tricycle also has a vibrant café-bar, an adjoining repertory cinema and an art gallery, making the journey to Kilburn well worth the trek.*
Festival Hall Belvedere Road, SE1 You needn't dress up or feel at all intimidated at this concert hall for the people. There are two superb resident orchestras. *(See p129)*	**Laban Centre** Creekside, SE8 Two performance spaces for avant-garde dance are set in a state-of-the-art building. *(See p130)*	
Royal Opera House Bow Street, WC2 London's most lavish setting for operatic productions and performances by the Royal Ballet has a high-class atmosphere. *(See p118)*	**>>** *The Clore Studio at the Royal Opera House is an additional space for experimental contemporary dance.*	**Donmar Warehouse** 41 Earlham Street, WC2 A mixture of cerebral drama and big-name actors has been key to the success of the Donmar. It's an intense, intimate space. *(See p118)*
		Royal National Theatre South Bank, SE1 Of the National's three auditoria, the Cottesloe studio is the most versatile space for small-scale, experimental productions. *(See p129)*
		Almeida Almeida Street, N1 A beguilingly light and airy foyer-café leads onto a brooding auditorium where brilliant, nerve-jangling drama is the norm. *(See p126)*

TOP CHOICES – *performance*

GIG VENUES	JAZZ & BLUES	COMEDY

Borderline
Orange Yard, Manette Street, WC2
Enjoy the sweaty fun as new bands thrash out their songs. US bands often get their first UK footing here too. *(See p119)*

606 Club
90 Lots Road, SW10
This stalwart of the British jazz scene is set in a basement in Chelsea. Book a table. *(See p123)*

Hackney Empire
Mare Street, E8
Long-established as a venue for comedy, the Empire attracts well-known comics such as Paul Merton, Jenny Eclair and Bill Bailey. *(See p125)*

Shepherd's Bush Empire
Shepherd's Bush Green, W12
This mid-scale hall with an excellent sound system is especially suited to gigs by solo artists. *(See p123)*

Comedy Store
1a Oxendon Street, SW1
At this legendary club, energetic stand-up comedy is performed to an audience that takes no prisoners. *(See p121)*

12 Bar Club
22–3 Denmark Street, WC2
Tiny it may be, but on a good night this venue, set among the music shops of "Tin Pan Alley", has an electric atmosphere. *(See p119)*

Ronnie Scott's
47 Frith Street, W1
London's best-loved jazz venue. Stick around for the late-night sessions, when musicians pull out all the stops. *(See p121)*

Comedy Café
66–8 Rivington Street, EC2
Situated in one of the liveliest parts of town, the Comedy Café provides drinks, snacks and laughs by the bucket-load. *(See p125)*

Ocean
270 Mare Street, E8
Quality sound systems, spaces for bands of all sizes, and a lively bar are among the strengths of this purpose-built venue. *(See p125)*

>> *The pub circuit is a big part of the music scene for hard-working bands trying to make their mark. Check out the Hope & Anchor on Upper Street, Islington – a bar with great rock heritage.*

Jazz Café
5 Parkway, NW1
The Jazz Café provides a broad mix of jazz-influenced music – everything from funky Roy Ayers to lyrical rapper Q-Tip. *(See p127)*

Royal Opera House *ballet & opera* `9 G3`
Bow Street, Covent Garden, WC2 • 020 7304 4000
>> www.royaloperahouse.org
Tours: three daily at 10:30, 12:30 and 2:30

Shared by the Royal Ballet and Royal Opera, the Opera House is a magnificent theatre, the tiers of its auditorium rising to precipitous heights, topped off with a richly decorated ceiling. The ballet programme offers classical pieces with a few modern works. *Romeo and Juliet*, *Onegin* and *Don Quixote* were 2004 productions. In the same year, operatic performances included *Faust*, *Peter Grimes* and *Tosca*. Tickets range from under £5 (restricted view bench seats up in the gods) to more than £150. On Mondays, some seats are offered at huge discounts.

The Linbury Studio is a modest alternative for experimental dance and small ensemble concerts. On Mondays, free lunchtime recitals are held here or in the Crush Room, one of the Opera House's many spaces for eating, drinking and socializing.

Poetry Café *hub of poetry life in London* `9 G3`
22 Betterton Street, WC2 • 020 7420 9887
>> www.poetrysociety.org.uk Open 11–11 Mon–Fri, 6:30–11 Sat

This is a good café in its own right, the fare ranging from Marmite on toast and a cup of tea to decent wine. It's also the venue for readings, poetry and jazz nights, open-mike slots and poetry slams. Come here to find out about the more itinerant poetry events around town, too.

Donmar Warehouse *innovative theatre* `9 F3`
41 Earlham St, WC2 • 020 7845 5815
>> www.donmarwarehouse.com

Now under the directorship of Michael Grandage, the Donmar continues the success it achieved under Sam Mendes, who persuaded Nicole Kidman and other stars to perform on stage here. Productions have included Tom Stoppard's new version of Pirandello's *Henry IV* and Harold Pinter's *Old Times*.

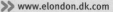

12 Bar Club *live gigs in a tiny room*   9 F2
22–3 Denmark Street, WC2 • 020 7916 6989
≫ www.12barclub.com Club open from 8pm daily

Hosting several acts each night in an upstairs room accessed via a tight alley, the 12 Bar is a great place to hear the ballads of an accomplished singer-songwriter. That said, it also puts on a frenetic London Callin' night (last Sat of the month), which draws on the capital's punk and ska heritage.

Arts Theatre *popular & offbeat drama*   9 F3
Great Newport Street, WC2 • 020 7836 3334
≫ www.artstheatre.com

Following a varied life over the last few decades, the Arts Theatre is trying to regain its touch for cutting-edge drama – a reputation it had in the days when it premiered Samuel Beckett's English-language version of *Waiting For Godot. Hurricane*, a show celebrating snooker legend Alex Higgins, was a more recent hit.

ENO @ The Coliseum *opera in English*   9 G4
St Martin's Lane, WC2 • 020 7632 8300
≫ www.eno.org

Now back in its superbly revamped building, the English National Opera continues with its mission to present opera in the English tongue. To further popularize the art form, 500 seats are available for just £10 on weekdays. There are great views across Trafalgar Square from the public area on the top floor.

Borderline *tomorrow's rock stars today*   9 F3
Orange Yard, Manette Street • 020 7534 6970
≫ www.borderline.co.uk

A small venue (capacity under 300) with a big reputation – bands such as REM, Oasis, Blur and Pulp have played at this hot and sweaty little club. More than this, though, it's a place for new bands to break through and for stalwarts of the US circuit to find a British audience.

Mean Fiddler *small venue, great sound* `9 F3`
168 Charing Cross Road, WC2 • 020 7434 9592
»» www.meanfiddler.com

The Mean Fiddler puts on fewer gigs and more obscure names than the famous Astoria next door, but the proximity of musicians and audience, and the quality of the sound system ensure that it's an ideal place to catch up-and-coming bands. Waggish hip-hop crew Goldie Lookin' Chain was the perfect tonic in 2004.

Soho Theatre *literary haunt* `9 F3`
21 Dean Street, W1 • 020 7478 0100
»» www.sohotheatre.com

Not only a theatre but also a scriptwriting centre, this modern venue in the heart of Soho takes plenty of risks with new writers. Expect the work to be fresh, enthusiastic and maybe rough around the edges. It's also a comedy venue, with leading circuit regulars Jason Byrne and Mark Thomas gracing the stage.

Curzon Soho *art-house cinema* `9 F3`
99 Shaftesbury Ave, W1 • 020 7734 2255
»» www.curzoncinemas.com

The Curzon screens the best international releases and special features, such as seasons of Eastern European films or short art films. Few other cinemas would screen Eduardo Paolozzi's *14-minute History of Nothing*. Sunday is repertory day, offering such classics as *Alphaville* or *Rear Window*.

Buying Tickets for West End Shows

As a general rule, the cheapest tickets are sold at theatre box offices. If a show is sold out, you might be able to buy returns just before a performance. More expensive seats will usually be available through a STAR-regulated ticket agent. London has just one official discounted tickets booth, in the middle of **Leicester Square**, offering tickets on the day of the performance (open 10–7 Mon–Sat, 12–3:30 Sun). For further information: **www.official londontheatre.co.uk** has play summaries and tickets (it's linked with a pamphlet available at most theatres); **www.thisistheatre.com** provides details about performances and the history of venues; **www.londontheatre.co.uk** has seating plans and links to booking agencies.

Ronnie Scott's *jazz stalwart* 9 F3
47 Frith Street, W1 • 020 7439 0747
>> www.ronniescotts.co.uk Open 8:30pm–3am Mon–Sat
(music starts 9:30), Sun 7:30–11

Some of the big jazz names from the US may now
favour larger venues such as the Festival Hall or the
Barbican, but you can't beat the intensity of being
just a few feet away from a group of musicians when
they hit a groove or start pushing their skills to the
limits. On a good night, Ronnie Scott's offers just
such an experience and thereby hangs on to its
reputation as the best jazz club in London.

There are two music sessions most nights. Food is
served during the first. In the late-night session, with
the audience's hunger sated, attention can focus
more fully on the music. In turn, the musicians often
produce their best performances after midnight.

Upstairs is a dance venue, where DJs spin Afro-
Cuban rhythms as the soundtrack for salsa, or 70s
and 80s funk and soul for the Big City Groove nights.

The Other Cinema *cosy film house* 9 F3
11 Rupert Street, W1 • Info 020 7437 0757
Booking 020 7734 1506

A cineaste's dream, The Other Cinema is like a private
viewing room, with plush seats and deep, comfy
sofas at the back. It's a cinema with eclectic
programming, showing an array of cult and world
cinema, sometimes in themed seasons. There's a tiny
bar outside the auditorium for a pre-film apéritif.

Comedy Store *radical club comes of age* 9 F4
1a Oxendon St, SW1 • 0870 060 2340
>> www.thecomedystore.co.uk

The Store opened in 1979 as a punkish riposte to the
gag-merchants who then dominated Britain's comedy
landscape, and it helped to create a new genre of free-
wheeling stand-up. It's a more conventional venue
these days, but something of that initial spirit persists
with the Sunday and Wednesday improv nights.

Performance

>>> >>> >>>

The Place *thrilling moves* `3 F5`
17 Duke's Road, WC1 • 020 7387 0031
>> www.theplace.org.uk

The Place is home to the London Contemporary Dance School and the Richard Alston Dance Company. The primary stage is the Robin Howard Dance Theatre, where you can see the work of recent graduates as well as that of established choreographers and companies from around the world.

St John's *chamber music* `15 G2`
Smith Square, SW1 • 020 7222 1061
>> www.sjss.org.uk

An elegant Baroque church of 1728 provides a beautiful setting for its schedule of classical music, as well as an acoustically excellent one. The Academy of Ancient Music and the London Chamber Orchestra perform regularly, and there's a very reasonable Thursday lunchtime concert series (tickets £5).

Wigmore Hall *supreme classical venue* `8 C2`
36 Wigmore St, W1 • 020 7935 2141
>> www.wigmore-hall.org.uk

World-renowned for recitals, Wigmore Hall should be the first destination for lovers of classical and early music. The concert hall was built in 1901, its architect Thomas Collcutt making extensive use of marble and alabaster for the walls and flooring, which greatly contributes to the room's harmonics. The fine quality of resonance has attracted some of the world's most acclaimed musicians and composers over the decades, including Saint-Saëns, Prokofiev, Francis Poulenc, Benjamin Britten and Jacqueline du Pré.

Major artists continue to be drawn here; recent performers have included the Hilliard Ensemble, Angela Hewitt and Joanna Macgregor. The Wigmore also attracts a very loyal audience, especially appreciative of the hall's intimacy. In addition to daily evening performances, there are Monday lunchtime recitals and coffee concerts on Sundays *(see p13)*.

Electric Cinema *plush film house* `6 D3`
191 Portobello Rd, W11 • 020 7908 9696
>> www.the-electric.co.uk

A beautifully renovated, single-screen cinema, with the most comfortable audience seating in London. You can put your feet up on footstools, sit back in a wide leather chair, and casually reach across to your drink on a side table. This is Club-Class cinema-going, with a bar for wine, beer and snacks at the back (which closes 5 minutes before films begin) and two-seater sofas on which the romantically inclined can snuggle up. The programming is excellent too, with choice films from around the world, as well as the best of Hollywood's auteurs. On Sunday afternoons, the cinema screens low-priced double-bill features.

Another string to the Electric's bow is its next-door brasserie, which is open from 8am for breakfasts, then rolls on throughout the day and evening, serving up perfect brasserie food, from club sandwiches and whitebait to lamb chops and char-grilled fish.

606 Club *jazz with food and drink* `13 G5`
90 Lots Rd, SW10 • 020 7352 5953
>> www.606club.co.uk Open nightly

Geared towards the British jazz scene (and, yes, there is one), this cosy basement bar-restaurant club – with brick walls, café furniture and low lighting – is open to non-members if you book for a meal. This is the only way to get a drink as well, and a fee is added to the bill for the music.

Shepherd's Bush Empire *hot gigs* `6 A5`
Shepherd's Bush Green, W12 • 020 8354 3300
>> www.shepherds-bush-empire.co.uk

This one-time TV theatre is much loved by musicians requiring acoustic subtlety. Artists such as the blues-ish soul vocalist Ben Harper, London's new soul/jazz diva Amy Winehouse and the folk/country singer Gillian Welch have played here to critical acclaim. There are three or four live shows most weeks.

>> *The BBC Proms concert series is one of the world's largest classical music festivals* (see p11) `123`

Performance

Riverside Studios *arts innovation* `12 A4`
Crisp Road, W6 • 020 8237 1111
>> www.riversidestudios.co.uk

Riverside Studios is a small arts centre with great
scope and ambition. A repertory cinema offers nightly
double bills of world movies, while two performance
spaces serve up a wide array of international fare,
from Colombian dance to Iranian theatre. The café-bar
has a pleasant terrace overlooking the Thames.

Barbican *cultural gathering place* `10 C1`
Silk Street, EC2 • 0845 120 7550
>> www.barbican.org.uk

A major arts centre to rival the South Bank *(see p129)*,
the Barbican was hewn from Brutalist concrete in a
radical piece of urban planning. Beyond breezy
walkways and concourses overlooked by apartments,
the interior public spaces are open and welcoming.
There's an excellent concert hall, a distinctly loungy
cinema (independent, art house and repertory), a
theatre and an experimental drama space, the Pit.

The concert hall is home to the accomplished
London Symphony Orchestra and also hosts contemporary classical music, rock gigs and jazz – recent
artists have included Joe Zawinul, Hugh Masekela,
Herbie Hancock and Sonny Rollins. The Barbican
Theatre stages a mix of drama and dance. *The Black
Rider* – a collaboration by author William Burroughs,
musician Tom Waits and director Robert Wilson –
premiered here in 2004, starring Marianne Faithfull.

The Spitz *live bands* `11 F1`
109 Commercial Street, E1 • 020 7392 9032
>> www.spitz.co.uk
Open 11am–midnight Mon–Sat, 10am–10:30pm Sun

An arty bar and music venue in an increasingly lively
part of town, The Spitz is set in a room above
Spitalfields Market *(see p161)*. Relax to some rootsy
sounds or submit to an acoustic onslaught from some
avant-garde electro wizard of the knobs and dials.

Hackney Empire *restored theatrical gem* `5 H1`
Mare Street, E8 • 020 8985 2424
>> www.hackneyempire.co.uk

Having undergone a massive £15 million refurbishment, the Hackney Empire is back in business. The interior, designed by music hall architect Frank Matcham in 1901, is a superb piece of Victorian showmanship. A multicultural hodge-podge of influences from India, Italy and the Middle East is rendered into tiers that subtly reflect the social hierarchy of the time: plenty of curvy ornamentation for the rich; a lick of paint and a side entrance for the poorer patrons.

The fanciful setting makes any night out here feel special, but the programme of events deserves equal praise for its mission to bring every kind of entertainment to a downtrodden part of town. Comedy, which was the strongest element pre-refurb, now vies with opera, jazz, classical, cabaret, drama and dance. A few international acts feature among local and national companies.

Comedy Café *food, drinks and laughter* `5 E5`
66–8 Rivington Street, EC2 • 020 7739 5706
>> www.comedycafe.co.uk Open from 7:30pm Wed–Sat

One of London's best places for stand-up. There's usually a couple of established acts such as Nick Revell, Julia Morris or Milton Jones in the line-up. The club's rather American in feel, with orderly table seating, pitchers of beer and burgers rather than pints and packets of crisps. Wednesday is open-mike spot.

Ocean *superb live venue* `5 H1`
270 Mare St, E8 • 020 8533 0111
>> www.ocean.org.uk Bar open 10am–late daily (from 6pm Sun)

One of London's newest and best live music clubs, Ocean offers a state-of-the-art sound system and various spaces (medium, small and tiny) for gigs. One night you might witness the antics of Lee Scratch Perry, the next it might be 1980s throwbacks Level 42. There's a separate DJ-bar (Aqua) at street level.

Performance

Walthamstow Dog Track *fast canines*
Chingford Road, E4 • 020 8498 3300 • ◉ Walthamstow
Central, then bus 97, 357, 215 or W11
》 www.wsgreyhound.co.uk Racing on Tue, Thu & Sat

Sightings of celebrities such as Brad Pitt or Claudia
Schiffer down the "Stow" demonstrate the new-found
appeal of greyhound racing. Place bets from the
comfort of the Paddock Grill or mix it up with the
commoners in the Popular Enclosure. *(See also p16.)*

Sadler's Wells *vibrant dance theatre* `4 A4`
Rosebery Avenue, EC1 • 0870 737 7737
》 www.sadlers-wells.com

A superb modern theatre, Sadler's Wells is primarily a
dance venue, though it does feature opera as well.
Choreographer/dancer Michael Clark produced two
acclaimed works in 2003 and 2004, and the venue
has also showcased Argentinian tango, the Rambert
Dance Company and the Dance Theatre of Harlem.

Scala *live bands, club nights and more* `3 H4`
275 Pentonville Road, N1 • 020 7833 2022
》 www.scala-london.co.uk

The Scala positions itself as an alternative venue,
putting on a mix of live acts (indie, world music and
unsigned bands), as well as a staple of adventurous
club nights. The Scala's events often have more than
one focus on a given night, so live bands may well
share the spotlight with DJs and film screenings.

Almeida *pioneering theatre* `4 B2`
Almeida Street, off Upper St, N1 • 020 7359 4404
》 www.almeida.co.uk

The Almeida had a revamp in 2002, acquiring Michael
Attenborough as creative director along with a smart
new foyer and café-bar. Attenborough's tenure has
overseen the hugely acclaimed *Festen* and world
premiere of Sebastian Barry's *Whistling Psyche*. The
auditorium is a stark, serious and resonant space.

King's Head Theatre Bar *pub-theatre* `4 B2`

115 Upper Street, N1 • 020 7226 8561
>> www.kingsheadtheatre.org

A good pub on Islington's Upper Street has the added attraction of a tiny little theatre out the back. You can order a pre-theatre dinner as well, for a full evening's entertainment. Performances range from newly penned works to well-worn classics. Many stars have played here, including Ben Kingsley and Alan Rickman.

Union Chapel *atmospheric gigs* `4 B1`

Compton Avenue, N1 • Info 020 7226 1686; tickets from Reckless Records on Upper St or at www.wegottickets.com
>> www.unionchapel.org.uk

The Union Chapel, a working Congregational church, is a wonderfully Gothic setting for live gigs. Sit beneath its dramatic arches and soak up the atmosphere with Hungarian folk groups or creative pop musicians such as Björk. It also hosts occasional comedy nights.

Jazz Café *showcase for musical innovators* `2 D3`

5 Parkway, NW1 • 020 7916 6060
>> www.jazzcafe.co.uk Open 7pm–1am Mon–Sat, 7pm–2am Fri & Sat, 7pm–midnight Sun

Not only jazz, but also soul, funk, world, latin, R&B and hip-hop are performed here, so the Jazz Café's remit is broad indeed. What the performers tend to share is musical inventiveness. So, if it's a hip-hop night, you're less likely to see a mainstream artist such as Jäy–Z than you are to witness the lyrical flow of Q-Tip or the psychedelic ramblings of The Pharcyde.

As popular with performers as it is with regulars, the Jazz Café welcomes back time and again the big names of the jazz/funk/soul world, such as Gil Scott Heron and Roy Ayers (who's practically made the place his second home). In terms of creature comforts, the Jazz Café on the balcony offers European cuisine, while the downstairs bar, located in the livelier, dancier area right in front of the stage, does a brisk trade in beers and cocktails.

>> *The Almeida Restaurant, opposite the theatre, has moderately priced modern European cuisine*

Performance

Jongleurs *comedy in comfort*

`2 D2`

Middle Yard, Chalk Farm Road, NW1 • 0870 787 0707
>> www.jongleurs.com

The Jongleurs empire started in Battersea just over
20 years ago. Having undergone a revamp, the
Camden branch is the smartest operation, rolling out
a mix of decent fast food, jugs of beer and laughs
aplenty. Established comics – such as Sean Meo,
Adam Hills and Gina Yashere – are regulars.

Hampstead Theatre *fresh new plays*

Eton Avenue, NW3 • 020 7722 9301 • ⊖ Swiss Cottage
>> www.hampsteadtheatre.com

Ensconced in a brand new light and airy home, the
Hampstead Theatre now has a larger auditorium, with
about 300 seats, and an extra studio space for its
most experimental work. Its ethos, however, remains
unchanged, and so it will continue to develop and
promote new writing and young actors.

Everyman *superior cinema*

`1 A5`

5 Holly Bush Vale, NW3 • 0870 066 4777
>> www.everymancinema.com

This is cinema-going at its most sophisticated. The
auditorium has an upper balcony of leather seats and
cushions, plenty of leg room and excellent sight lines
– so no having to stare at the silhouette of someone's
coiffured hair instead of the action on screen. Indeed,
the Everyman has the feel of a private club, with two
comfortable lounges and a bar offering a good
selection of whiskies, beers and wines, and a little
tapas menu, in addition to the two screening rooms.

You could easily idle away an afternoon or evening
here without even seeing a film, instead playing
rounds of backgammon, chess, jenga or mikado – a
selection of games available from the reception desk.
However, it would be a shame to forego the pleasures
of an excellent cinema programme, which takes the
pick of new films and a second look at recent releases,
and also offers classics and themed seasons.

To find venues accessible to disabled people, check >> www.elondon.dk.com

Tricycle *experimental drama*
269 Kilburn High Rd, NW6 • 020 7328 1000 • ⊖ Kilburn
≫ www.tricycle.co.uk

Comprising a theatre, cinema, gallery and café-bar, the Tricycle is best known for its political and some- times satirical plays. Musapha Matura's *Playboy of the West Indies* and Irish comedy *Stones in His Pockets* are among the productions that had their first London runs at the Tricycle.

Royal National Theatre
`9 H4`

South Bank, SE1 • 020 7452 3400; bookings 020 7452 3000
≫ www.nationaltheatre.org.uk

Behind foyer areas arranged on several levels are three auditoria: the fan-shaped Olivier Theatre; the smaller Lyttelton; and the Cottesloe, an experimental studio space. The programme accommodates classical and popular theatre – from big productions to experimental drama – and spectacular musicals.

South Bank Centre *music, music, music*
`9 H4`

Belvedere Road & South Bank, SE1 • 020 7960 4242
≫ www.rfh.org.uk

The South Bank Centre comprises three contrasting music venues: the **Festival Hall** for symphonies, the **Queen Elizabeth Hall** for chamber music and the **Purcell Room**, which specializes in solo and small ensemble performances. Rock/pop and jazz events are also hosted, including the annual Meltdown Festival each June/July. Two symphony orchestras are resident: the world-renowned Philharmonia and the highly praised London Philharmonic. The smaller London Sinfonietta also plays regularly.

The South Bank Centre is superb at putting on free entertainment too, most events taking place in the foyer/bar area and ballroom of the Festival Hall. The **Commuter Jazz** series is a regular Friday slot from 5pm.

Note that in summer 2005, the Festival Hall starts the next stage of its renovation, which will affect parts of the building for several months. *(See also p164.)*

Performance

National Film Theatre *movies galore* 9 H4
South Bank, SE1 • 020 7928 3232
>> www.bfi.org.uk

This repertory cinema excels in themed seasons – some populist (Audrey Hepburn), others more for art-house aficionados (early Buñuel and Cocteau shorts). It's the main venue for the London Film Festival too *(see p11)*. Three screens provide serene conditions for film-viewing: no rustling sweet papers here.

Old Vic *theatrical transatlantic crossover* 10 A5
The Cut, SE1 • Box office 020 7928 7616
>> www.oldvictheatre.com

Built in 1818, the Old Vic is one of London's oldest theatres still in use and can list Laurence Olivier, John Gielgud, Vivien Leigh and Alec Guinness among its thespian credentials. With Kevin Spacey now at the helm as artistic director, the ambition is to transfer successful productions from here to Broadway.

Shakespeare's Globe *Tudor revival* 10 C4
Bankside, SE1 • 020 7401 9919
>> www.shakespeares-globe.org Theatre season: May–Sep

Recreating the ambience of Shakespearean theatre, the Globe is largely roofless, hence the summer-only season of the Bard's plays. There's bench seating in the middle and upper galleries; otherwise you have to stand, and will be encouraged to chip in with earthy comments rather than just polite applause.

Laban *dance for the 21st century* 16 A3
Creekside, SE8 • Box office 020 8469 9500
>> www.laban.org

Housed in a prestigious building by Herzog & de Meuron (architects of Tate Modern), Laban is a centre for dance education and performance. Two venues, the Bonnie Bird and Studio theatres, offer contemporary dance and physical theatre, sometimes mixed with electronic media, such as video projections.

Ritzy *Brixton's picture palace*
Coldharbour Lane, SW2 • 020 7733 2229 • ⊖ Brixton
» www.picturehouses.co.uk

Hugely popular with Brixtonians, the Ritzy is as much
a place to meet up and hang out as a cinema per se;
its upstairs café-bar is great for lounging to easygoing
tracks laid down by the DJs. But with five screens, the
Ritzy also has a diverse programme, mixing popular
new releases with highlights from world cinema.

Battersea Arts Centre *in the studio*
Lavender Hill, SW11 • 020 7223 2223 • ⊖ Clapham Junction
» www.bac.org.uk

A centre for experimental performance, BAC likes to
emphasize the merits of collaboration and interdisci-
plinary productions. With several studio spaces, a
main theatre and a café-bar that's an occasional
venue for poetry events, BAC ensures that there's
never a dull moment in leafy southwest London.

Rivoli Ballroom *a swirling time warp*
350 Brockley Rd, SE4 • 020 8692 5130
⊖ Crofton Park (from Blackfriars)

This wonderful Edwardian dance hall has an arched
ceiling, chandeliers and old-fashioned side-room
bars. Events are oddments from different eras: it has
hosted the faux sophistication of Club Montepulciano
(nights of crooning cabaret acts and light gambling),
as well as salsa evenings, jive nights and trad jazz.

Tickets for Sporting Events

If you want to see the big football clubs, such as
Arsenal and Chelsea, try official **club websites** first,
then agencies such as **www.footballtickets.eu.com**
or **www.frontrowpromotions.com**. Individuals post
tickets for sale on **www.thegumtree.com**. You can
also use web agencies for international rugby
matches played at Twickenham (**www.rfu.com**).

London has two major cricket grounds: the Oval and
Lord's *(see p107)*. Getting tickets for international
Tests usually requires booking a month in advance
or handing over vast sums (£200 or more) to an
agency such as **www.londonticketshop.co.uk**. To
catch the tennis action at Wimbledon, you need to
queue in the morning or pay the exorbitant prices
commanded by agencies for Centre Court matches.

pubs, bars & clubs

Pubs remain the city's main drinking institutions, but swish cocktail lounges and funky DJ bars are stealing more and more of the limelight. Meanwhile, the dance scene maintains a blistering pace, its focus now moving from mega-clubs such as Ministry of Sound to more esoteric venues such as 93 Feet East and Herbal in Shoreditch. From creaking old taverns to style bars, London's got it covered.

DJ BARS	GAY BARS & CLUBS	A QUIET PINT

Cherry Jam
58 Porchester Road, W2
Check out Cherry Jam's regular Friday night event, Outernational, for "indigenous grooves" from Latin America and Africa. *(See p141)*

Heaven
Under the Arches, Villiers Street, WC2
It's been going a long time and there's no reason to stop now – Heaven offers Saturday night's most full-on party. *(See p136)*

>> *Weekday afternoons are a good time to visit some of the old pubs in The City, such as the Lamb Tavern in Leadenhall Market (Map 10 D3).*

The Social
5 Little Portland Street, W1
A relaxed upstairs lounge bar contrasts with the basement, where DJs keep upping the beats-per-minute count. *(See p140)*

Vauxhall Tavern
372 Kennington Lane, SE11
A pub that's been turned into a weekend cabaret venue for high-camp Saturdays and lazy Sundays. *(See p153)*

Loungelover
1 Whitby Street, E1
Stretching expectations of what constitutes a DJ bar, Loungelover embraces opulence, with overblown decor and fancy cocktails. *(See p149)*

Fridge
1 Town Hall Parade, SW2
The regular gay night is Fusion on the 2nd and 4th Fridays of the month; Orange makes an occasional Sunday appearance. *(See p153)*

The Lamb
94 Lamb's Conduit Street, WC1
Though often busy with local university and hospital staff in the evenings, this welcoming pub is a relaxed place for an afternoon pint. *(See p141)*

Vibe Bar
Old Truman Brewery, 91–5 Brick Lane, E1
In this former East End brewery, DJs seek out anything that might have a niche audience: from 80s fetish pop to "acid fried beats". *(See p148)*

Trade at Turnmills
63b Clerkenwell Road, EC1
Itinerant club night Trade is an irregular feature at Turnmills for late-night, early-hours hedonism. *(See p146)*

Pride of Spitalfields
3 Heneage Street, E1
The kind of traditional local pub where you can sit undisturbed at the bar, absorbing the surrounding conversations and banter. *(See p148)*

The Crown
116 Cloudesley Road, N1
Tranquillity is the watchword at this Islington pub, set on a quiet road, with a relaxing interior, friendly staff, and great beers and food. *(See p151)*

>> *Browse www.gaytoz.com and www.aromadome.com for full listings and information about gay bars, venues and club nights.*

Greenwich Union
56 Royal Hill, SE10
The Union's back garden is a serene spot to enjoy one or more of the Meantime Brewery's chocolate or fruit-based beers. *(See p155)*

HISTORIC PUBS

Trafalgar Tavern
Park Row, SE10
Charles Dickens, Dr Johnson and many politicians of the 19th century were lured by the famous whitebait suppers at this inn. *(See pp155 & 174)*

The Lamb & Flag
33 Rose Street, WC2
One of the oldest public houses in central London, The Lamb was a venue for bare-knuckle boxing in the 17th century. *(See p137)*

Black Friar
174 Queen Victoria Street, EC4
The name and site recall a Dominican monastery, but the interior is more of an Art Nouveau curiosity. *(See p144)*

French House
49 Dean Street, W1
The French connection was established in World War II, when the bar served as an "office" for De Gaulle's government in exile. *(See p139)*

>> *The best website for information and an honest assessment of London pubs is www.fancyapint.com.*

THE COCKTAIL HOUR

Lobby Bar
1 Aldwych, WC2
The capacious interior of the Lobby Bar is sleekly furnished and very upmarket. Drinks are expertly mixed and served without fuss. *(See p136)*

Blue Bar
Berkeley Hotel, Wilton Place, SW1
Polished cocktails and fine malts are served at this cool and elegant Wedgwood-blue bar. *(See p142)*

Trailer H
177 Portobello Road, W11
Strong, fruity cocktails are the hallmark of Trailer H, more a place for fun and high times than for reserve and sophistication. *(See p143)*

TOP CLUBBING

Herbal
10–14 Kingsland Road, E2
No fancy interior here – just a great sound system and a cast of DJs who search out the best in funky house, jungle and eastern breaks. *(See p147)*

93 Feet East
150 Brick Lane, E1
This multi-space club and bar, with a courtyard for summer evenings, is the place to seek out new developments in musical styles. *(See p148)*

Fabric
77a Charterhouse Street, EC1
One of London's biggest clubs, Fabric pushes its musical direction into all dance music territories, from hip-hop to elecro-beats to nu jazz. *(See p145)*

>> *For an accessible weekly round-up of clubbing in London, check out DJ Lottie's previews in the* Metro Life *supplement of* The Standard *newspaper on Thursdays.*

Notting Hill Arts Club
21 Notting Hill Gate
A club for the indie/dance crossover. Come for arty bands, DJ nights and the punk reverie of Death Disco. *(See p144)*

Lobby Bar *sophisticated cocktails*

9 H3

1 Aldwych, WC2 • 020 7300 1000

>> www.onealdwych.com Open 9am–11pm (10am–10:30pm Sun)

Located within the high-ceilinged lobby of a contemporary luxury hotel is this ultra-stylish cocktail bar. Sofas and high-backed chairs are arranged around an oversized wooden boatman. Uniformed staff mix magnificent Martinis, Bellinis and Collins, and deliver superior satay and sushi to a well-heeled clientele.

Heaven *gay nirvana*

9 G4

Under the Arches, Villiers Street, WC2 • 020 7930 2020

>> www.heaven-london.com Open from 10pm Mon, Wed & Sat

Set deep in the vaults of a railway bridge, Heaven is a gay clubbing institution. The regular slots are a dress-up-and-play Popcorn night on Mondays; Fruit Machine on Wednesdays (house, R&B and "pure pop"); and the full-on Saturday party night. Men and women, gays and straights – all are welcome.

Gordon's Wine Bar *atmospheric cellar*

9 G4

47 Villiers Street, WC2 • 020 7930 1408

Open 11am–11pm (noon–10:30pm Sun)

Tatty, candlelit and clandestinely romantic, Gordon's is an old favourite with Londoners. You'll rarely find a free table in this dusty former wine cellar between Charing Cross and Embankment stations, but the ambience makes up for the lack of comfort. With all the vintage publicity posters, smoky alcoves and rickety furniture, it feels like a relic from the 1940s.

A small bar dispenses an excellent range of reasonably priced wines, plus port, Madeira and a few sherries (there are no beers or spirits). Most customers part with £10 for a bottle of acceptable house red, but there's enough choice higher up the price scale to attract the connoisseur. A separate food counter offers a selection of cheeses and salads. The basement gives access to a row of terrace tables along Watergate Walk, a spot that's always busy on summer evenings.

The American Bar *Art Deco relic* `9 G4`

Savoy Hotel, Strand, WC2 • 020 7836 4343
>> www.the-savoy.co.uk Open 2pm–1:30am Mon–Sat

A pioneering cocktail bar from the early 20th century. Authentic Art Deco details and the bar's classy location on the first floor of the Savoy Hotel have helped to attract decades of celebrity custom. It first gained global renown during American Prohibition, when wealthy folk from across the Atlantic demanded a higher standard of drink than was common in London at the time. Britain's first Martini was mixed here, and an entire Savoy cocktail book was compiled in 1930. Its most successful era was after World War II, when head bartender Peter Dorelli would concoct cocktail masterpieces. Ernest Hemingway and Ira Gershwin were among the rich and famous patrons.

Today's drinks list is extensive, if within traditional limitations, and pricey – all cocktails are £9 or more. There's also a selection of malt whiskies. Smart dress (including jacket and tie) is required.

Atlantic Bar & Grill *cocktail bar* `9 E4`

20 Glasshouse Street, W1 • 020 7734 4888
>> www.atlanticbarandgrill.com
Open noon–3am Mon–Fri, 6pm–3am Sat. DJs at weekends

All mirrors and pillars, the Atlantic occupies the Art Deco ballroom of the former Regent Palace Hotel. Mixing master Dick Bradsell created the splendid cocktail list; he is honoured with a smaller bar in his name next door.

Lamb & Flag *historic public house* `9 G3`

33 Rose Street, WC2 • 020 7497 9504
Open 11am–11pm (noon–10:30pm Sun)

In the 17th century, bare-knuckle fights were staged in the backroom of this Covent Garden old-timer – hence the pub's former name, the Bucket of Blood. Its old beams and panelling, creaky stairs and quirky signs attract quite a few tourists, but locals are also drawn by the selection of quality cask ales.

Bar Rumba *basement DJ bar* `9 F3`
36 Shaftesbury Avenue, W1 • 020 7287 2715
Open 5pm–3:30am Mon–Fri, 7pm–6am Sat, 8pm–1am Sun.
Adm fee after 11pm

A well-established late-opening fixture of Soho nightlife, this is not a glamorous place, but the musical pedigree is impressive. Many of the world's top DJs have spun here for a cosmopolitan crowd. Drinks are reasonably priced.

The Endurance *Soho pub* `9 E3`
90 Berwick Street, W1 • 020 7437 2944
Open noon–11pm daily

Sandwiched between second-hand record shops by Berwick Street Market, the Endurance has a fine range of beers and wines, and superb food at lunchtimes. The mixed, music-oriented clientele creates a lively ambience around a simple, one-bar interior. Classic punk and indie are on the jukebox.

Madame Jo-Jos *Soho cabaret club* `9 E3`
8–10 Brewer Street, W1 • 020 7734 3040
» www.madamejojos.com Open Tue–Sat evenings

This plush old theatre has been used as a location in various films, including Stanley Kubrick's *Eyes Wide Shut* (the scene where Tom Cruise meets the pianist and tries to elicit the code word for an orgy). Club nights include a regular Friday slot for Keb Darge's Legendary Deep Funk, in which you'll encounter some rare 45s and, usually, some acrobatic jazz- and break-dancers shaking to the beats. On Saturday, the Groove Sanctuary offers nu jazz, Latin and deep house.

Madame Jo-Jos is best known for drag cabaret, and on Saturday evenings the Kitsch Cabaret takes place from 7 to 10pm. The excellent Kitty Cartier indulges in sharp-tongued repartee with the audience, then carouses them with show tunes and hits from the 1960s on. It's a big party, with raucous hen night groups, jocular banter and the odd flash of old Soho flesh from hired strippers.

French House *literary, gallic pub* `9 F3`
49 Dean Street, W1 • 020 7437 2799
Open noon–11pm daily

This one-room cabin has a legendary past. Owned by the Belgian Berlemont family before World War I, The York Minster, as it was then known, enjoyed three golden eras. First came the cabaret days, when the great musical stars of Parisian *chanson* relaxed here between shows. Then the French Resistance used it as a London base for its clandestine operations. (De Gaulle and his Free French schemed in a room above the bar.) It became known as the French House at this time. In the 1950s, writers Dylan Thomas and Brendan Behan were among the celebrated regulars.

The Berlemonts and the bohemians have gone, but a hangover from those boozy, literary days remains. Beer is not served in pints, but in glasses. Wine, cider from Brittany, pastis and champagne are all popular; classic French labels are also sold by the half-bottle. A framed photo of De Gaulle still has pride of place.

The Player *sexy basement bar* `9 E3`
8 Broadwick Street, W1 • 020 7494 9125
>> www.theplyr.com Open 5:30pm–midnight (to 1am Fri & Sat). Adm fee after 9pm Thu, Fri & Sat

This small bar is now part of the excellent Match chain, renowned for its cocktail expertise. You can expect high-volume music, slick service (many punters tip the waiters) and professional Martinis. Pre-booking a table is usually necessary.

Jerusalem *cheap eats & quality lagers* `9 E2`
33–34 Rathbone Place, W1 • 020 7255 1120
Open all day from noon Mon–Fri (to 1am Thu, Fri), 7pm–1am Sat. Adm fee after 10pm Fri & Sat

At lunchtime the long wooden tables of this dark basement bar/restaurant heave with media folk from Soho. By night, the bare brickwork vibrates with a thriving subterranean club scene; in between, a trendy, post-work crowd dives into pitchers of beer.

>> *Never ask for a "beer" – it's lager or bitter, preferably ordered by name*

Market Place *Continental terrace scene* `9 E2`
11 Market Place, W1 • 020 7079 2020
Open 11am–11pm (to 1am Thu–Sat)

The Market Place prides itself on a roster of great DJs. It's part of the highly regarded Cantaloupe group *(see p47)*, which ensures a creative array of food and cocktails, and unusual international beers. Having to queue for entry is a drawback. (See how many asymmetrical haircuts you can spot while waiting.)

Mash *bar-diner with long opening hours* `8 D2`
19–21 Great Portland Street, W1 • 020 7637 5555
Open 7:30am–2am Mon–Fri; 11am–2am Sat

Tongue-in-cheek retro chic defines the look. The bar's back wall exposes huge vats of the Mash range of house beers (draught pilsner, wheat, fruit or stout varieties). There are cocktails on offer, too, and sophisticated snacks, because the kitchen also caters for a high-standard restaurant upstairs.

Zeta Bar *swish hotel lounge bar* `8 C5`
Mayfair Hilton Hotel, 35 Hertford Street, W1 • 020 7208 4067
» www.zeta-bar.com Open Mon–Sat evenings (to 1am Mon & Tue, to 3am Wed–Sat). Adm after 11pm

Foxy décor, innovative cocktails and clubby music at conversational volume help make the Hilton's bar a destination in its own right. Better still, bar prices, for Mayfair, are far from outrageous. The polished clientele can enjoy oysters and Thai fish cakes too.

The Social *diner by day, club bar by night* `8 D2`
5 Little Portland Street, W1 • 020 7636 4992
» www.thesocial.com
Open noon–11pm Mon–Thu, noon–1am Fri & Sat

Daytime sees this street-level cabin café serve honest fodder (burgers, pies etc), as well as beer, hot drinks and the occasional cocktail. After dark, the area downstairs becomes a DJ bar of renown. Live acts have included Primal Scream and Badly Drawn Boy.

Cherry Jam *DJ bar* `7 F2`
58 Porchester Road, W2 • 020 7727 9950
» www.cherryjam.net Open 6pm–2am Mon–Sat;
4pm–midnight Sun. Adm after 8pm

This is co-owned by Ben Watt of Everything But The
Girl fame. In the early evening the place is fairly quiet
and acts as a modest hangout for local hipsters.
Bands or record decks start playing after about 9pm.
Drinks include bottled beers, cocktails and coffee.

Lamb *characterful old pub* `9 H1`
94 Lamb's Conduit Street, WC1 • 020 7405 0713
Open 11am–11pm Mon–Sat; noon–4pm, 7–10:30pm Sun

A curio between Clerkenwell and Bloomsbury, the
Lamb is approaching its 300th anniversary, though
what is preserved is a masterpiece from the Victorian
era. Details include framed caricatures, etched glass
and delicate screens giving customers privacy. The
antique Polyphone music box is still in working order.

The End *steely cool club* `9 G2`
18 West Central St, WC1 • 020 7419 9199
» www.the-end.co.uk Open from 10pm; to 3am Mon & Wed;
to 4am Thu; to 6am Fri & Sat

Down in the vaults of a former post office, The End is
stylish in a minimalist way, with a kicking main room
and a slightly more laid-back lounge, where Rob
Mello and guests provide a mesmerizing concoction
of electronic funk and house. Great sound system.

Nag's Head *London's most eccentric pub* `14 B1`
53 Kinnerton Street, SW1 • 020 7235 1135
Open 11am–11pm (noon–10:30pm Sun)

The intimate layout and interior oddities of this neighbourhood pub, set in a cobbled cul-de-sac, hark back
to the early 1800s, when the place provided lodgings
for stablehands. An excellent choice of traditional ales,
fine food, a jazzy soundtrack and civilized atmosphere help ensure a solid core of amiable regulars.

» *Many pubs do not serve food in the afternoons, after 2pm or 3pm*

Blue Bar *hotel bar of the highest standard* `14 B1`
Berkeley Hotel, Wilton Place, SW1 • 020 7235 6000
Open 4pm–1am Mon–Sat

The Blue Bar at the Berkeley Hotel is a triumph of detail. Touches of Rococo and Art Deco blend into an eye-pleasing backdrop of stucco and Wedgwood blue in an interior of restrained style. An equally polished bar staff quietly dispenses bowls of warmed nuts and large, spicy olives as guests peruse an extensive list of cocktails, champagnes, Highland and Island malt whiskies and fine wines. Cocktails such as a classic Martini or champagne-based drinks are perfect in mix and presentation.

American customers often opt for a classic malt and a cigar. (The cigars are displayed in a modest cabinet by the bar lined with champagne buckets.) The snack menu offers modern tapas dishes, which are as delicately presented as everything else here. On leaving, customers receive the same impeccably discreet nod that greeted them on the way in.

Townhouse *easy-going style bar* `14 A1`
31 Beauchamp Place, SW3 • 020 7589 5080
» www.lab-townhouse.com Open 4pm–midnight Mon–Fri,
noon–midnight Sat, 4–11:30pm Sun

This chic bar, set in a three-storey Georgian townhouse, serves cocktails created by famed mixologist Douglas Ankrah. There are more than 100 to consider, making for a tricky choice if your attention is further distracted by the classic movies projected silently on to a wall.

Apartment 195 *upmarket lounge bar* `14 A4`
195 King's Road, SW3 • 020 7351 5195
» www.apartment195.co.uk Open from 4pm Mon–Sat

This exclusive style bar has created a much-needed buzz down the King's Road. Members and stylish guests mingle in the cocktail lounge, salon and TV room, sipping professionally mixed classic cocktails (moderately priced), fine wines and classy beers. Phone to reserve a table on Fridays and Saturdays.

Lonsdale *concept bar of renown* `6 D3`

44–8 Lonsdale Road, W11 • 020 7727 4080
>> www.thelonsdale.co.uk
Open 6pm–midnight daily (to 11:30pm Sun)

A recipient of many Best Bar awards, the Lonsdale scores top marks for its décor, superior drinks and tapas-style snacks. Beyond the starchy doormen, the atmosphere is loungy and laidback – even though you know that the "just got out of bed" look sported by all present took hours to create. The interior, designed by leading bar architects Fusion, features futuristic, aged-bronze hemispheres on the walls, and steel bobbles in the smaller upstairs bar.

The famous cocktail list has been designed by London mixologists Dick Bradsell and Henry Besant. Martinis (choose from elderflower, rose petal, marmalade and other variants) are joined by fresh Raspberry Mules, Earl Grey Fizzes (delicate tea, mixed with bisongrass vodka and prosecco), Diane Von Furstenbergs (vodka, fruit, vanilla) and 60 others.

Trailer H *modest basement bar* `6 C2`

177 Portobello Road, W11 • 020 7727 2700
Open 5pm–late Tue–Fri, 6pm–late Sat

The H stands for "happiness"; indeed, the drinks list here is as good as it gets. House specials are lurid-coloured *tiki* cocktails, which look as innocuous as fruit smoothies but, boy, do they kick. Zombies are limited to two per person. It's the ideal venue for an apéritif before going to the Electric Cinema *(see p123)*.

Golborne Grove *pub/bar/restaurant* `6 C1`

36 Golborne Road, W10 • 020 8960 6260
>> www.groverestaurants.co.uk   Open 11am–midnight daily

Golborne Road is London's "Little Casablanca", busy with Moroccan eateries and shops. The landscape is less colourful at its western end, but relief is offered by this popular establishment, which offers excellent food (international) from a daily changing menu, a fine wine list and all the usual beers and spirits.

Notting Hill Arts Club *acoustic pioneers* `7 E4`

21 Notting Hill Gate, W11 • 020 7460 4459
>> www.nottinghillartsclub.com Open 6pm–1am Mon–Wed,
6pm–2am Thu & Fri, 4pm–2am Sat, 4pm–1am Sun

NHAC is always searching for new and exciting music
and art, and programmes a diverse range of club
nights, film screenings and live bands. Wednesdays
are for nostalgics, though, as Death Disco crashes
through some punk and indie rock.

Windsor Castle *al fresco pints* `7 E5`

114 Campden Hill Road, W8 • 020 7243 9551
Open noon–11pm Mon–Sat, noon–10:30pm Sun

This characterful and friendly old pub is a prime
summer destination, thanks to its leafy beer garden
at the back. Fish and chips and traditional pub grub
always seem to taste that much better in the open air.
At less clement times of the year, drinkers cosy up in
a warren of oak-panelled rooms.

Black Friar *extraordinary interior* `10 B3`

174 Queen Victoria Street, EC4 • 020 7236 5474
Open 11:30am–11pm Mon–Fri; noon–4pm Sat

An unusual and much-loved landmark, the Black Friar
was built in Victorian style on the site of a former
Dominican monastery. An extravagant early-20th-
century Art Nouveau makeover left an interior with
marble surfaces, mirrored alcoves and decorative
monks. Grab a seat before the after-work crowd arrives.

Notorious Pubs & Literary Haunts

In the first half of the 20th century, the **Fitzroy Tavern**
was a shrine of London bohemia, frequented at one
time or another by writers Dylan Thomas and George
Orwell, magician Aleister Crowley and chief hangman
Albert Pierrepoint. South of Oxford Street is the
Pillars of Hercules, which is found in Dickens' *A Tale
of Two Cities* (1859) and was a favourite meeting
point in the 1980s for authors such as Ian McEwan.
On the same street is the **Coach & Horses**, with the
self-proclaimed "rudest landlord in Soho". Hard-
drinking journalist Jeffrey Bernard was a regular
here. The nearby **French House** *(see p139)* has also
been favoured by literary hellraisers and troubled
souls, including poet and novelist Sylvia Plath.
For individual pub details, *see p228.*

Vertigo *London's highest bar* `10 D2`
Level 42, Tower 42, 25 Old Broad Street, EC2 • 020 7877 7842
» www.vertigo42.co.uk Open by reservation only

Book in advance and dress smartly, and join City
executives at the top of the former NatWest Tower
for an unparalleled view of the capital. A choice of
30 brands of champagne, 10 fine wines and a range
of classy, seafood-based dishes helps to heighten
the experience even further.

Café Kick *homage to the beautiful game* `4 A5`
43 Exmouth Market, EC1 • 020 7837 8077
Open noon–11pm Mon–Fri, 1–11pm Sat & Sun

A continental-style café-bar where the main draw is
classic Rene Pierre table football. Groups of young
twentysomethings crowd the tables, animatedly
flicking wrists and voicing their triumphs. European
football memorabilia, bottled beers, wines and snacks
from southern Europe add to the cosmopolitan mix.

Fabric *hedonistic clubbing at its finest* `10 B1`
77a Charterhouse St, EC1• 020 7336 8898
» www.fabriclondon.com Open 9.30pm–5am Fri,
10pm–7am Sat, Sun: check website for details

With three great rooms and sound systems that make
your legs shake, Fabric is quite possibly the best club
in London – at least, that's how it feels when you're in
it. Club nights aren't all about big name DJs, but it's
hard not to be impressed by a line-up of turntablists
and musicians which might include James Lavelle,
Craig Richards, DJ Spinbad, Fila Brazillia or Roots
Manuva. When he's not over at Herbal *(see p147)*,
Goldie sometimes makes an appearance with his
Metalheadz crew for an onslaught of junglist drum 'n'
bass. Fabric's musical focus is house and techno on
Saturdays and breakbeat, hip-hop and drum 'n' bass
for Friday's FabricLive session, but you'll also hear
electro and nu jazz. FabricLive has also been
instrumental in bringing to London's attention live acts
such as Norway's Röyksopp.

Pubs, Bars & Clubs

Fluid *the perfect start to an all-nighter* `10 B1`
40 Charterhouse Street, EC1 • 020 7253 3444
>> www.fluidbar.com Open noon–midnight Mon–Wed,
noon–2am Thu & Fri, 7pm–2am Sat. Adm Fri & Sat)

Fluid is a delightfully kitsch DJ bar with Japanese details – screen prints, Asahi beer, rice-wine cocktails, even a photo-sticker booth. With its retro video games and superb soundtrack (leftfield beats, jazz dub, chunky house), it's the ideal pre-club bar.

Jerusalem Tavern *old English pub* `10 B1`
55 Britton Street, EC1 • 020 7490 4281
Open 11am–11pm Mon–Fri, 5pm–11pm Sat, noon–5pm Sun

A simple, small wooden coffee house dating from the early 18th century is now the flagship outlet for North Suffolk's excellent St Peter's Brewery. Unusual fruit beers and classic ales are served, while fine pub lunches are provided for habitués of Clerkenwell looking for a little respite from the area's DJ bars.

Turnmills *dance club* `10 B1`
63b Clerkenwell Rd, EC1 • 020 7250 3409
>> www.turnmills.com Open 6:30pm–midnight Tue, 10pm–4am Thu, 10:30pm–7:30am Fri, 10pm–6am Sat

An industrial-gothic interior with low ceilings gives Turnmills a deep, dark and sweaty feel once the up-for-it crowd gets into the groove. The club's rooms include two main dance floors and some chill-out areas; the music tips towards house and clubby R&B.

Cargo *live music & all-day drinking* `5 E5`
83 Rivington St, EC2 • 020 7739 3440
>> www.cargo-london.com Open 6pm–1am Mon, noon–1am Tue–Thu, noon–3am Fri, 6pm–3am Sat, 1pm–midnight Sun

Under the railway arches of Shoreditch, Cargo is a daytime bar-café, a live music venue and a dance club all in one. International sounds get an airing at Champions of Sound (Fridays), and Cargo's occasional mini festivals also promote diverse, global music.

Herbal *mixed bag of music* `5 E4`
10–14 Kingsland Rd, Shoreditch, E2 • 020 7613 4462
>> www.herbaluk.com
Open 9pm–2am Mon & Wed–Sun, 8pm–1am Tue

This is a club that's got all its priorities right: an old warehouse building that's left largely untouched; comfy bar with wooden floors and windows overlooking the street; a superior sound system; and, best of all, a menu of musical flavours that pulls the initiated back again and again.

One of the best (irregular) nights is Eastern Drum and Breaks: in the main dance area you can lose yourself in some intense London-style tabla breaks, while upstairs in the bar the mood is mellower, for more Anglo-Asian experiments in sound. Other great nights include the monthly Hospitality, for a less-abrasive form of drum 'n' bass, and Starf*cker for funky house and a light smattering of 1980s porn music. Herbal's guest DJs have included Grooverider, Artful Dodger, Gilles Peterson, Mr Thing and Goldie.

Hoxton Square Bar `5 E5`
& Kitchen *groundbreaking style bar*
2–4 Hoxton Square, N1 • 020 7613 0709
Open 11am–midnight Mon–Sat, 11am–11:30pm Sun

Formerly the Lux Bar (when it kick-started London's style-bar revolution), HSB&K now has even more bare concrete space and battered old sofas to lounge on. Decent, simple bar food and good European lagers are served. Grab a window seat before the evening rush.

Mother/333 *DJ bar and club* `5 E5`
333 Old Street, EC1 • 020 7739 5949
>> www.333mother.com Open 8pm to 3 or 4am nightly

The first-floor Mother bar opens at 8pm nightly; closing time depends on what's on. Club 333 downstairs joins up with Mother on weekend nights for sweaty fun and a real mix of music. You'll find a friendly crowd, while top-notch DJs such as Andrew Weatherall and Smilex keep the mood upbeat.

>> *DJ bars and clubs usually charge admission after 9 or 10pm, and stay open into the early hours*

Vibe Bar *bohemian DJ bar*   `11 F1`
Old Truman Brewery, 91 95 Brick Lane, E1 • 020 7377 2899
» www.vibe-bar.co.uk Open 11am–11:30pm Mon–Thu & Sun,
11am–1am Fri–Sat. Adm fee after 8pm Fri & Sat

Spread around various poky spaces in a former brewery, this arty venue doubles up as a successful DJ bar
and live music outlet, and has helped to regenerate
the cultural life of the Brick Lane area *(see p160).* The
main room may look makeshift – haphazard furniture,
murals, an old piano and a DJ shack – but the Vibe is
a well-run, multidisciplined organization attracting
customers from all income brackets.

A menu of curries, kebabs and salads helps wash
down standard beers and strong cocktails. One side
room is sometimes given over to obscure board
games from the Indian Subcontinent; there's Internet
access, too. The best space is a cobbled courtyard
(covered and heated in winter), which lends an al
fresco, continental air to this otherwise truly cross-
cultural London experience.

Pride of Spitalfields *East End boozer*   `11 F1`
3 Heneage Street, E1 • 020 7247 8933
Open 11am–11pm Mon–Sat, noon–10:30pm Sun

A solid, honest-to-goodness pub, located on a side
road off Brick Lane. Many come here for a swift drink
before visiting a nearby curry house. Traditional ales
include Crouch Vale Best, Fuller's ESB and London
Pride, plus obscure guest ales. Authentic jellied eels
come free on Sunday lunchtimes.

93 Feet East *bar & evening club*   `11 F1`
150 Brick Lane, E1 • 020 7247 3293
» www.93feeteast.co.uk Open 5–11pm Mon–Thu, 5pm–1am
Fri, noon–1am Sat, noon–10:30pm Sun

You know this place must be a bit special, because it
manages to draw in a regular crowd despite restricted
opening hours. Success is due to a searching music
policy, mixing live acts, visuals and great DJs, plus
cool bar areas and a courtyard too.

Golden Heart *artists' haunt* `11 F1`
110 Commercial Street, E1 • 020 7247 2158
Open 11am–11pm Mon–Sat, noon–10:30pm Sun

Popularized by the 1990s crop of young British artists,
this smoky Victorian institution of dark-wood panelling and traditional ales is also a favourite of workers
from Shoreditch market. This gives the pub the feel of
a genuine "local". In summer, there is outside seating.
Be warned: the bar staff are notoriously abrupt.

Loungelover *hedonistic bar* `5 F5`
1 Whitby Street, E1 • 020 7012 1234
Open 6pm–midnight Mon–Thu, 6pm–1am Fri, 7pm–1am Sun

The latest innovative designer bar, set beside Les
Trois Garçons *(see p47)*, is anything but miminalist.
A camp interior of chandeliers and bizarre bric-a-brac
is complemented by l over-themed cocktails and
champagne frosts, delivered by a studiously trendy
bar staff. Book a table in advance at weekends.

Prospect of Whitby *ancient inn on the Thames*
57 Wapping Wall, E1 • 020 7481 1095 • ⊖ Wapping
Open 11:30am–11pm Mon–Sat, noon–10:30pm Sun

London's oldest riverside pub, still with its flagstone
floor and pewter-covered bar counter, was a
smugglers' inn in the 16th century, and later served
liquid refreshment to Samuel Pepys and Charles
Dickens. Today, it is enjoyed by locals and visitors
alike, lured by real ales and views from the terrace.

The Grapes *another historic riverside boozer*
76 Narrow Street, E14 • 020 7987 4396 • Limehouse DLR
Open noon–3 & 5:30–11 Mon–Fri, noon–11 Sat, noon–10:30 Sun

As wonky and haphazard as when Charles Dickens
described it in *Our Mutual Friend* (1864), this
creaking wooden pub still boasts its riverside
platform terrace. Today, it also has a first-class fish
restaurant upstairs, and excellent seafood-oriented
bar snacks. Real ales are on offer, too.

>> *The best London beers are Fuller's (who brew London Pride and ESB) and Young's (Special)*

Medicine Bar *very popular DJ bar*   `4 B2`
181 Upper Street, N1 • 020 7704 9536
Also at 89 Great Eastern Street, EC2
» www.medicinebar.net
Open 5pm–midnight Mon–Thu, 5pm–2am Fri, noon–2am Sat,
noon–midnight Sun. Adm after 9pm Fri & Sat; DJs Thu–Sun

This enormously successful clubby bar on Islington's
main street has now spawned a branch in hipper
Shoreditch, but the original venue cannot be beaten.
The formula is quite simple: take an ornate bar of the
traditional pub variety; around it, create a laid-back
interior of subtle lighting, tatty sofas and greenery;
make sure you keep dispensing spot-on cocktails and
standard beers at very reasonable prices; and, finally,
hire a DJ to mix up a storm.

The sounds encompass jazz funk, soul, hip-hop,
jazzy drum 'n' bass and house. There's a modest
chill-out room, and on summer evenings the
adjoining passage is filled with tables. The
atmosphere is sexy and slightly bohemian; the
clientele second-generation clubbers, who've
sampled all kinds of nightlife and feel at home with
something less full-on than a proper club night.

Admirably unpretentious, the Medicine Bar's only
snag is its very popularity and infectious spirit. Two
hundred people jigging around the narrow main bar
on a busy night leaves little room for manoeuvre.
Those people swanning to the head of the queue and
enjoying discounts have gone to the trouble of
obtaining a membership card – check the venue's
funky website for details of this and forthcoming DJs.

Embassy Bar *very cool bar*   `4 B2`
119 Essex Road, N1 • 020 7226 7901
Open 5pm–11pm daily (to 1am Fri & Sat)

While nearby Upper Street is big with party crowds,
Essex Road's Embassy Bar draws the discerning.
Behind an all-black exterior is a small bar room with a
central, semi-circular counter and an outer ring of
black leather furniture for lounging. Downstairs,
there's a basement bar with a dance floor.

The Crown *organic gastropub* `4 A3`
116 Cloudesley Road, N1 • 020 7837 7107
Open noon–11pm Mon–Sat, noon–10:30pm Sun

Fuller's Brewery made a wise choice when they
decided to give this standard local a serious upgrade
in the late 1990s. Set in a tranquil street surrounded
by grand townhouses, The Crown's catchment area
was undergoing a serious demographic shift. Soon
the newly rusticated interior was filled with discerning
high-income professional couples, ably catered to by
an open kitchen *au fait* with chargrilled meats and
continental sauces. The quality of wine on offer has
improved beyond recognition, and cocktails, too, are
of a standard (and a price) expected in the West End.
The character of the original pub has been kept, with
the etched-glass panels and a beautifully carved oak
bar. The menu, chalked up on a board, invariably
features a couple of safe standards, not least a
superb Sunday roast. A patio comes into good use in
summer, and children are welcome all year round.

Island Queen *elegant old pub* `4 B3`
87 Noel Road, N1 • 020 7704 7631
Open noon–11pm Mon–Sat, noon–10:30pm Sun

A haunt of actors and canal-side residents, the Island
Queen is a study in decorum and good taste. Ships'
figureheads set against dark wood and etched glass
are attractive features of this venerable establishment. It is also appreciated for its fine ales (such as
London Pride) and the pool table in the snug.

Pineapple *a locals' local*
51 Leverton Street, NW5 • 020 7284 4631 • ⊜ Kentish Town
Open 11am–11pm Mon–Sat, 11am–10:30pm Sun

The Pineapple is a gem of a pub, hidden away in
the backstreets of Kentish Town. A cool, arty crowd
served by cool, arty barstaff in cool, arty surroundings are the key elements. It also has real ales
(including the sought-after Marston's Pedigree),
good music and a conservatory.

Pubs, Bars & Clubs

Lock Tavern *DJ-run Brit pub* `2 D2`
35 Chalk Farm Road, NW1 • 020 7482 7163
Open noon–11pm Mon–Sat, noon–10:30pm Sun

This landmark venue in Camden (not by the Lock, iron-ically) offers textbook lessons in how to run a modern, urban public house. Once a grimy Victorian city pub, it has been renovated by a music-minded team keen to appeal to discerning all-comers. The Lock retains the comforts of a local pub – leather furniture in the main downstairs bar, armchairs around the fireside in the upstairs one – and runs an excellent kitchen, providing what is best described as British tapas, reasonably priced and catering to vegetarians.

Fine ales are poured alongside standard lagers, and sunk with abandon at weekends. The beer garden (covered and heated in winter) and roof terrace overlooking Camden Market buzz with savvy young urbanites, happy to waste entire Sundays here. That's when DJs play all day, with international "names" doing a turn once in a while.

Anchor Bankside *historic riverside pub* `10 C4`
34 Park Street, SE1 • 020 7407 1577
Open 11am–11pm Mon–Sat, 11am–10:30pm Sun

Its heavy beams and bare stonework bore witness to such famous figures as Dr Samuel Johnson in the 18th century. Today, the Anchor's proximity to the Globe and Tate Modern makes it popular with visitors to London. The riverside terrace is a draw in summer, but the cosy interior is at its best in winter.

Mac Bar *hip DJ hangout* `3 E2`
102 Camden Road, NW1 • 020 7485 4530
≫ www.macbar.co.uk Open noon–11 Mon–Sat, noon–10:30 Sun

A brash cocktail-and-DJ bar of high repute, the Mac Bar represents a bright beacon of change in Camden's somewhat stilted pub life. Here, a sharp crowd gathers around the maroon furniture, enjoying superbly mixed cocktails and equally well mixed musical accompani-ments (DJs Fridays and Saturdays, jazz Wednesdays).

Check out how to mix the coolest cocktails with ≫ www.elondon.dk.com

Vauxhall Tavern *high camp fun & laughs*   `15 H4`
372 Kennington Lane, SE11 • 020 7737 4043
Open 9pm–2am Sat, noon–midnight Sun

Saturday is the big night here, when Duckie – a gay London institution – features cabaret, punk, post-punk and electro spun on the decks by London Readers Wifes (sic). Between the main acts, hostess Amy Lamé *(right)* orchestrates a quiz or two. Sundays are for lounging with Slags Chillout DJ set.

Ministry of Sound *branded superclub*
103 Gaunt Street, SE1 • 020 7378 6528 • ⊖ Elephant & Castle
≫ **www.ministryofsound.com** Open 10:30pm–5am Fri, 11pm–7am Sat; check website for other club nights

Many die-hard clubbers now shun the Ministry (in part for its megalomaniacal branding), but you'd be a fool to ignore one of its big nights, when the likes of Little Louie Vega from Masters At Work or London's very own Norman Jay take to the decks – bliss.

Fridge/Fridge Bar *Brixton institutions*
1 Town Hall Parade, SW2 • 020 7326 5100 • ⊖ Brixton
≫ **www.fridge.co.uk** Fridge open 10pm–6am Fri & Sat; Fridge Bar open 11am–midnight daily (to 3am Fri & Sat)

Saturday's Love Muscle is the regular, pumped-up gay night. On every other Friday, Fusion keeps things fast and sweaty for clubbers of all persuasions until dawn. The Fridge Bar has its own club – try the occasional 'Til Shiloh night, for dub, and roots and culture.

Beer Gardens

Few city-centre pubs have beer gardens, but there are plenty further afield where Londoners revel in a combination of beer and sun at the first warming of the weather. One of the largest gardens belongs to the **Freemason's Arms** just off Hampstead Heath, and there's a smaller, prettier garden attached to the nearby historic **Spaniards Inn**. Islington residents drink under open skies at the countryfied **Albion**; while over in Camden, the defiantly urban **Lock Tavern** *(see opposite)* boasts a roof terrace. Pick of the South London pubs for al-fresco boozing is the **Windmill**, which has Clapham Common as its garden. The **Royal Inn on the Park** is a fine East London pub on the edge of Victoria Park. For individual pub details, *see p228.*

Pubs, Bars & Clubs >>>>>

Bug Bar & Lounge *DJs in the crypt*
The Crypt, Brixton Hill, SW2 • 020 7738 3366 • ⊖ Brixton
>> www.bugbrixton.co.uk Open 8pm–1am Thu, 8pm–3am Fri
& Sat, 8pm–late Sun. Adm Sat after 9pm

This destination DJ bar and club, located in a
spacious stone crypt beneath Brixton's St Matthew's
Church, has undergone a recent upgrade after seven
years of gritty, Gothic hedonism. The old décor,
redolent of a student party, has gone, and in its place
more stylish, leather furniture has been spread over
the basement space. The lighting, too, is more in tune
with a lounge interior than low-key dive, and the Bug
has even allowed itself the new epithet "& Lounge".

  The music is still excellent (from breakbeats on
Saturdays to Wednesday's Singers and Poets night),
and the dance floor in the Bug's club room has lost
none of its raw energy. Reasonably priced cocktails and
a loyal core of regulars – plus a surprising number
happy to travel across the river for a night here – ensure
that the Bug is in no danger of over-gentrification.

Dogstar *DJ bar with attitude*
389 Coldharbour Lane, SW9 • 020 7733 7515 • ⊖ Brixton
Open noon–2am daily (to 4am Fri & Sat)

Dogstar is a large, loud dance bar, revered for having
kick-started the Brixton nightlife revolution in the
mid-1990s. A younger generation now meets under
the overhead projectors, but the formula is pretty
much the same: late, late nights, flavoured spirits and
some serious partying. Expect a queue at weekends.

Riverside Pubs

The **Founders Arms**, a modern brick bunker near
Tate Modern, is the most central Thames-side pub.
For more atmosphere and a riverside terrace, try
Anchor Bankside, which dates from 1775. Further
east, other historic riverside pubs include the
Prospect of Whitby, **The Grapes** *(both p149)* and,
in Greenwich, the **Trafalgar Tavern** *(see opposite)*.

Hammersmith boasts a string of pubs linked by a
riverside walkway. Best of the bunch is **The Dove**,
which began life in the 18th century as a coffeehouse
and has Britain's smallest bar. The nearby **Blue
Anchor** is where Gwyneth Paltrow engaged in silly
drinking games in *Sliding Doors*. Richmond has
perhaps the finest riverside pubs, notably the **White
Cross**. For individual pub details, *see pp228–9*.

Bread & Roses *family-oriented pub*
68 Clapham Manor St, SW4 • 020 7498 1779 • ⊖ Clapham North
Open noon–11pm Mon–Sat, noon–10:30pm Sun

This pub is run by the Workers' Beer Company, which lines up its own house ale alongside other quality varieties, and names its potent cocktails after famous revolutionaries. The pub food is wholesome, and children are unusually well catered for, with a day-time crèche and play area.

Prince of Wales *a pub with character*
38 Old Town, SW4 • 020 7622 3530 • ⊖ Clapham Common
Open 5–11pm Mon–Fri, 1–11pm Sat, 1–10:30pm Sun

The Prince of Wales is an eccentric pub, full of curios accumulated by a former landlord after a lifetime at sea. Superb ales feature strongly, although finding the space to enjoy them amid all the junk can be a problem. The pub attracts South London's bohemian dreamers, and serenades them with alternative music.

Greenwich Union *own-brew place* `16 B3`
56 Royal Hill, SE10 • 020 8692 6258
Open 11am–11pm Mon–Sat, 11am–10:30pm Sun

Interesting house beers are available at this establishment, run by the Meantime Brewing Company. They include the company's Union brand, alongside raspberry and chocolate varieties and traditional Central European brews. There's excellent food, regular live jazz, a front terrace and a back garden.

Trafalgar Tavern *historic ale house* `16 C1`
Park Row, SE10 • 020 8858 2437
Open 11:30am–11pm Mon–Sat, noon–10:30pm Sun

This has been a Greenwich institution for 150 years or more, its walls lapped by the Thames, and its grand, high-ceilinged rooms dotted with maritime memorabilia. Real ales and Czech lagers are a fixture in the three main bar areas, although the back bar by the adjoining restaurant is more suited to fine wine.

Brixton and Clerkenwell rank alongside Soho as London's best spots for nightlife

streetlife

Markets are the pulse of local neighbourhoods such as Notting Hill, Spitalfields and Borough. Elsewhere, it is the bars, shops, galleries and cafés that provide the spark – as in Hoxton, where locals spill out of the pubs and onto the pavements at the first glimmer of sunshine. Other areas, notably Brixton and Soho, come into their own after nightfall.

Streetlife

Soho *24-hour party people*　9 F3

The densely packed district between Oxford Street to the north and Chinatown to the south is a hive of activity day and night. **Old Compton Street**, Soho's main thoroughfare, represents London at its most sexually relaxed – almost every bar and café along the road (from **G-A-Y** to **Comptons**) has a predominantly gay clientele. There is a wider, international appeal to adjoining streets, where you find the **French House** *(see p139)*, the **Gay Hussar** (No. 2 Greek St) and the non-stop, caffeine-fuelled **Bar Italia** (Frith Street; *see also p19*), in which Italian football plays on the screen whenever possible.

Wardour Street is busier, with some good food stops, such as **Satsuma, Mezzo** and **Spiga**, but the grittiest and most varied part of Soho lies between **Brewer** and **Broadwick** streets. Brewer is home to **Madame Jo-Jos** *(see p138)* and **The Escape Bar** (gay dance acts); style books (**Soho's Original Book Shop**) and gay erotica (**Prowler Soho**); **Randall & Aubin** for seafood and champagne; and **Lina Stores**, one of the few remaining Italian delicatessens in Soho (along with **Camisa** at No. 61 Old Compton Street).

Walker's Court leads through to **Berwick Street**, passing sleazy 1960s institution **Raymond Revue** bar and a concentration of sex shops and peep shows. Berwick retains a lively street market and is renowned for its record shops. **Vinyl Junkies** shares premises with **Daddy Kool** in a daily soul vs. reggae sound clash. And **Sister Ray** and **Selectadisc** offer a mixed bag of music styles, old and new.

Rainy nights and Soho go hand in hand, but if you find yourself here on a bright summer's day, pick up something sweet at **Patisserie Valerie** *(see p26)* and head for prim **Soho Square** or the spruced up **St Anne's Churchyard**. Here you can laze the afternoon away, until the lure of sweaty bars and loud music drags you back into the melee.

Portobello Road *shops, stalls & cafés* `6 D3`

Antiques market open 7:30am–5:30pm Sat;
general market & shops 9am–5pm Mon–Sat (to 1pm Thu)

This is one of the most characterful streets in London. A mile-long walk along its north-south axis takes you from pastel-hued Notting Hill cottages and quaint little antiques shops to a blankets-on-the-floor street market in the shadows of the Westway flyover. The area was lowly in the 1950s, and bohemian in the 1960s and 1970s. Today it remains – despite the influence of well-heeled local celebrities and films such as *Notting Hill* – eclectic, vibrant and fun.

The southern end of the road is at its busiest best on Saturdays, when the antiques market holds sway. The quaint shops have a preponderance of well-oiled cricket bats, ancient golf clubs, tanned leather foot-balls and old curling stones destined for re-use as doorstops. A clutter of Victoriana – enamel signs, painted buckets and faded flags – can be trawled through at **Alice's** (No. 86). Close by, refreshment is readily available at the **Earl of Londsdale** on the corner of Westbourne Grove or the **Fluid Juice Bar** on Elgin Crescent. Just beyond the **Electric Cinema** *(see also p15)* and its brasserie, Blenheim Crescent cuts across Portobello. Situated here are two excellent bookshops, **Blenheim Books** and the **Travel Bookshop**, which has a good selection on London.

The **general market** (with a nice stall for olives and breads) takes place below the flyover. Here, the **Market Bar** is always good for a lager or cocktail. **Café Grove** opposite has a first-floor terrace.

North of the Westway is **Portobello Green** *(see p83)* and a rambling Saturday market that peters out as it reaches the Golborne Road. Here funky clothes shops *(see p85)* and antique furniture shops spill out onto the pavements, and there are some good bars and eateries: **Bed** for drinks from early evening, **Galicia** for tapas; **Golborne Grove** *(see p143)* as the requisite gastropub; **Lisboa Patisserie** *(see p42)*; and **George's Portobello Fish Bar** for takeaways.

Streetlife

>> >> >>

Westbourne Park *upmarket Notting Hill* `6 D3`

The joys of this characterful West London enclave are split between the leisurely shops of **Westbourne Grove**, and the eateries on **Westbourne Park Road**.

The Grove is a place for boutique-browsing on sunny days. Its focal point, strangely, is a Piers Gough-designed turquoise-brick public toilet building, reminiscent of the Art Nouveau Métro entrances of Paris. A flower kiosk, **Wild at Heart**, is built into the structure. Nearby shops include **Joseph** (No. 236), **Agnès B** (No. 235), **Camper** (No. 214), **Jigsaw** (No. 192) and **Anne Wiberg's** "trash couture" (No. 170). A 5-minute stroll up Chepstow Road – passing or otherwise the **Prince Bonaparte** – takes you to Westbourne Park Road. To your left are **The Oak** gastropub and **Lucky 7**, a groovy diner-type place for soups, sandwiches, hot dogs, beers and shakes. And to your right, the wonderful **Cow** and its friendly rival **The Westbourne**, both gastropubs of renown. For a quieter meal, there's **Rosa's**, a simple, almost rustic dining room at No. 69.

Brick Lane *curry houses & style shops* `11 F1`

Once synonymous with fantastic cheap curry houses, Brick Lane in London's East End has a more diverse character these days. The restaurants are still there – **Preethi**, **Le Taj**, **Café Naz**, **Bengal Cuisine**, **Meraz Café** on Hanbury Street, to name a few – though price rises and touting have tainted their image. North of the **Truman's Brewery** there is now a cluster of fashion outlets, stylish furniture shops and hip cafés and bars. The most interesting clothes shops are in Dray Walk on the old brewery site – **Junky**, **Public Beware** and **Gloria's Super Deluxe**. Nearby, **93 Feet East** and the **Vibe Bar** *(see p148)* soak up the evening crowds.

A daytime visit is best on Sundays, when the trashy morning market brings throngs of people to the streets here, but any evening is good for wandering between the neon-signed curry houses and maybe stopping in for a pint at the old-fashioned **Pride of Spitalfields** *(see p148)*. For more about shopping in Brick Lane and nearby **Cheshire Street**, see p88.

Spitalfields Market *fashion & furniture* `11 F1`
020 7247 8556
Open 10:30–4:30 Mon–Fri; 10–5 Sun

Currently London's most exciting market, Spitalfields – set in a historic building just east of the City – is jam-packed on Sundays with stalls selling everything from organic vegetables to retro furniture. Fashion has become its greatest strength, though – look out for the Vivienne Westwood-inspired **Grunge Vogue** and a young designer called **Kim**. Flower stalls, such as **Chayapa Flowers**, add to the fun, and permanent stalls such as **Arkansas Café** (barbecued steaks and roast poultry) provide tasty nourishment.

Weekdays are much quieter, but the market continues and on Thursdays trades almost exclusively in fashion. Lamb Street to the north and Brushfield Street to the south are home to interesting vintage furniture outlets, quality poster shops and traditional British food shop **A Gold** *(see p87)*. The **Market Coffee House** is perfect for a moment of repose.

Columbia Road *East End flower market* `5 F4`

From the break of dawn on Sunday mornings, this short stretch of narrow East London road rouses itself into a vibrant flower- and foliage-filled market. Stall traders shout about their bargain trays of bedding plants and wait for the late-rising urbanites to turn up for exotica in the form of banana plants and tree ferns. Snack stalls and cafés offer breakfasts, brunches and early lunches and, when that's done, the **Birdcage** pub on the corner of Columbia Road and Cosset Road is on hand to slake mid-morning thirsts. If that doesn't take your fancy, there's **Laxeiro** tapas bar at the other end of the market, **Stingray Global Café** for oversize pizzas or the more secretive **Nelson's Head** pub, tucked away on Horatio Street.

Alongside the horticulture, Columbia Road's shops offer a nice line in furniture (old, retro and new) as well as ceramics and funky light shades. By early afternoon, the crowds disperse, most carrying a pet-sized piece of the great natural world back to their city flats.

For information about all Brick Lane's curry houses, see www.bricklanerestaurants.com

Hoxton *bohemian Shoreditch* `5 E5`

It's indisputably London's coolest area for an artsy crowd – and Hoxton's bubble is far from bursting. Designers, artists and other creative types saw the potential in this down-at-heel district in the mid-90s, converting derelict buildings into studios and live-work lofts. A smattering of bars followed. Now the streets around Hoxton Square and Charlotte Road are lined with hip restaurants, clubs, design shops and galleries.

Hoxton wakes up late, and the daytime streets can feel quite lazy, especially at weekends when people saunter between the galleries. Jay Jopling's **White Cube**, situated on the square, is the biggest gallery; **The Agency** (ring the buzzer at 18 Charlotte Road) is one of the longest established. There's also a great contemporary arts bookshop, **ARTWORDS**, at 65 Rivington Street. Arrive late in the afternoon, take up a seat at one of the bars and watch the throngs gather as the sky darkens. **The Bricklayer's Arms** on Charlotte Road is an old stalwart, while **Zigfrid** has Chesterfield sofas and large windows framing the square.

Ktchn (35 Charlotte Rd) does excellent European/Middle Eastern salads to take-away. Many of the bars serve decent food (**Cantaloupe**, *see p47*, and the **Great Eastern Dining Room**, *see p48*), **Hoxton Square Bar and Kitchen**, *see p147*, and again, Zigfrid). For a little more formality, head for the **Rivington Bar and Grill** (Rivington St) or **Home** on Leonard Street. On Curtain Road and Shoreditch High Street, the bars have more of a boyish feel to them, with much evidence of pool tables (**Elbow Room** and **Pool**, opposite each other on Curtain Road). **Bar Kick** on Shoreditch High Street has table football. **Juno**, next door, has a variety of nostalgic games for those who grew up in the age of *Space Invaders* and *Pac Man*.

Round the corner on Kingsland Road is **Dream Bags/ Jaguar Shoes**, a name left over from previous occupants. Befitting the bar's bohemian New York style, Leonard Cohen doesn't so much play from the speakers as seep from the crumbling plasterwork. For the late-night, early-morning crowd, there are the clubs **Herbal**, **Cargo** and **Mother/333** *(see pp146–7)*.

Camden Lock *Camden Market's best spot* `2 D2`

The roadway from Camden Tube to Chalk Farm Road Tube is awash with stalls dishing out T-shirts, cheap fashionwear and all manner of smoking paraphernalia. The nicest part of **Camden Market**, though, is at its furthest reaches, in and around the railway arches of **Stables Market**. Here, you'll find a good mix of retro-style clothes, furniture and curios. There's also "goth" gear and techno clubwear – the latter in the clublike space of **Cyberdog**, where a bar serves guarana drinks and fruity "detox" concoctions. The music gets evermore manic, and the whiff of incense and cooking hangs everywhere.

The snacks served by the market food stalls are just belly-fillers, though. If you want a more carefully prepared meal and a drink, head across Chalk Farm Road to the **Lock Tavern** *(see p152)*, or to its near neighbour the **Loch Fyne Oyster Bar**. **The Enterprise**, a free house (pub) right outside Chalk Farm Road station, serves up a good pint.

Borough *London's larder by the river* `10 D4`

With the rumble and clatter of trains passing overhead, **Borough Market** (open noon–6pm Fri and 9am–4pm Sat) on the South Bank brightens the shadows of Southwark's railway arches with bright red and yellow awnings spread above stalls selling Spanish hams, local breads, French cheeses, and wild game from the Highlands of Scotland. This is the belly of modern London, a neighbourhood crammed with the warehouses of food importers. As well as buying food to take away, market regulars can munch on juicy venison burgers, washed down with a pint at the **Market Porter**, **The Wheatsheaf** or the **Globe Tavern**. Day-trippers tend to take a more leisurely lunch, with a meal at **Fish!** or round the corner at **Cantina Vinopolis**.

Though most signs point to **Southwark Cathedral** and the **Thameside Walk**, it's worth exploring a few of Borough's dark old streets, which yield up great pubs, such as the historic **George Inn**, just off Borough High Street, and the **Royal Oak** on Tabard Street.

The South Bank *riverside culture* `10 A4`

At the heart of an arching, river-hugging cultural quarter, the South Bank Complex includes the **South Bank Centre** *(see p129)*, **Hayward Gallery** *(see p109)* and **Royal National Theatre** *(see p129)*. Tucked under Waterloo Bridge are the **NFT** *(see p130),* its lively **Film Café** and some browsable second-hand bookstalls.

Few people are indifferent to the Brutalist/ International Style architecture of these buildings, and the National Theatre in particular is often vilified – unjustly so, given the fantastic interior spaces, which include many café, bar and foyer areas for socializing and free entertainment. The Long Bar at the National, for example, hosts an excellent pre-theatre programme of World Music in the early evening.

To the west of this complex is the touristy area around the **London Eye** *(see p18)*. To the east, along the riverbank, is the quieter, prettier area of **Gabriel's Wharf** – a kind of middle-class shanty town, with pizzerias and crafts shops, a place to hire bicycles (**London Bicycle Tour Co**) and **Riverside Therapies** for a shiatsu or Swedish back rub. Further east, crafts continue at the **Oxo Tower Wharf** *(see p91)*, also home to its namesake restaurant *(see p54)*.

Tate Modern *(see p111)* brings thousands to Bankside daily, along the riverside walk, across the **Millennium Bridge** from the direction of the City and St Paul's, or by riverboat *(see p100)*. Theatregoers off to **Shakespeare's Globe** *(see p130)* and visitors to **Vinopolis** (a wine museum with a good bistro) swell the numbers further. Two pubs on hand, **The Anchor** *(see p154)* and the **Founders Arms**, get very busy in summer. Venture just a little further along the river to the freshly scrubbed **Southwark Cathedral**, and you will find plenty of great pubs and decent cafés, and the superb food market at **Borough** *(see p163)*.

Northcote Road *neighbourhood food market*
🚇 Clapham Junction
Market open 9–5 Thu, Fri & Sat

Clapham's market road is at its jolliest on Saturdays. London's foodies are well served by delicatessens, shops and stalls selling designer kitchenware, cheeses, artisan breads, meats and fresh fish. Make up a picnic to take to nearby Clapham Common or eat at the superb **Gourmet Burger Bar** (No. 44). For a drink, it has to be **The Eagle** on Chatham Road.

Brixton *lively days & even livelier nights*
At the southern end of the Victoria Tube line, Brixton is home to a mix of cultures and social groups. This diversity is reflected in the shops, cafés, restaurants, bars and clubs. Busy with a lively market by day, it is, however, at night that Brixton comes into its own, when it draws in a youthful, partying crowd.

The **Dogstar** *(see p154)*, **Living** and the **Fridge Bar** *(see p153)* all get going early, as do the local eateries – **Ichiban** for sushi, **Fujiyama** and the **Satay Bar** for noodles and rice dishes, and **Bamboula** for Caribbean food. For an unusual dining experience, try the camp Baroque of **Café Goya**; the excellent Caribbean cooking at the **Brixtonian Havana Club** (which also stocks more than 200 rums!); or the atmospheric **Bug Restaurant**, which shares St Matthew's crypt with the **Bug Bar & Lounge** *(see p154)*.

As the night draws on, the streets are criss-crossed with people heading in different directions: the **Brixton Academy** for live bands; the **Juice Bar** for poetry nights; the **Ritzy** *(see p131)* for films; **Tongue & Groove** and **Neon** for cocktails in a clubby vibe; or the pulsating **George IV** DJ bar on Brixton Hill. **Mass**, **Substation South** (gay) and the **Fridge** (mixed, *see p153*) are the big clubs with all-nighters on Fridays and Saturdays. Throughout the night, buses head back into central London from outside the Fridge, and there's a black cab rank outside the cinema. But many revellers stay until 6am, spilling out onto Brixton's green by the church in the early morning sunlight.

havens

Sometimes you just need to steal away from the accelerated pace of city life. A wealth of parks makes London one of the world's greenest cities. But, even in the centre of town, there are many other places that offer solace and respite. Spas and massage provide deep relaxation, and you will also find secret courtyards, old stone churches and tranquil woodland cemeteries in which to stroll or contemplate.

Havens

Temple *serene courtyards of the judiciary* 10 A3
Off Fleet Street, EC4 • Tours 020 7797 8241
>> www.innertemple.org.uk or www.middletemple.org.uk

Background noise drops to the level of polished shoes clipping across worn flagstones as soon as you venture through the small archway of Inner Temple Lane. Take a slow stroll around the interconnected courtyards of the Inner and Middle Temples, surrounded by the chambers of law firms established here since the mid-14th century. Before that time, the area belonged to the Knights Templar; the statue by Temple Church *(see p98),* which depicts two knights sharing a horse, recalls the vows of poverty made by that military brotherhood when it was formed in 1117.

By the side of Middle Temple's Elizabethan Banqueting Hall is the perfect oasis of Fountain Court, its gnarled trees propped up by posts around a small pool and fountain, with plane trees towering overhead. Beyond here, lawns (usually open 12:30–3pm Mon–Fri) stretch down towards the Thames.

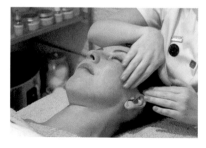

Indian Head Massage *free your mind* 9 G3
169 Drury Lane, WC2 • 020 7831 0830
>> www.farmacia123.com Head massage on Wed

The Indian head massage technique uses pressure, finger taps and light flicks to release tension. The masseuse will concentrate on your head and neck, but may work all the way down to the tips of your toes in order to find the source of tension. You may experience some discomfort here and there, but, by the end of the half-hour session, you should feel a deep sense of relaxation.

Victoria Embankment Gardens *breathing space* 9 G4

Though small, these gardens are a treasure for anyone wishing to steal away from the hurly-burly of the city. A small café rustles up all-day breakfasts, and music plays from the bandstand in summer, while workers on their lunch break soak up the sunshine. Look for the implausibly placed watergate – the land around here was claimed from the Thames in 1862.

Elemis Day Spa *queenly pampering* 8 D3
2–3 Lancashire Court, W1 • 020 8909 5060
>> www.elemis.com Open from 10am daily

Both men and women are welcome at this spa, which is renowned for discreet ocean wraps, Japanese silk facials, stone therapies, Balinese borehs and dozens of other exotic rituals. A "rasul" with mud in a steam room is the cheapest option, but you must book several weeks in advance or hope for a cancellation.

Bunhill Fields Burial Ground *Blake's resting place* 10 D1
City Road & Bunhill Row, EC1 • 020 8533 6482
Open 7:30am–7pm Mon–Fri, 9:30–sunset Sat & Sun (4pm closing Oct–Mar)

Close to the Barbican and a short walk from the buzz of Hoxton, Bunhill Fields is a remarkably quiet and shady spot. A pathway cuts through its little wooded burial ground, where the tombs of writers William Blake, Daniel Defoe and John Bunyan take pride of place. To the side of the graves is a glade-like lawn – a magical place to stretch out on a summer's day and listen to the birdsong.

St Olave's Recitals *a melodious hour* 11 E3
Hart Street, EC3 • 020 8533 6482
Recitals Wed & Thu 1–2pm; donations welcome

Sitting in the cool of a stone church and listening to one of St Olave's free lunchtime recitals is a splendid way to relax into a contemplative mood. London's 17th-century diarist Samuel Pepys cherished St Olave's, though he often slept through sermons. There's a pretty little churchyard at the Seething Lane entrance.

The Royal Parks

There are nine Royal Parks in all, some of them far from the city centre, in places such as Richmond and Greenwich *(see p174)*. Of the central parks **St James's** is the oldest, and is considered by many to be the most elegant. It separates Crown (Buckingham Palace) and State (the Houses of Parliament) with a swathe of grassland and a lake fringed by languid willows. The biggest is **Hyde Park**, though technically its western end – where you'll find the Serpentine Gallery *(see p101)* and the Orangery *(see p170)* – is **Kensington Gardens**. **Regent's Park** has attractive formal gardens as well as wide open spaces, used to host open-air theatre and concerts. Both Hyde Park and Regent's Park offer guided nature walks. For details, visit www.royalparks.gov.uk.

Holland Park *genteel charm* `6 D5`

The former grounds of a Jacobean country house, Holland Park holds a variety of delights, including woodland walks, formal English gardens and a splendid French restaurant. The house itself stands at the centre of the park, but, never having recovered from bomb damage in World War II, it now serves mainly as a backdrop to outdoor performances on summer evenings.

The outbuildings have fared better, with the Garden Ballroom now home to Marco Pierre White's Belvedere restaurant (modestly priced for a set lunch). If your appetite or wallet are not up to that, look for the pleasant café offering simpler fare that has taken root next to one of the garden walls.

The Rose Garden is perhaps the greatest sensorial delight of the formal gardens, while the Kyoto Garden, severe when laid out in 1991, has mellowed into a serene corner. The call of peacocks as they strut around their domain adds to the charm of the park.

Porchester Spa *Art Deco retreat* `7 F3`
Queensway, W2 • 020 7792 2919
Open 10am–10pm daily; call for details of men-only, women-only & mixed sessions

This beautiful Art Deco day spa of the 1920s is great value and attracts a complete mix of people. Enjoy a Swedish massage or Moroccan glove body scrub, along with unlimited access to Turkish baths, Russian steam rooms and an icy plunge pool. Snacks are served in the frigidarium (cool room) upstairs.

Orangery *antidote to museum fatigue* `7 F5`
Kensington Gardens, W8 • 020 7376 0239
Open Mar–Oct 10–6; Nov–Feb 10–5; tea served from 3pm

Set next to Kensington Palace, the graceful Orangery, dating from 1704, is a light-filled, yet cool retreat. Add to this the glorious gardens and the chance to enjoy a leisurely summer lunch or afternoon tea at this superior café, and you have ample reward for a morning spent shopping or in the museums of Kensington.

Chelsea Physic Garden *herbal cures* `14 B4`

Swan Walk, SW3 • 020 7376 3910
>> www.chelseaphysicgarden.co.uk
Open Apr–Oct: noon–5 Wed, 2–6 Sun & special events

A gateway bristling with knotted vegetation leads you into the secluded world of a garden in which the beauty and fragrance of the plants are matched by their restorative qualities. Established by the Society of Apothecaries in 1673, this was the herbal medicine cabinet of its day, and still operates as a research centre. Though dripping with blooms and bursting with verdant foliage, the World Medicine Garden and other areas retain a scientific orderliness, with small cards indicating the curative properties of each specimen. The pomegranate turns out to be quite a fruit – not only has it been used to purge envy, but it is also thought to be a reasonable cure for worms.

Sit in one of the tranquil spots where chairs have been set, and you'll soon appreciate the simpler restorative qualities of this unique English garden.

Little Venice *canal boats, cafés and bars* `7 G1`

Blomfleld Road & Warwick Crescent, W2
Boat trips: London Waterbus Company, 020 7482 2660

Little Venice centres on the junction of two canals: Regent's Canal, which links to the Thames, and the Grand Union, which extends all the way to Birmingham. Until relatively recently, this area was known as Browning's Pool, in honour of the 19th-century poet Robert Browning, who lived nearby. The tranquil waterways are a delightful city oasis, overlooked by Rembrandt Gardens, and dotted with colourful houseboats, barges and pleasure craft. Locals sit and gaze at the scene, while boat owners potter about their cheerily decorated vessels.

The neighbourhood has several nice eateries. One of the best is **The Bridge House Canal Theatre Café** on Delamere Terrace. This serves tasty food, and there's also live comedy, music and theatre upstairs. You can also board a ferry at Little Venice, and take a 50-minute trip through Regent's Park to Camden.

>> *For some ideas for a leisurely breakfast in Little Venice,* see p12

Hampstead Heath *ancient heathland* `1 C2`

This vast, elevated expanse of grassy slopes and woodlands, bordered on all sides by North London's wealthiest residential districts, is a magnificent remnant of real countryside within walking distance of the Tube. Londoners travel up here – in droves on Sundays – to gaze down upon their city, breathe deep and shake off urban stresses.

For a satisfying exploration of the Heath, try a circular walk from Hampstead village. Starting at the Tube station, wander through the quiet back roads past historic houses where luminaries such as John Keats *(see p108)*, George Orwell and H G Wells once lived. Crossing East Heath Road, you then step into the wilds, initially following a wide track through the woods. The destinations of the many crisscrossing paths are not easy to fathom, and it's best to meander in a vaguely northeasterly direction, through woodlands up to **Kenwood House** *(see p108)*, home to the Iveagh Bequest, with a café in the old coach house. Just beyond the house, in the direction of Highgate, are fantastic views. From these lofty heights, central London unfolds in a smoky blue haze along the shallow valley of the Thames, the distant towers and construction cranes of the City and Docklands contrasting with the slope of long grass at your feet.

Follow the path down the open slope and turn right at the bottom of South Wood, which forms the boundary of the Kenwood estate. From here, the path will take you back to Hampstead, past playing fields and old duelling grounds. Return to the welcoming pubs of Hampstead – **The Freemason's Arms** (Downshire Hill), **The Flask** (Flask Lane), **Ye Olde White Bear** (Well Road) and the **Holly Bush** (Holly Bush Steps).

Highgate Woods *woodland ramble*

A short walk up Muswell Hill Road from Highgate Tube station brings the woods into view: to your left, **Highgate Wood** proper; to your right, the dell of **Queen's Wood**. Both are rich in oak and hornbeam and the sound of birdsong – about 70 species of birds have been spotted here. Either wood is blissful for an hour or so of rambling on footpaths. Highgate Wood is more open, the wide paths eventually giving way to a playing field and the pleasant **Oshobasho Café** (open 8:30am–6pm or dusk if earlier). The more densely forested Queen's Wood has a **Weekend Café** (10–6 Sat & Sun), charmingly set amid the trees in a cottage with a verandah.

Having cleared mind and lungs, reintroduce yourself to city life gradually by way of **Highgate Village**. Drop by the **Flask** (corner of The Grove and Highgate West Hill), which serves English ales and Belgian monastery brews, and good pub food. Also pay a visit to **Highgate Cemetery** *(see p105)*, off Swain's Lane.

Abney Park Cemetery *graveyard for dissenters*
Stoke Newington Church Street, N16 • ⊜ Stoke Newington
⊜ **Angel or King's Cross, then bus 73**
≫ **www.abney-park.org.uk** Open daylight hours daily

Neglected for much of the 20th century, Abney Park is a gothic fantasy – gravestones broken and scattered, statues toppled and overrun with ivy, and green tendrils grasping to reclaim the ground. This natural tide has been only partially stemmed by recent interventions to clear pathways, and it remains a wild and enchanting woodland. Among the religious nonconformists buried here the most famous is William Booth, founder of the Salvation Army.

The main entrance, with its dramatic Egyptian gateway, is on Stamford Hill, but the more secretive way in is via a small gate on Church Street. The inner reaches – where you'll eventually reach a decrepit chapel – can feel very remote, and if you are visiting alone you may feel safer at the weekend, when it becomes the haunt of local families.

Havens

Greenwich Park *panoramic views* `16 C3`
Greenwich, SE10 • Park Office: 020 8858 2608
>> www.royalparks.gov.uk/parks/greenwich_park
Open from 6am daily

A walk around this breezy, partly formal, partly wild park, which stretches from the historic dockyards at Greenwich up the hill to Blackheath, offers fine views of London. From the top of the park, you can see the Thames wend through the metropolis, its banks giving rise to some of the densest clusters of development at Docklands, The City and Westminster.

Between the moored *Cutty Sark* at Greenwich Pier and Wren's **Old Observatory** at the top of the hill, the park's main paths are usually thronged with visitors, but stray from them and you can soon lose the crowds. Beyond the Observatory, heading south, you'll find a cricket green, the wilds of a deer park,

formal gardens and even Roman earthworks to explore. But if you don't want to lose sight of the river, head east to another promontory, One Tree Hill, on the Maze Hill side of the park. From here, there are views across to the Observatory and down to the **Old Royal Naval College** (the **Queens House**, *see p112*, is mostly obscured by a clump of trees at the foot of the hill). Beyond this looms Canary Wharf, the brown, silty Thames looping at its feet.

Walk down one of the meandering pathways, past the children's playground and then towards a gate that brings you out onto Park Row. You can either head to the Thames end of the road for a drink and a plate of whitebait at the **Trafalgar Tavern** *(see p155)* or take an immediate right for a quieter drink at **The Plume of Feathers**. Either way, it's good to finish off a walk in Greenwich with a riverside stroll back to the pier.

Kew Gardens *World Heritage beauty spot*

Kew • 020 8332 5655 • ⊖ ⊕ Kew Gardens

≫ www.kew.org Open 9:30–6 Mon–Fri, 9:30–7 Sat & Sun

The extensive, astonishingly lovely Royal Botanical Gardens are stocked with mature specimens of rare (and ordinary) trees, plants and flowers collected over hundreds of years from the remotest corners of the world. From the Tube and train station it's a well-signed 5-minute walk along leafy residential streets to the main, Victoria Park entrance. Maps, supplied with your tickets, place everything clearly.

The scale of Kew means that it is not difficult to find private space. The gardens comprise both wild and formal areas – gentle woodlands; pristine formal lawns and beds overflowing with ever-changing floral displays; ornamental lakes stocked with wildfowl; elegant glass-houses; and an eclectic collection of buildings including the landmark Pagoda.

Near the entrance, the beautiful, steamy **Palm House** (1848) is popular, but you can ascend a spiral staircase to the quieter elevated walkway. The **Princess of Wales Conservatory**, a mix of dry and moist habitats, also draws a crowd, but is worth a saunter in May during the orchid festival. **Queen Charlotte's Cottage** dates from the 18th century and was a favourite spot of this queen. She and husband King George III would picnic here. It remains a perfect idyll for a lazy afternoon munching sandwiches. If you are lucky, you may be serenaded by a blackbird from the branches of a silver birch. If you've neglected to bring a picnic, the **Orangery** is the best of several eating options, serving simple meals and cakes.

Between the Orangery and the river is the formal **Queen's Garden** – a place where statues punctuate walls of manicured hedges, laburnum drips from covered walkways and small fountains bubble. **Adm**

≫ *In Kew, consider a meal at the expensive but excellent Glasshouse (020 8940 6777) by the station*

hotels

In this eclectic city, your choice of accommodation sets the tone for your visit. Would you like a classy residence in Chelsea, close to the boutiques? Or is high-voltage Covent Garden, right in the centre, more your style? Perhaps you'd like to sample the edgy glamour of Notting Hill or the laid-back cool of Clerkenwell. Hotel rates are quite high, but there's memorable accommodation for all budgets.

TOP CHOICES – *hotels*

ROMANTIC HIDEAWAYS	SPAS & SPORTS	GASTRONOMIC
Blakes 33 Roland Gardens, SW7 Blakes' sumptuous rooms are perfect for lounging and loving. Wedding packages are available if you want to take things further. *(See p185)*	**The Dorchester** Park Lane, W1 The impressive Art Deco spa at this superbly appointed hotel offers a range of luxurious treatments and a well-equipped gym. *(See p183)*	**Claridge's** Brook Street, W1 Claridge's has the best hotel restaurant in town. Celebrated chef Gordon Ramsay serves up the Michelin-starred nosh. *(See p183)*
Hamilton House 14 West Grove, Greenwich, SE10 The pretty honeymoon suite in this Georgian house has breathtaking views of the Thames snaking past Greenwich. *(See p189)*	**Crescent Hotel** 49–50 Cartwright Gardens, WC1 Guests have access to the tennis courts opposite, and can even borrow racquets. *(See p181)*	
The Portobello Hotel 22 Stanley Gardens, W11 Luxurious furnishings include round beds, Moroccan cushions and a Victorian claw-foot tub right in the middle of the room... *(See p186)*	**One Aldwych** 1 Adlwych, WC2 Underwater music plays through the hotel's 18-m (60-ft) pool. There's also high-tech equipment and free personal training in the gym. *(See p180)*	>> *Prices quoted for hotels in London may or may not include VAT (17.5% tax), so always check when getting a quote.*
>> *If you are flexible about the dates of your stay, www.hoteldirect.co.uk/london offers a quick and easy way to find some of the best discounts on rooms in London's hotels.*	**London Bridge Hotel** 8–18 London Bridge Street, SE1 Free entry to the adjoining gym is among the facilities here. You could also just as easily go for a jog by the river. *(See p189)*	**Great Eastern Hotel** Liverpool Street, EC2 Design guru and restaurateur Terence Conran has installed five fabulous eateries at this hotel. Aurora is best of the lot. *(See p187)*
Miller's Residence 111a Westbourne Grove, W2 A precious find, this atmospheric, antiques-crammed guesthouse is lit by candles after dark. *(See p186)*		**The Metropolitan** It may not be part of the hotel itself, but acclaimed modern Japanese restaurant Nobu sits atop the cool and stylish Metropolitan. *(See p182)*

For online services that book hotels at all prices, see >> www.elondon.dk.com

STYLE STATEMENTS

Hazlitt's
6 Frith Street, W1
Hazlitt's is true to its period heritage, right down to the paint colours, carved bedsteads and old-fashioned WCs. *(See p181)*

Malmaison
Charterhouse Square, EC1
Contemporary furnishings and specially commissioned photographs set the style for this chic yet afford-able small chain hotel. *(See p187)*

Abbey House
11 Vicarage Gate, W8
Comfortable, Victorian-style rooms are the defining feature of an elegant address. Shared facilities keep the prices down. *(See p186)*

The Zetter
86–8 Clerkenwell Road, EC1
This loft hotel, converted from a warehouse, is decked out with 70s furniture, hand-printed panels and top-notch showers. *(See p188)*

BEST OF THE BARGAINS

>> If you are looking for an alternative to a hotel, www.yourstay.com/london offers well-appointed apartments for short-term rental.

Travel Inn, County Hall
Belvedere Road, SE1
Reliable chain accommodation is brought to a fantastic location here, just steps away from the London Eye and Saatchi Gallery. *(See p189)*

Dover Hotel
42–4 Belgrave Road, SW1
It's seriously cheap, but the Dover has satellite TV and modern ensuite facilities in every room. *(See p183)*

VIEWS & LOCALES

Covent Garden Hotel
10 Monmouth Street, WC2
In the middle of Covent Garden, this hotel can't be beaten when it comes to combining style and a central location. *(See p180)*

The Franklin
28 Egerton Gardens, SW3
Reserve a room at the back of this Knightsbridge townhouse hotel to overlook the tranquil, residents-only gardens. *(See p184)*

Holiday Inn Express, Old Street
275 Old Street, EC1
In hip Hoxton, this is the perfect base if you intend spending your days bar- and gallery-hopping, and your nights in the clubs. *(See p189)*

>> www.hotels-london.co.uk is an online booking agency that also has lists of useful web links, last-minute deals and special offers.

One Aldwych *contemporary grand hotel* `9 H3`

1 Aldwych, WC2 • 020 7300 1000
>> www.onealdwych.co.uk

The neo-grand design of this hotel became an instant hit with the style-conscious when it opened in the late 1990s. Occupying a former newspaper HQ on one corner of the Aldwych, it gives monumental elegance a modern edge. Staff wear lavender shirts designed by cool Savile Row tailor Richard James, and the walls are adorned with 350 original works of art. The rooms are surprisingly quiet, given the hotel's central position. Their styling is contemporary yet colourful, with silk drapes and plush upholstery. The suites at the front of the building, under a coppered cupola, are circular. Every detail has been considered: flowers are changed daily, and the terrazzo-stone bathrooms have heated floors and mini TVs. The health club surpasses most hotel gyms, with personal trainers on call and a pool with underwater music.

The Lobby Bar *(see p136)*, with its high ceiling, arched windows and dramatic sculptures, is always lively. There are two well-regarded restaurants, Axis and the less formal Indigo (both modern European cuisine), and a chic coffee bar. **Expensive**

Covent Garden Hotel *theatreland retreat* `9 F3`

10 Monmouth Street, WC2 • 020 7806 1000
>> www.coventgardenhotel.co.uk

Its location in London's Theatreland makes this cosy hotel a favourite with actors and others in the film and performing arts industries. The luxurious screening room gets plenty of use. Rooms are individually decorated in updated English style, one with a vast four-poster bed. **Expensive**

Hazlitt's *authentic period hotel* `9 F3`
6 Frith Street, W1 • 020 7434 1771
» www.hazlittshotel.com

The Soho home of 18th-century essayist William Hazlitt is true to its heritage while providing 21st-century comforts. The panelled rooms contain fireplaces, antique headboards and rolltop baths, yet there's also air-conditioning and Internet access. The drawing room has books signed by literary guests. **Expensive**

Charlotte Street Hotel *artistic digs* `9 E2`
15 Charlotte Street, W1 • 020 7806 2000
» www.charlottestreethotel.com

Set amid Charlotte Street's eclectic restaurants, this understated hotel combines original works by "Bloomsbury set" artists, reflecting the legacy of its location, with modern gadgets such as mini TVs in the luxurious granite bathrooms. The bar buzzes with media folk, and there's a swanky screening room. **Expensive**

Crescent Hotel *tidy guesthouse* `3 F5`
49–50 Cartwright Gardens, WC1 • 020 7387 1515
» www.CrescentHotelofLondon.com

The best of several small hotels occupying a Georgian crescent near University College, the Crescent is smart and well kept. There are TVs in the bedrooms, a guests' lounge and a cheerful breakfast room with a characterful old cast-iron cooker. Guests may use the tennis courts in the garden opposite. **Cheap**

Generator *futuristic budget hotel* `3 G5`
Compton Place, off Tavistock Place, WC1 • 020 7388 7666
» www.generatorhostels.com

London's biggest backpackers' hostel is decked out in stainless steel and neon. Accommodation is no-frills: bed down in a communal dorm or pay a little more for a private room. However, with a bar open until 2am, karaoke and a 24-hour Internet café, the young guests aren't here just to rest. **Cheap**

» *Expensive: over £200 for a double room per night; moderate: £120–200; cheap: £10–120*

The Metropolitan *cool & contemporary* 8 C5
Old Park Lane, W1 • 020 7447 1000
>> www.metropolitan.co.uk

This minimalist upstart caused a stir when it joined the luxury line-up overlooking Hyde Park in 1997; it was the first new hotel to open on Park Lane for two decades. Its understated chic hasn't dated a bit. Armani-clad staff waft around the cream lobby, with its 1930s-inspired club chairs. Rooms are contemporary yet comfortable, with blond-wood furniture, harmonious pale fabrics, and plenty of light (London weather permitting) streaming through the plate-glass windows. The Metropolitan has all the amenities you would expect from a top-class hotel – glamorous marble bathrooms, Internet access, CD players, DVDs on request – plus some fabulous "extras" that make it a bit more special. The health club offers holistic treatments using the natural COMO Shambhala products devised at the hotel's Caribbean sister resort. As a guest, you're assured entry to the tiny members-only Met Bar – a notorious celebrity hotspot in the 1990s, which still draws a cool clientele. The Michelin-starred modern Japanese restaurant Nobu *(see p34)* is literally on your doorstep. **Expensive**

Durrants *authentic Georgian pile* 8 B2
George Street, W1 • 020 7935 8131
>> www.durrantshotel.co.uk

Established in 1790, Durrants, in trendy Marylebone, is appealingly old-fashioned. The hotel has a warren of rooms spread across several terraced houses. Antiques and old prints feature heavily. Bathrooms, thankfully, are comfortably modern. The restaurant and bar have the air of a gentlemen's club. **Moderate**

Dorset Square *English country chic* 8 B1
39 Dorset Square, NW1 • 020 7723 7874
>> www.dorsetsquare.co.uk

Overlooking a lovely garden square – the site of the world's first cricket ground – this sprawling Regency house has a rustic feel, with distressed wood, floral fabrics and a cosy drawing room. The restaurant serves modern European cuisine. Marylebone Village and Regent's Park are a stroll away. **Expensive**

Dover Hotel *well-maintained modern B&B* 15 E3
42–4 Belgrave Road, SW1 • 020 7821 9085
>> www.dover-hotel.co.uk

Just up the road from Victoria Station and well placed for the pubs and cafés of Pimlico, this welcoming B&B in a grand stucco-fronted terrace offers an ensuite shower, WC and satellite TV in every room. It may not be fancy, but its rooms are refreshingly modern and immaculately clean. **Cheap**

Topham Belgravia *essentially English* 14 D2
28 Ebury Street, SW1 • 020 7730 8147
>> www.tophams.co.uk

Run by the Topham family for over 60 years, the hotel occupies five 19th-century houses in an upmarket Belgravia street. In terms of decor, it's like staying with an elderly aunt (think chintz and china cabinets), but it's cosy and characterful, and has an elegant restaurant. **Moderate**

Grand Old Dames

Just off smart shopping strip Bond Street, **Claridge's** has long been favoured by European royalty, and now lures gourmets with Michelin-starred chef Gordon Ramsay's eponymous restaurant. Opened in 1889 to accommodate theatre-goers, **The Savoy**, on the Strand, has numerous show business connections, and its legendary American Bar *(see p137)* was the birthplace of the dry Martini. For unashamed indulgence, the grandiose **Dorchester** overlooking Hyde Park boasts an Art Deco spa and nearly three staff to every guest room. Rooms at the **Ritz**, on Piccadilly, are sumptuous in Louis XVI style. Its 1930s Rivoli Bar has been splendidly restored. For details of all hotels, *see p229.*

Our price categories are based on hotel "rack" rates, but big discounts are frequently available

City Inn Westminster *unpretentious* `15 F3`
30 John Islip Street, SW1 • 020 7630 1000
≫ www.cityinn.com

Around the corner from Tate Britain and handy Millbank Pier *(see p99)*, this slick, design-conscious newcomer is part of a small chain. It offers many of the facilities of a luxury hotel – DVD players, broadband Internet, bathrobes – without any attitude. Deals on the website make it even more of a bargain. **Moderate**

The Franklin *understated English townhouse* `14 A2`
28 Egerton Gardens, SW3 • 020 7584 5533
≫ www.franklinhotel.co.uk

Located in a quiet Knightsbridge street, the Franklin offers an opportunity to see how the other half lives. It's like staying in the private home of an affluent family, complete with framed portraits, antiques, fine English fabrics and secluded residents' gardens at the back. **Moderate**

Mayflower *affordable "boutique" style* `13 E3`
26–8 Trebovir Road, SW5 • 020 7370 0991
≫ www.mayflower-group.co.uk

This affordable gem, in a grand terrace in busy Earl's Court, has recently been refurbished. Now each room has its own style, which might be contemporary, antique or slightly Oriental. Touches of luxury include marble bathrooms and balconies off some rooms. **Cheap**

Five Sumner Place *spacious & attractive* `13 H3`
5 Sumner Place, SW7 • 020 7584 7586
≫ www.sumnerplace.com

Set in a white stuccoed terrace, this immaculately maintained hotel is well placed for the museums and shops of South Kensington. Although decorated in an unremarkable traditional English style, the rooms are comfortable, and large by London standards. Breakfast is served in a pretty conservatory. **Moderate**

Blakes *sumptuous designer hideaway*   `13 G3`
33 Roland Gardens, SW7 • 020 7370 6701
» www.blakeshotels.com

Opened in the early 1980s by socialite designer
Anouska Hempel, Blakes is London's original
boutique hotel. Its effortless sense of style and
discreet Kensington location have attracted the rich
and famous from the beginning.

In contrast to Hempel's homage to minimalism in
her eponymous hotel, The Hempel, Blakes is a riot of
beautiful furniture and curios; a living textbook for
designers and aficionados of interiors, packing in a
wide array of styles. The lobby has a colonial air, with
bamboo furniture, antique birdcages and vintage
Louis Vuitton trunks. The individually designed
bedrooms, with sweeping draperies and exceptional
items of antique furniture and artifacts – many of
which were acquired by Hempel on her travels –
range in theme from opulent Oriental to Baroque
Italian. The restaurant is in the basement, its cuisine
a blend of East and West. Adjoining it are Blakes Bar
and the Chinese Room – a dark, mysterious lounge,
dressed with an elaborate screen, banquettes
and cushions. **Expensive**

The Colonnade *informal grand house*   `7 F1`
2 Warrington Crescent, W9 • 020 7286 1052
» www.theetoncollection.com

There's an air of posh informality about this hotel,
which comprises two Victorian mansions near Little
Venice *(see p171)*. Open since the 1930s, it's been
extensively refurbished. Most rooms are comfortably
opulent, some with four-poster beds. The sea-themed
"Cabin" has a bunk bed and portholes. **Moderate**

The Portobello *divinely decadent* `6 D3`
22 Stanley Gardens, W11 • 020 7727 2777
>> www.portobello-hotel.co.uk

Join the list of rock and film stars who have stayed at this over-the-top Notting Hill townhouse. Many rooms are themed – Moroccan, Japanese, Colonial – with exciting features such as round or four-poster beds and Victorian bathtubs (Alice Cooper kept his boa constrictor in one). **Moderate**

Miller's Residence *unusual guesthouse* `7 E3`
111a Westbourne Grove, W2 • 020 7243 1024
>> www.millersuk.com

A discreet entrance off busy Westbourne Grove leads to one of London's most atmospheric hotels. Owned by antiques expert Martin Miller, it's crammed with bric-a-brac and unusual pieces. There's a free bar and snacks are available in the cluttered drawing room, which is candlelit at night. **Moderate**

Abbey House *superior b&b* `7 E5`
11 Vicarage Gate, W8 • 020 7727 2594
>> www.abbeyhousekensington.com

This friendly B&B in a grand Victorian house near Kensington High Street has been owned by the same family for 25 years. It is refurbished annually and offers spotlessly clean, comfortable accommodation with shared facilities. All rooms have orthopaedic mattresses and colour TVs. **Cheap**

Booking a Hotel

Book as far as possible in advance for the best rates and widest choice. Special deals often feature on hotel websites and sites of the many Internet-based agencies. Try **www.visitlondon.com** – the website of the official tourist board – which has reviews, discounted rates and links to dozens of London hotels. The **British Hotel Reservation Centre** operates a 24-hour booking service by phone (020 7340 1616) and online (**www.bhrc.co.uk**). The agency **www.pinkhotels.com** specializes in finding rooms at gay- and lesbian-friendly hotels. Always check the booking details. Many hotels do not include VAT (17.5%) in the quotation, but add it to the final bill. Some quotes are per person, others are per room. Check, too, whether breakfast is included.

Great Eastern *Conran-styled grand hotel* `11 E2`
Liverpool Street, EC2 • 020 7618 5000
» www.great-eastern-hotel.co.uk

Built in the golden age of rail travel, the magnificent 19th-century hotel next to Liverpool Street station was recently given a makeover by the Conran Group – the design consultancy of style guru Terence Conran. The result is a dramatic marriage of Victorian grandeur (marble staircases, soaring ceilings, ornate plasterwork) with 21st-century design (contemporary colour schemes, modern furniture, high-tech facilities). Exciting works of contemporary art are displayed throughout, some on loan from nearby Whitechapel Gallery. The Conran aesthetic runs to the bedrooms, which are furnished with his own designs and original pieces by Eames and Arne Jacobson. Black-and-white tiled bathrooms come complete with natural Ren products, and all the requisite high-tech business facilities are available. The well-equipped gym is set in a former Masonic temple.

With his restaurateur's hat on, Conran has also made this a serious dining destination. There are no fewer than five eateries, the best of which is the glamorous Aurora, with a stunning original stained-glass ceiling dome. The modern brasserie Terminus is a less formal place – noisy, vibrant and fun. **Expensive**

Malmaison *French-inspired mini-chain* `10 B1`
Charterhouse Square, EC1 • 020 7012 3700
» www.malmaison.com

This converted Victorian nurses' residence maintains its reputation for contemporary luxury at a great price. CD players and minibars stocked with French wines come as standard in the chic, spacious rooms. A buzzing brasserie and high-tech gym complete the thoroughly modern package. **Moderate**

The Zetter *eclectic loft style* `10 B1`
86–8 Clerkenwell Road, EC1 • 020 7324 4444
➤➤ www.thezetter.com

Clerkenwell is an area known for its cool loft apartments, and it now has a loft hotel. Converted from a 19th-century warehouse, the Zetter has five floors set around a central atrium, and rooms featuring huge factory windows and exposed brick. The décor is an eclectic mix: reconditioned 1970s furniture, hand-printed panels, slick modern elements such as state-of-the-art showers, and cosy touches such as hot-water bottles. Old Penguin paperbacks and free copies of design magazine *Blueprint* provide inspiring bedtime reading. Instead of minibars, vending machines on each floor dispense everything from toothpaste to champagne; just insert your room card and the charge is put on the tab. The top-floor studios have sundecks with views across the city. The hotel's modern Italian restaurant, with tables on St John's Square in summer, is a destination in its own right. **Moderate**

The Rookery *historic hideaway* `10 B1`
Peter's Lane, Cowcross Street, EC1 • 020 7336 0932
➤➤ www.rookeryhotel.com

The Clerkenwell sister of Hazlitt's *(see p181)* occupies six Georgian houses and shops (faded butcher's and baker's signs are still visible). Decorated with quirky antiques, it retains many original features, such as flagstone floors in the hall and ceiling beams in some bedrooms, while offering all mod cons. **Expensive**

La Gaffe *unpretentious Hampstead B&B* `1 A4`
107–11 Heath Street, NW3 • 020 7435 8965/4941
➤➤ www.LaGaffe.co.uk

Set above an Italian restaurant amid Hampstead's winding lanes and quaint cottages, this small, family-run inn is very reasonably priced. It's style isn't much to speak of – more provincial B&B than smart hotel – but La Gaffe is handy for the local boutiques and, of course, the Heath *(see p172)*. **Cheap**

London Bridge Hotel `10 D5`

8–18 London Bridge Street, SE1 • 020 7855 2200
>> www.londonbridgehotel.com

Close to Borough Market *(see p163)*, this hotel has comfortable, if somewhat corporate-style, accommodation. "Executive" rooms are better, with more contemporary fittings. Guests can enjoy free entry to the adjoining Fitness First health club, and there's a decent Malaysian restaurant in-house. **Moderate**

Mercure London `10 B4`
City Bankside *modern Euro-style chain*

77–9 Southwark Street, SE1 • 020 7902 0800
>> www.mercure.com

This spare, modern hotel is geared mainly towards business travellers, but cheap weekend deals and its position near the Tate Modern and South Bank make it attractive to tourists. There's a small gym, and a stylish restaurant with an extensive wine list. **Moderate**

Hamilton House *elegant village retreat* `16 C4`

14 West Grove, Greenwich, SE10 • 020 8694 9899
>> www.hamiltonhousehotel.co.uk

Nautical buffs will delight in the seafaring pedigree of this Georgian house overlooking Blackheath – handy for Greenwich Park and its various historical sites. The décor makes use of pale colours and antique-effect bedspreads. Some rooms have breathtaking views of the Thames. **Moderate**

Chains

If you're after budget accommodation, it's worth considering a chain hotel: the rooms may be bland, but there won't be any nasty surprises, and, increasingly, you can stay in some of London's hottest areas. **Holiday Inn** (www.holiday-inn.com) has an affordable Express branch amid the hip bars of Hoxton (275 Old St, EC1). An outpost of cheap chain **Travel Inn** (www.travelinn.co.uk) is housed in the former County Hall – steps away from the London Eye and South Bank complex. For river views, however, you'll have to stay at the pricier **Marriott** (www.marriott.com), which shares the building. More upmarket is the **London Docklands Hilton** (www.hilton.com), which has a pool, river views from some rooms and cheap special offers.

London Street Finder

Almost every listing in this guide includes a boxed page and grid reference to the maps in this section. The few entries that fall outside the area covered by these maps give transport details instead. The main map below shows the division of the Street Finder, along with postcodes.

Key to Street Finder

- ▪ Sight/public building
- ⊖ Underground station
- ⊖ Railway station
- ⊖ Coach station
- ⊖ River boat pier
- ⓘ Tourist information office
- ✚ Hospital with casualty unit
- ⊖ Police station
- ✚ Church
- ✡ Synagogue
- ☾ Mosque
- ⊗ Post office
- ═ Railway line
- ▬ Pedestrian street
- ▬ Motorway

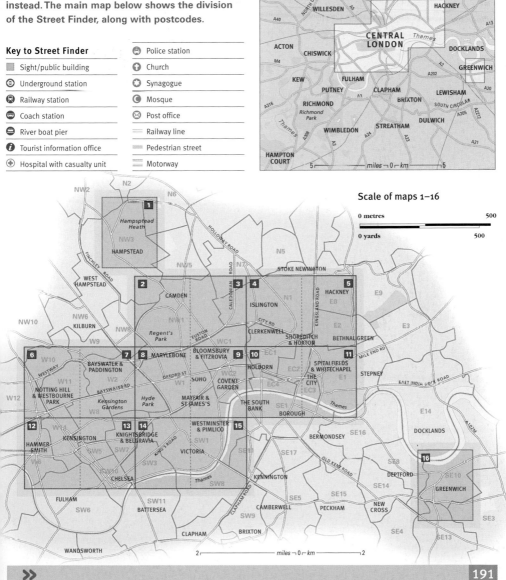

Greater London

HIGHGATE
HAMPSTEAD
WEMBLEY
WILLESDEN
HACKNEY
Hackney Marshes
ACTON
CHISWICK
CENTRAL LONDON
Thames
DOCKLANDS
GREENWICH
KEW
FULHAM
PUTNEY
CLAPHAM
LEWISHAM
RICHMOND
Richmond Park
BRIXTON
SOUTH CIRCULAR
DULWICH
WIMBLEDON
STREATHAM
HAMPTON COURT

Scale of maps 1–16

0 metres   500
0 yards   500

Map areas:
1 Hampstead Heath / HAMPSTEAD
2 Camden
3, 4 Islington / Clerkenwell
5 Hackney
6 Notting Hill & Westbourne Park
7 Bayswater & Paddington
8 Marylebone
9 Bloomsbury & Fitzrovia
10 Holborn
11 Spitalfields & Whitechapel / The City
12 Hammersmith
13 Kensington
14 Knightsbridge & Belgravia
15 Westminster & Pimlico / Victoria
16 Greenwich

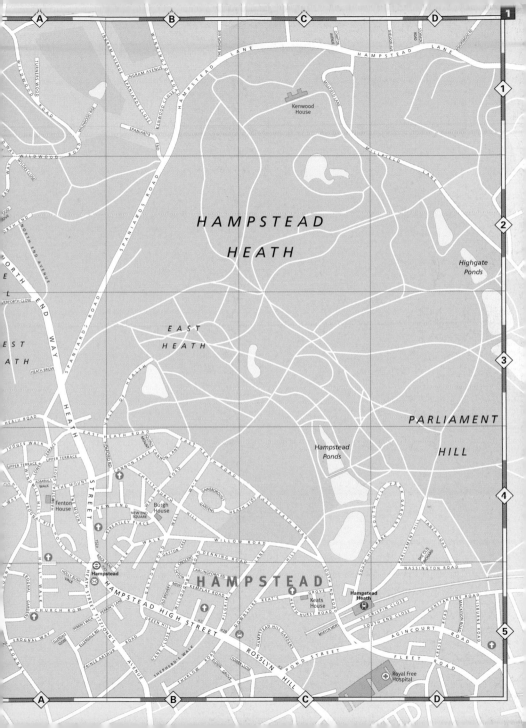

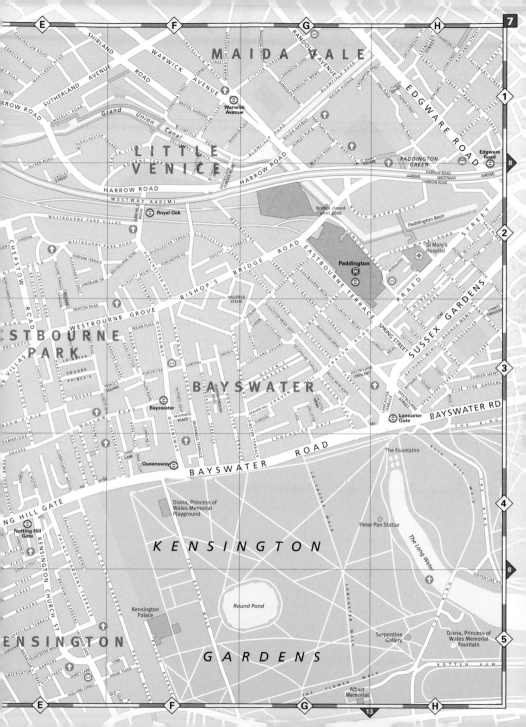

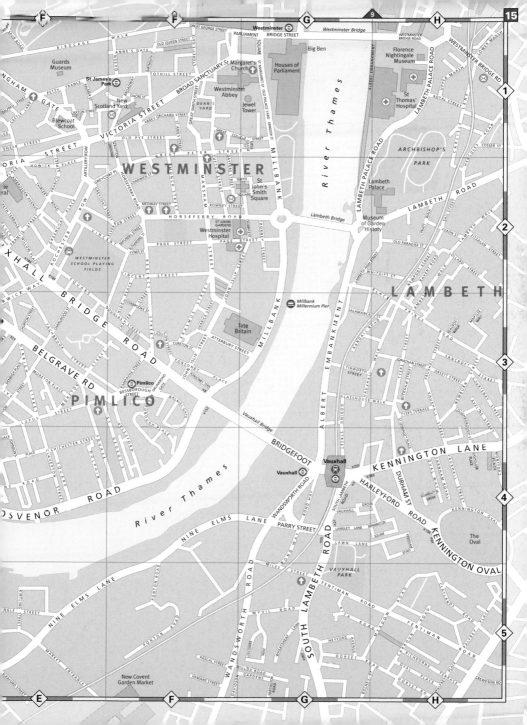

Index of Main Streets

aQuaint (p61)
38 Monmouth St (Map 9 F3)
Fashion

Aram (p60)
110 Drury Lane (Map 9 G3)
Interiors

Blackwell's (p65)
100 Charing Cross Road
(Map 9 F3)
Books

Borders (p65)
Charing Cross Road (Map 9 F3)
Books

Burro (p60)
29 Floral Street (Map 9 G3)
Fashion

Camper (p60)
Floral Street (Map 9 G3)
Fashion

Coco de Mer (p61)
23 Monmouth St (Map 9 F3)
Lingerie

Diesel StyleLab (p60)
Floral Street (Map 9 G3)
Fashion

Forbidden Planet (p63)
179 Shaftesbury Ave (Map 9 F2)
Books

Foyles (p65)
Charing Cross Road (Map 9 F3)
Books

Gay's the Word (p64)
66 Marchmont St (Map 3 G5)
Books

Helter Skelter (p65)
4 Denmark Street (Map 9 F2)
Books

Kiehl's (p61)
29 Monmouth St (Map 9 F3)
Health & Beauty

Kirk Originals (p60)
29 Floral Street (Map 9 G3)
Shoes & Accessories

Koh Samui (p61)
65–7 Monmouth St (Map 9 F3)
Fashion

Magma (p62)
8 Earlham Street (Map 9 F3)
Books

Maharishi (p60)
19a Floral Street (Map 9 G3)
Fashion

Marchpane (p64)
Cecil Court (Map 9 F3)
Books

Neal's Yard Dairy (p62)
17 Shorts Gardens (Map 9 G3)
Food

Nigel Williams (p64)
Cecil Court (Map 9 F3)
Books

Paul Smith (pp60 & 84)
Floral Street (Map 9 G3)
Fashion

PJ Hilton (p64)
Cecil Court (Map 9 F3)
Books

Poste Mistress (p61)
261–3 Monmouth St (Map 9 F3)
Shoes & Accessories

Ray's Jazz (p65)
Foyles Bookshop, Charing
Cross Road (Map 9 F3)
Music

Shipley (p65)
70 Charing Cross Rd (Map 9 F3)
Books

Shipley Media (p65)
80 Charing Cross Rd (Map 9 F3)
Books

Size? (p62)
17–19 Neal Street (Map 9 G3)
Fashion

Stage Door Prints (p64)
9 Cecil Court (Map 9 F3)
Prints & Posters

Storey's (p64)
3 Cecil Court (Map 9 F3)
Prints & Posters

The Tintin Shop (p60)
34 Floral Street (Map 9 G3)
Prints & Posters

Vertigo (p60)
22 Wellington St (Map 9 G3)
Prints & Posters

The Wild Bunch (p62)
Earlham Street (Map 9 F3)
Florist

Fitzrovia

FCUK (p85)
396 Oxford Street (Map 9 E2)
Fashion

Topshop (p68)
Oxford Circus (Map 9 D2)
Fashion

Marylebone

Anello & Davide (p72)
20–21 St Christoper's Place
(Map 8 C3)
Shoes & Accessories

Calmia (p73)
52–4 Marylebone High St
(Map 8 C1)
Health & Beauty

Carluccio's (p72)
St Christopher's Pl (Map 8 C3)
Food

Daunt Books (p74)
83 Marylebone High St (8 C1)
Books

La Fromagerie (p74)
2–4 Moxton Street (Map 8 C2)
Food

John Lewis (p79)
278–306 Oxford St (Map 8 D3)
www.johnlewis.com
Department Store

Madeleine Press (p74)
90 Marylebone High St
(Map 8 C1)
Fashion

Margaret Howell (p72)
34 Wigmore Street (Map 8 C2)
Fashion

Marimekko (p72)
16–17 St Christopher's Place
(Map 8 C3)
Interiors

Mint (p73)
70 Wigmore Street (Map 8 C2)
Interiors

Mulberry (p72)
11–12 Gees Court (Map 8 C3)
Fashion

Osprey (p72)
St Christopher's Pl (Map 8 C3)
Shoes & Accessories

Paul Rothe (p73)
35 Marylebone Lane (Map 8 C2)
Food

Selfridges (p71)
400 Oxford Street (Map 8 C3)
Department Store

Sixty 6 (p73)
66 Marylebone High St
(Map 8 C1)
Fashion

Skandium (p74)
86–7 Marylebone High Street
(Map 8 C1)
Interiors

Whistles (p72)
12 St Christopher's Place
(Map 8 C3)
Fashion

Mayfair & St James's

b Store (p67)
6 Conduit Street (Map 8 D3)
Shoes & Accessories

Browns (p70)
23–7 South Molton Street
(Map 8 D3)
Fashion

Fenwick (p79)
63 New Bond Street (Map 8 D3)
www.fenwick.co.uk
Department Store

Fortnum & Mason (p79)
181 Piccadilly (Map 9 E4)
www.fortnumandmason.com
Department Store

Georgina Goodman (p69)
12–14 Shepherd St (Map 8 D5)
Shoes & Accessories

Jigsaw (p85)
126 New Bond St (Map 8 D3)
Fashion

Karen Millen (p85)
262–4 Regent St (Map 8 D3)
Fashion

N Peal (p70)
37 & 71 Burlington Arcade
(Map 9 E4)
Fashion

Oki-ni (p68)
25 Savile Row (Map 9 E3)
Fashion

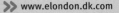

Ronnie Scott's (p121)
47 Frith Street (Map 9 F3)
Music Venue

Soho Theatre (p120)
21 Dean Street (Map 9 F3)

Westminster & Pimlico

St John's Smith Square (p122)
Smith Square (Map 15 G2)
Concert Hall

Pubs, Bars & Clubs

Bloomsbury

Lamb (p141)
94 Lamb's Conduit St (9 H1)
Pub

Covent Garden

The American Bar (p137)
Savoy Hotel, Strand (Map 9 G4)
Bar

The End (p141)
18 West Central St (Map 9 G2)
Bar

Gordon's Wine Bar (p136)
47 Villiers Street (Map 9 G4)
Bar

Heaven (p136)
Villiers Street (Map 9 G4)
Club

Lamb & Flag (p137)
33 Rose Street (Map 9 G3)
Pub

Lobby Bar (p136)
1 Aldwych (Map 9 H3)
Bar

Soho

Atlantic Bar & Grill (p137)
20 Glasshouse St (Map 9 E4)
Bar

Bar Rumba (p138)
36 Shaftesbury Ave (Map 9 F3)
Bar

Coach & Horses (p144)
29 Greek Street (Map 9 F3)
Pub

The Endurance (p138)
90 Berwick Street (Map 9 E3)
Pub

Escape Bar (p158)
10a Brewer Street (Map 9 E3)
Bar

French House (p139)
49 Dean Street (Map 9 F3)
Pub

G-A-Y (p158)
30 Old Compton St (Map 9 F3)
Bar/Club

Madame Jo-Jos (p138)
8–10 Brewer Street (Map 9 E3)
Club

Pillars of Hercules (p144)
7 Greek Street (Map 9 F3)
Pub

The Player (p139)
8 Broadwick Street (Map 9 E3)
Bar

Fitzrovia

Fitzroy Tavern (p144)
16 Charlotte Street (Map 9 E2)
Pub

Jerusalem (p139)
33–4 Rathbone Pl (Map 9 E2)
Bar

Market Place (p140)
11 Market Place (Map 9 E2)
Bar

Mash (p140)
19–21 Great Portland Street
(Map 8 D2)
Bar

The Social (p140)
5 Little Portland St (Map 8 D2)
Bar

Mayfair & St James's

Zeta Bar (p140)
Mayfair Hilton Hotel,
35 Hertford Street
(Map 8 C5)
Bar

Havens: Parks & Gardens

Covent Garden

Victoria Embankment
Gardens (p168)
Victoria Embankment &
Villiers Street (Map 9 G4)

Holborn

Temple (p168)
Off Fleet Street (Map 10 A3)

Havens: Spas & Treatments

Covent Garden

Farmacia Urban Healing (p168)
169 Drury Lane (Map 9 G3)

Mayfair & St James's

Elemis Day Spa (p169)
2–3 Lancashire Ct
(Map 8 D3)

Hotels

Bloomsbury

Crescent Hotel (p181)   £
49–50 Cartwright
Gardens (Map 3 F5)

Generator (p181)   £
Compton Place (Map 3 G5)

Covent Garden

Covent Garden Hotel   £££
(p180)
10 Monmouth St (Map 9 F3)

One Aldwych (p180)   £££
1 Aldwych (Map 9 H3)

Fitzrovia

Charlotte Street Hotel   £££
(p181)
15 Charlotte Street
(Map 9 E2)

Marylebone

Dorset Square (p183)   £££
39 Dorset Square
(Map 8 B1)

Durrants (p182)   ££
George Street (Map 8 B2)

Mayfair & St James's

The Metropolitan (p182)   £££
Old Park Lane (Map 8 C5)

Soho

Hazlitt's (p181)   £££
6 Frith Street (Map 9 F3)

Westminster & Pimlico

City Inn
Westminster (p184)   ££
30 John Islip Street (Map 15 F3)

Dover Hotel (p183)   £
42–4 Belgrave Rd (Map 15 E3)

West

Restaurants

Bayswater & Paddington

Magic Wok (p43)   £
61 Queensway (Map 7 F3)
Chinese

Maroush Gardens (p36)   ££
1–3 Connaught St (Map 8 A3)
Middle Eastern

Satay House (p43)   £
13 Sale Place (Map 7 H2)
Malaysian

Chelsea & Fulham

Chutney Mary (p40)   £££
535 King's Rd (Map 13 G5)
Indian

Gordon Ramsay (p34)   £££
68–9 Royal Hospital Road
(Map 14 B4)
European

Lots Road Pub &   ££

Dining Room (p40)
114 Lots Road (Map 13 G5)
Gastropub

The Painted Heron (p40)   ££
112 Cheyne Walk (Map 13 H5)
Indian

Tom Aikens (p39)   £££
43 Elystan Street (Map 14 A3)
European

Tendido Cero (p40)   ££
174 Old Brompton Rd
(Map 13 G3)
Spanish

Hammersmith

The Gate (p41)   ££
51 Queen Charlotte Street
(Map 12 A3)
Vegetarian

West

Restaurants *continued*

The River Café (p41)   £££
Rainville Road (Map 12 A5)
Italian

Kensington & Earl's Court

Orangery (p170)   ££
Kensington Gardens (Map 7 F5)
Café

Knightsbridge & Belgravia

Foliage (p37)   £££
Mandarin Oriental,
66 Knightsbridge (Map 8 B5)
European

Hunan (p38)   ££
51 Pimlico Road (Map 14 C3)
Chinese

Noura (p38)   ££
16 Hobart Place (Map 14 D1)
Middle Eastern

Racine (p39)   ££
239 Brompton Rd (Map 14 A2)
French

Zafferano (p39)   £££
15 Lowndes Street (Map 14 B1)
Italian

Zuma (p38)   £££
5 Raphael Street (Map 14 A1)
Japanese

Notting Hill & Westbourne Park

E&O (p42)   ££
14 Blenheim Cres (Map 6 C3)
Oriental

Lisboa Patisserie (p42)   £
57 Golborne Road (Map 6 C2)
Café

Lonsdale (p143)   ££
44–8 Lonsdale Road
(Map 6 D3)
Gastropub

Rosa's (p160)   ££
69 Westbourne Park Road
(Map 7 E2)
European

S&M Café (p42)   £
268 Portobello Rd (Map 6 D3)
Café

The Westbourne (p160)   ££
101 Westbourne Pk Villas (7 E2)
Gastropub

Shopping

Chelsea & Fulham

Antiquarius (p80)
131–41 King's Rd (Map 14 A4)
Vintage Furniture

The Conran Shop (p78)
81 Fulham Road (Map 14 A2)
Interiors

Designers Guild (p80)
267 & 277 King's Rd (Map 14 A4)
Interiors

Jimmy Choo (p77)
169 Draycott Ave (Map 14 A3)
Shoes & Accessories

Joseph (p77)
77 Fulham Road (Map 13 H3)
Fashion

Kate Kuba (p79)
22 Duke of York Square (14 B3)
Shoes & Accessories

Korres (p79)
124 King's Road (Map 14 A3)
Health & Beauty

Oliver Sweeney (p79)
29 King's Road (Map 14 B3)
Shoes & Accessories

Knightsbridge & Belgravia

Anya Hindmarch (p76)
15–17 Pont Street (Map 14 B2)
Shoes & Accessories

The Chocolate Society (p76)
36 Elizabeth St (Map 14 C2)
Food

Erickson Beamon (p76)
38 Elizabeth St (Map 14 C2)
Shoes & Accessories

Harrods (p79)
87–135 Brompton Road
(Map 14 B1) www.harrods.com
Department Store

Harvey Nichols (p79)
109–25 Knightsbridge (14 B1)
www.harveynichols.com
Department Store

Jo Malone (p75)
150 Sloane Street (Map 14 B2)
Health & Beauty

Lulu Guinness (p77)
3 Ellis Street (Map 14 B2)
Shoes & Accessories

Maria Grachvogel (p75)
162 Sloane Street (Map 14 B2)
Fashion

Neisha Crosland (p77)
8 Elystan Street (Map 14 A3)
Interiors

Patrick Cox (p75)
129 Sloane Street (Map 14 B2)
Shoes & Accessories

Philip Treacy (p76)
69 Elizabeth St (Map 14 C2)
Shoes & Accessories

Poilane (p76)
46 Elizabeth St (Map 14 C2)
Food

Les Senteurs (p76)
71 Elizabeth Street (Map 14 C2)
Health & Beauty

Tracey Boyd (p76)
42 Elizabeth St (Map 14 C2)
Fashion

Woodhams (p76)
45 Elizabeth St (Map 14 C2)
Florist

Notting Hill & Westbourne Park

202 (p80)
202 Westbourne Gro (Map 7 F3)
Fashion

Bill Amberg (p81)
10 Chepstow Road (Map 7 E2)
Shoes & Accessories

Blenheim Books (p159)
11 Blenheim Cres (Map 6 C3)
Books

Coco Ribbon (p84)
21 Kensington Park Road
(Map 6 C3)
Fashion

The Cross (p85)
141 Portland Road (Map 6 C4)
Fashion

Duchamp (p82)
75 Ledbury Road (Map 6 D3)
Fashion

Graham & Green (pp85 & 90)
4 & 10 Elgin Crescent
(Map 6 C3)
Interiors

Honest Jon's (p83)
278 Portobello Rd (Map 6 D3)
Music

Intoxica! (p83)
231 Portobello Rd (Map 6 D3)
Music

J&M Davidson (p81)
42 Ledbury Road (Map 6 D3)
Fashion

JW Beeton (p82)
48–50 Ledbury Rd (Map 6 D3)
Fashion

Marilyn Moore (p84)
7 Elgin Crescent (Map 6 C3)
Fashion

Miller Harris (p81)
14 Needham Road (Map 7 E3)
Health & Beauty

Nick Ashley (p82)
57 Ledbury Road (Map 6 D3)
Fashion

Paul Smith (pp60 & 84)
120 & 122 Kensington Park
Road (Map 6 D4)
Fashion

Portobello Market (p159)
Map 6 D3
Market

Preen (p83)
Unit 5 Portobello Green
(Map 6 C2)
Fashion

Rellik (p85)
8 Golborne Road (Map 6 C1)
Fashion

Rough Trade (p81)
130 Talbot Road
(Map 6 D3)
Music

Simon Finch Rare Books (p82)
61a Ledbury Rd (Map 6 D3)
Books

Space.NK (p80)
127–31 Westbourne Gr (7 F3)
Health & Beauty

Travel Bookshop (p159)
13–15 Blenheim Cres (6 C3)
Books

Willma (p84)
339 Portobello Rd (Map 6 C2)
Shoes & Accessories

Art & Architecture

Kensington

Brompton Cemetery (p105)
Lillie Road (Map 13 E4)

Brompton Oratory (p101)
Brompton Road (Map 14 A2)
Church

Kensington Palace (p96)
Palace Avenue (Map 7 F5)

Leighton House Museum (p103)
12 Holland Park Rd (Map 12 D1)

Linley Sambourne House (p102)
18 Stafford Terrace (Map 13 F1)
Historic Building

Natural History Museum (p102)
Exhibition Road (Map 13 H2)

Science Museum (p102)
Exhibition Road (Map 13 H2)

Serpentine Gallery (p101)
Kensington Gdns (Map 7 H5)
Art Gallery

V&A (p102)
Exhibition Road (Map 13 H2)
Museum

Performance

Chelsea & Fulham

606 Club (p123)
90 Lots Road (Map 13 G5)
Music Venue

Hammersmith

Riverside Studios (p124)
Crisp Road (Map 12 A4)
Arts Centre

Notting Hill & Westbourne Park

Electric Cinema (p123)
191 Portobello Rd (Map 6 D3)

Shepherd's Bush

Shepherd's Bush Empire (p123)
Shepherd's Bush Green
(Map 6 A5)
Music Venue

Pubs, Bars & Clubs

Bayswater & Paddington

Cherry Jam (p141)
58 Porchester Road (Map 7 F2)
Bar

Chelsea & Fulham

Apartment 195 (p142)
195 King's Road (Map 14 A4)
Bar

Hammersmith

Blue Anchor (p154)
13 Lower Mall (Ⓔ Hammersmith)
Pub

The Dove (p154)
19 Upper Mall (Ⓔ Hammersmith)
Pub

Kensington

Windsor Castle (p144)
114 Campden Hill Rd (Map 7 E5)
Pub

Knightsbridge & Belgravia

Blue Bar (p142)
Berkeley Hotel,
Wilton Place (Map 14 B1)
Bar

Nag's Head (p141)
53 Kinnerton St (Map 14 B1)
Pub

Townhouse (p142)
31 Beauchamp Pl (Map 14 A1)
Bar

Notting Hill & Westbourne Park

Golborne Grove (p143)
36 Golborne Road (Map 6 C1)
Bar

Lonsdale (p143)
44–8 Lonsdale Rd (Map 6 D3)
Bar

Notting Hill Arts Club (p144)
21 Notting Hill Gate (Map 7 E4)
Club

Trailer H (p143)
177 Portobello Rd (Map 6 C2)
Bar

Havens: Parks & Gardens

Chelsea & Fulham

Chelsea Physic Garden (p171)
Swan Walk (Map 14 B4)

Kensington

Holland Park (p170)
Map 6 D5

Havens: Spas & Treatments

Bayswater & Paddington

Porchester Spa (p170)
Queensway (Map 7 F3)

Hotels

Bayswater & Paddington

The Colonnade (p185) ££
2 Warrington Cres (Map 7 F1)

Chelsea & Fulham

Blakes (p185) £££
33 Roland Gdns (Map 13 G3)

Five Sumner Place (p184) ££
5 Sumner Place (Map 13 H3)

Kensington

Abbey House (p186) £
11 Vicarage Gate (Map 7 E5)

Mayflower (p184) £
26–8 Trebovir Rd (Map 13 E3)

Knightsbridge & Belgravia

The Franklin (p184) £££
28 Egerton Gdns (Map 14 A2)

Topham Belgravia (p183) ££
28 Ebury Street (Map 14 D2)

Notting Hill & Westbourne Park

Miller's Residence (p186) ££
111a Westbourne Gr (Map 7 E3)

The Portobello (p186) ££
22 Stanley Gardens (Map 6 D3)

City & East

Restaurants

The City

Club Gascon (p47) £££
57 West Smithfield (Map 10 B2)
French

Smiths of Smithfield ££/£££
(p45)
67–77 Charterhouse St
(Map 10 B2)
European

Sutton Arms (p45) ££
6 Carthusian St (Map 10 B1)
Gastropub

Clerkenwell

Fish Central (p45) £
149–51 Central St (Map 4 C5)
British

Flâneur Food Hall (p45) ££
41 Farringdon Rd (Map 10 A1)
European

Moro (p44) ££
34–6 Exmouth Mkt (Map 4 A5)
Spanish/North African

St John (p46) £££
26 St John Street (Map 4 B5)
British

Strada (p43) ££
8–10 Exmouth Market,
www.strada.co.uk (Map 4 A5)
Italian

Hackney

Green Papaya (p48) £
191 Mare Street (Map 5 H1)
Vietnamese

Shoreditch & Hoxton

Cantaloupe (p47) ££
35 Charlotte Road (Map 5 E5)
Mediterranean

Index by Area

 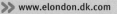

Fabric (p145)
77a Charterhouse St
(Map 10 B1)
Club

Fluid (p146)
40 Charterhouse St
(Map 10 B1)
Bar

Jerusalem Tavern (p146)
55 Britton Street (Map 10 B1)
Pub

Turnmills (p146)
63a Clerkenwell Rd (Map 10 B1)
Club

Hackney

Royal Inn on the Park (p153)
Grove Road (Ⓔ Bethnal Green)
Pub

Shoreditch & Hoxton

333/Mother (p147)
333 Old Street (Map 5 F5)
Club

Bar Kick (p162)
127 Shoreditch High Street
(Map 5 E5)
Bar

The Bricklayer's Arms (p162)
63 Charlotte Road (Map 5 E5)
Pub

Cargo (p146)
83 Rivington Street (Map 5 E5)
Bar/Club

Elbow Room (p162)
97–113 Curtain Rd (Map 5 E5)
Bar

Herbal (p147)
10–14 Kingsland Rd (Map 5 E4)
Club

Hoxton Square Bar & Kitchen
(p147)
2–4 Hoxton Square (Map 5 E5)
Bar

Loungelover (p149)
1 Whitby Street (Map 5 F5)
Bar

Pool (p161)
104–8 Curtain Road (Map 5 E5)
Bar

Zigfrid (p162)
11 Hoxton Square (Map 5 E5)
Bar

Spitalfields & Whitechapel

93 Feet East (p148)
150 Brick Lane (Map 11 F1)
Club

Golden Heart (p149)
110 Commercial St (Map 11 F1)
Pub

Pride of Spitalfields (p148)
3 Heneage Street (Map 11 F1)
Pub

Vibe Bar (p148)
Old Truman Brewery,
91–5 Brick Lane (Map 11 F1)
Bar

Wapping & Docklands

The Grapes (p149)
76 Narrow Street (Ⓔ Wapping)
Pub

Prospect of Whitby (p149)
57 Wapping Wall (Ⓔ Wapping)
Pub

Hotels

The City

Great Eastern (p187)   fff
Liverpool Street (Map 11 E2)

Clerkenwell

Malmaison (p187)   ff
Charterhouse Sq (Map 10 B1)

The Rookery (p188)   fff
Peter's Lane, Cowcross Street
(Map 10 B1)

The Zetter (p188)   ff
86 Clerkenwell Rd (Map 10 B1)

North

Restaurants

Camden

Café Corfu (p50)   ff
7 Pratt Street
(Map 3 E2)
Greek

Lock Tavern (p152)   ff
35 Chalk Farm Rd (Map 2 D2)
Gastropub

Mango Room (p51)   ff
10 Kentish Town Rd (Map 2 D1)
Caribbean

El Parador (p50)   f
245 Eversholt St (Map 3 E4)
Spanish

Hampstead

Giraffe (see p221)   ff
International

The Wells (p51)   ff/fff
30 Well Walk (Map 1 B4)
Gastropub

Islington

The Drapers Arms (p49)   ff
44 Barnsbury St (Map 4 A2)
Gastropub

Gallipoli (p49)   f
102 Upper Street (Map 4 B2)
Turkish

The House (p49)   ff
63–9 Canonbury Rd (Map 4 B1)
Gastropub

Masala Zone (see p221)   f

Kilburn

Kovolam (p52)   f
12 Willesden Lane (Ⓔ Kilburn)
Indian

Primrose Hill

The Lansdowne (p51)   ff
90 Gloucester Ave (Map 2 C2)
Gastropub

Manna (p51)   ff
4 Erskine Road (Map 2 B2)
Vegetarian

Odette's (p50)   fff
130 Regent's Park Rd (Map 2 B2)
European

Shopping

Islington

After Noah (p89)
121 Upper Street (Map 4 B2)
Vintage Furniture

Annie's Vintage Clothes (p90)
Camden Passage (Map 4 B3)
Fashion

Aria (p89)
295–6 & 133 Upper Street
(Map 4 B2)
Interiors

Camden Lock Market (p163)
Map 2 D2

Caroline Carrier's (p90)
Pierrepont Arcade
Camden Passage (Map 4 B3)
Interiors

Comfort & Joy (p88)
109 Essex Road (Map 4 B3)
Fashion

Judith Lasalle (p90)
Pierrepont Arcade
Camden Passage (Map 4 B3)
Vintage Furniture

Labour of Love (p89)
193 Upper Street (Map 4 B2)
Fashion

Origin (p90)
Camden Passage (Map 4 B3)
Interiors

Rock Archive (p90)
110 Islington High St (Map 4 A3)
Prints & Posters

Scorah Pattullo (p89)
137 Upper Street (Map 4 B2)
Fashion

twentytwentyone (p89)
274 Upper Street (Map 4 B2)
Interiors

Primrose Hill

Anna (p90)
126 Regent's Park Rd (Map 2 B2)
Fashion

Graham & Green (pp85 & 90)
164 Regent's Park Rd (Map 2 B2)
Interiors

Primrose Hill Books (p90)
Regent's Park Road (Map 2 B2)
Books

Rachel Skinner (p90)
13 Princess Road (Map 2 B2)
Shoes & Accessories

Index by Area

Connect up with other parts of town via ⟩⟩ www.elondon.dk.com

Restaurants

Recommended places to eat, including cafés and pubs

Belgian

Belgo (p43) ££
50 Earlham Street (Map 9 F3)
www.belgorestaurants.co.uk
Centre/Covent Garden

British

Fish! (p163)
Cathedral Street (Map 10 D4)
South/Borough

Fish Central (p45) £
149–151 Central Street
(Map 4 C5)
City & East/Clerkenwell

Golden Hind (p34) £
73 Marylebone Lane
(Map 8 C2)
Centre/Marylebone

J Sheekey (p31) £££
28–32 St Martin's Court
(Map 9 F3)
Centre/Covent Garden

Lindsay House (p26) £££
21 Romilly Street (Map 9 F3)
Centre/Soho

Livebait (p53) £££
41–5 The Cut (Map 10 A5)
South/South Bank

Masters Super Fish (p53) £
191 Waterloo Road (Map 10 A5)
South/South Bank

Randall & Aubin (pp17 & 158)
14–16 Brewer Street
(Map 9 E3)
Centre/Soho

Rock & Sole Plaice (p29) £
47 Endell Street (Map 9 G3)
Centre/Covent Garden

Rosa's (p160)
69 Westbourne Pk Rd
(Map 7 E2)
*West/Notting Hill &
Westbourne Park*

Rules (p30) £££
35 Maiden Lane (Map 9 G3)
Centre/Covent Garden

St John (p46) £££
26 St John Street
(Map 4 D5)
City & East/Clerkenwell

Cafés

Arkansas Café (p161)
Spitalfields Market (Map 11 F1)
City & East/Spitalfields

Bar Italia (pp19 & 158) £
22 Frith Street (Map 9 F3)
Centre/Soho

Beigel Bake (p19) £
159 Brick Lane (Map 5 F5)
City & East/Spitalfields

**The Bridge House Canal
Theatre Café** (p171)
Delamere Terrace (Map 7 G1)
West/Bayswater & Paddington

Lisboa Patisserie (p42) £
57 Golborne Road (Map 6 C2)
*West/Notting Hill &
Westbourne Park*

Market Coffee House (p161)
Brushfield Street (Map 11 E1)
City & East/Spitalfields

Orangery (p170) ££
Kensington Gardens
(Map 7 F5)
West/Kensington

Patisserie Valerie (p26) £
44 Old Compton Street
(Map 9 F3) *Centre/Soho*

Paul (p29) £
20 Bedford Street (Map 9 G3)
Centre/Covent Garden

S&M Café (p42) £
268 Portobello Road
(Map 6 D3)
*West/Notting Hill &
Westbourne Park*

Caribbean

Mango Room (p51) ££
10 Kentish Town Road
(Map 2 D1)
North/Camden

Chinese

ECapital (p25) £
8 Gerrard Street (Map 9 F3)
Centre/Soho

Hakkasan (p27) £££
8 Hanway Place (Map 9 F2)
Centre/Fitzrovia

Hunan (p38) ££
51 Pimlico Road (Map 14 C3)
West/Knightsbridge & Belgravia

Magic Wok (p43) £
61 Queensway (Map 7 F3)
West/Bayswater & Paddington

Phoenix Palace (p36) £
3–5 Glentworth Street
(Map 8 B1)
Centre/Marylebone

Wong Kei (p25) £
41–3 Wardour Street (Map 9 E3)
Centre/Soho

European

Andrew Edmunds (p24) ££
46 Lexington Street (Map 9 E3)
Centre/Soho

Blueprint Café (p52) ££
Shad Thames (Map 11 F5)
South/Borough

Cantina Vinopolis (p163)
1 Bank End (Map 10 C4)
South/Borough

Le Caprice (p31) £££
Arlington House
Arlington Street (Map 9 E4)
Centre/Mayfair & St James's

Chez Bruce (p55) ££
2 Bellevue Road
(Wandsworth)
South/Wandsworth

Fifteen (p34) £££
15 Westland Place (Map 4 C4)
City & East/Shoreditch & Hoxton

Flâneur Food Hall (p45) ££
41 Farringdon Road
(Map 10 A1)
City & East/Clerkenwell

Foliage (p37) £££
Mandarin Oriental Hyde Park
Hotel, 66 Knightsbridge
(Map 8 B5)
West/Knightsbridge & Belgravia

Gordon Ramsay (p34) £££
68–9 Royal Hospital Road
(Map 14 B4)
West/Chelsea & Fulham

The Ivy (p34) £££
1 West Street (Map 9 F3)
Centre/Covent Garden

Odette's (p50) £££
130 Regent's Park Road
(Map 2 B2)
North/Primrose Hill

The Orrery (p35) £££
55 Marylebone Hight St
(Map 8 C1)
Centre/Marylebone

**Oxo Tower Restaurant, Bar &
Brasserie** (p54) £££
Top Floor, Oxo Tower Wharf
Barge House Street (Map 10 A4)
South/South Bank

Sketch (p34) £££
9 Conduit Street (Map 8 D3)
Centre/Mayfair & St James's

**Smiths of
Smithfield** (p45) ££/£££
67–77 Charterhouse St
(Map 10 B2)
City & East/The City

The Sugar Club (p25) £££
21 Warwick Street (Map 9 E3)
Centre/Soho

Tom Aikens (p39) £££
43 Elystan Street (Map 14 A3)
West/Chelsea & Fulham

The Wolseley (p32) £££
160 Piccadilly (Map 9 E4)
Centre/Mayfair & St James's

French

Club Gascon (p47) £££
57 West Smithfield (Map 10 B2)
City & East/The City

La Galette (p36) £
56 Paddington St (Map 8 C1)
Centre/Marylebone

Le Petit Max (p55) ££
Riverside Plaza
Chatfield Road (⊕ Clapham)
South/Clapham

Putney Bridge (p55) £££
2 Lwr Richmond Rd (⊕ Putney)
South/Putney

Racine (p39) ££
239 Brompton Rd (Map 14 A2)
West/Knightsbridge & Belgravia

Restaurants

Gastropubs

The Drapers Arms (p49)   ££
44 Barnsbury Street (Map 4 A2)
North/Islington

Duke of Cambridge (p15)
30 St Peter's Street (Map 4 B3)
North/Islington

The House (p49)   ££
63–9 Canonbury Rd (Map 4 B1)
North/Islington

The Lansdowne (p51)   ££
90 Gloucester Avenue
(Map 2 C2)
North/Primrose Hill

Lock Tavern (p152)   ££
35 Chalk Farm Raod (Map 2 D2)
North/Camden

Lonsdale (p143)   ££
44–8 Lonsdale Rd (Map 6 D3)
*West/Notting Hill &
Westbourne Park*

**Lots Road Pub &
Dining Room** (p40)   ££
114 Lots Road (Map 13 G5)
West/Chelsea & Fulham

Sutton Arms (p45)   ££
6 Carthusian St (Map 10 B1)
City & East/The City

The Wells (p51)   ££/£££
30 Well Walk (Map 1 B4)
North/Hampstead

The Westbourne (p160)
101 Westbourne Pk Villas
(Map 7 E2)
*West/Notting Hill &
Westbourne Park*

Greek

Café Corfu (p50)   ££
7 Pratt Street (Map 3 E2)
North/Camden

The Real Greek (p48)   ££
14–15 Hoxton Market
(Map 5 E5)
City & East/Shoreditch & Hoxton

Indian

Café Spice Namaste (p46)   ££
16 Prescot Street (Map 11 F3)
*City & East/Spitalfields &
Whitechapel*

Chutney Mary (p40)   £££
535 King's Road (Map 13 G5)
West/Chelsea & Fulham

Cinnamon Club (p37)   £££
Old Westminster Library
Great Smith Street (Map 15 F1)
Centre/Westminster & Pimlico

Kovolam (p52)   £
12 Willesden Lane (☺ Kilburn)
North/Kilburn

Masala Zone (p43)   £
9 Marshall Street,
020 7287 9966 (Map 9 E3)
Centre/Soho
80 Upper Street,
020 7359 3399 (Map 4 B3)
North/Islington

The Painted Heron (p40)   ££
112 Cheyne Walk (Map 13 H5)
West/Chelsea & Fulham

Rasa Samudra (p28)   ££
5 Charlotte street (Map 9 E1)
Centre/Fitzrovia

Red Fort (p27)   £££
77 Dean St (Map 9 F3)
Centre/Soho

Tamarind (p33)   £££
20 Queen Street (Map 8 D4)
Centre/Mayfair & St James's

International

Café Emm (p25)   £
17 Frith Street (Map 9 F3)
Centre/Soho

Giraffe (p43)   ££
46 Rosslyn Hill (Map 1 C5)
www.giraffe.net
North/Hampstead

**The Providores &
Tapa Room** (p35)   £££
109 Marylebone High St
(Map 8 C1) *Centre/Marylebone*

Rivington Bar and Grill (p162)
28–30 Rivington Street
(Map 5 E5)
City & East/Shoreditch & Hoxton

Italian

Cecconi's (p31)   £££
5A Burlington Gardens
(Map 9 E4)
Centre/Mayfair & St James's

Locanda Locatelli (p34)   £££
8 Seymour Street (Map 8 B3)
Centre/Marylebone

The River Café (p41)   £££
Rainville Road (Map 12 A5)
West/Hammersmith

Sardo (p29)   ££
45 Grafton Way (Map 9 E1)
Centre/Fitzrovia

Strada (p43)   ££
8–10 Exmouth Market
(Map 4 A5) www.strada.co.uk
City & East/Clerkenwell

Zafferano (p39)   £££
15 Lowndes Street (Map 14 B1)
West/Knightsbridge & Belgravia

Japanese

Donzoko (p24)   £
15 Kingly Street (Map 9 E3)
Centre/Soho

Hazuki (p31)   ££
43 Chandos Place (Map 9 G4)
Centre/Covent Garden

Itsu (p43)   ££
103 Wardour Street (Map 9 E3)
www.itsu.co.uk
Centre/Soho

Kiku (p33)   £££
17 Half Moon Street
(Map 8 D4)
Centre/Mayfair & St James's

Matsuri (p29)   £££
71 High Holborn (Map 9 H2)
Centre/Holborn

Nobu (p34)   £££
19 Old Park Lane (Map 8 C5)
Centre/Mayfair & St James's

Tsunami (p54)   £££
5 Voltaire Road
(☺ Clapham North)
South/Clapham

Wagamama (p43)   £
Lexington Street (Map 9 E3)
www.wagamama.com
Centre/Soho

Yo! Sushi (p43)   £
52 Poland Street
(Map 9 E3)
www.yosushi.co.uk
Centre/Soho

Zuma (p38)   £££
5 Raphael Street (Map 14 A1)
West/Knightsbridge & Belgravia

Korean

Kaya (p33)   ££
42 Albemarle Street (Map 8 D4)
Centre/Mayfair & St James's

Malaysian

Champor-Champor (p52)   ££
62 Weston Street (Map 10 D5)
South/Borough

Satay House (p43)   £
13 Sale Place (Map 7 H2)
West/Bayswater & Paddington

Mediterranean

Cantaloupe (p47)   ££
35 Charlotte Road (Map 5 E5)
City & East/Shoreditch & Hoxton

Middle Eastern

Maroush Gardens (p36)   ££
1–3 Connaught Street (8 A3)
West/Bayswater & Paddington

Noura (p38)   ££
16 Hobart Place (Map 14 D1)
West/Knightsbridge & Belgravia

Patogh (p37)   £
8 Crawford Place (Map 8 A2)
Centre/Marylebone

Al Sultan (p34)   ££
51–2 Hertford St (Map 8 C5)
Centre/Mayfair & St James's

Al Waha (p43)   ££
75 Westbourne Grove (7 E3)
*West/Notting Hill &
Westbourne Park*

North African

Mô (p34)   £
23 Heddon Street (Map 9 E3)
Centre/Mayfair & St James's

Original Tagines (p36)   ££
7A Dorset Street (Map 8 B2)
Centre/Marylebone

North American

Bodean's (p24)   ££
10 Poland Street (Map 9 E3)
Centre/Soho

>>   **£££ expensive**   **££ moderate**   **£ cheap**   (Price ranges: Restaurants, *see p25*, Hotels, *see p181*)

Restaurants

North American
continued

Eagle Bar Diner (p27) £
3–5 Rathbone Pl (Map 9 F2)
Centre/Fitzrovia

Oriental

E&O (p42) ££
14 Blenheim Cres (Map 6 C3)
*West/Notting Hill &
Westbourne Park*

**Great Eastern
Dining Room** (p48) ££
54–6 Great Eastern St
(Map 5 E5)
City & East/Shoreditch & Hoxton

Spanish

Fino (p28) ££
33 Charlotte Street (Map 9 E2)
Centre/Fitzrovia

Mar i Terra (p24) £
17 Air Street (Map 9 E3)
Centre/Soho

Mesón Don Felipe (p53) £
53 The Cut (Map 10 A5)
South/South Bank

Moro (p44) ££
34–6 Exmouth Mkt (Map 4 A5)
City & East/Clerkenwell

Navarro's (p28) £
67 Charlotte Street (Map 9 E1)
Centre/Fitzrovia

El Parador (p50) £
245 Eversholt St (Map 3 E4)
North/Camden

Tendido Cero (p40) ££
174 Old Brompton Rd
(Map 13 G3)
West/Chelsea & Fulham

Thai

Busaba Eathai (p43) ££
106–10 Wardour Street,
020 7255 8686 (Map 9 E3)
Centre/Soho
22 Store Street,
020 7299 7900 (Map 9 F2)
Centre/Bloomsbury

Patara (p33) ££
3 & 7 Maddox St (Map 8 D3)
Centre/Mayfair & St James's

Turkish

Gallipoli (p49) £
102 Upper Street (Map 4 B2)
North/Islington

Tas (p53) ££
33 The Cut (Map 10 A5)
South/South Bank

Vegetarian

The Gate (p41) ££
51 Queen Charlotte St
(Map 12 A3)
West/Hammersmith

Manna (p51) ££
4 Erskine Road (Map 2 B2)
North/Primrose Hill

Vietnamese

Green Papaya (p48) £
191 Mare Street (Map 5 H1)
City & East/Hackney

Viet Hoa (p48) £
70–2 Kingsland Rd (Map 5 E4)
City & East/Shoreditch & Hoxton

Shopping

Books

ARTWORDS (p162)
65 Rivington Street (Map 5 E5)
www.artwords.co.uk
City & East/Shoreditch & Hoxton

Blackwell's (p65)
100 Charing Cross Rd (Map 9 F3)
Centre/Covent Garden

Blenheim Books (p159)
11 Blenheim Crescent
(Map 6 C3)
*West/Notting Hill &
Westbourne Park*

Borders (p65)
Charing Cross Road (Map 9 F3)
Centre/Covent Garden

Calder Bookshop (p91)
51 The Cut (Map 10 A5)
South/South Bank

Daunt Books (p74)
83 Marylebone High Street
(Map 8 C1)
Centre/Marylebone

David Drummond (p64)
Cecil Court (Map 9 F3)
Centre/Covent Garden

Forbidden Planet (p63)
179 Shaftesbury Ave (Map 9 F2)
Centre/Covent Garden

Foyles (p65)
Charing Cross Road (Map 9 F3)
Centre/Covent Garden

Gay's the Word (p64)
66 Marchmont St (Map 3 G5)
Centre/Bloomsbury

Helter Skelter (p65)
4 Denmark Street (Map 9 F2)
Centre/Covent Garden

Henry Pordes (p65)
58–60 Charing Cross Road
(Map 9 F3)
Centre/Covent Garden

Magma (p62)
8 Earlham Street (Map 9 F3)
Centre/Covent Garden

Marchpane (p64)
Cecil Court (Map 9 F3)
Centre/Covent Garden

Nigel Williams (p64)
Cecil Court (Map 9 F3)
Centre/Covent Garden

PJ Hilton (p64)
Cecil Court (Map 9 F3)
Centre/Covent Garden

Primrose Hill Books (p90)
Regent's Park Road
(Map 2 B2)
North/Primrose Hill

Quinto (p65)
48a Charing Cross Rd (Map 9 F3)
Centre/Covent Garden

Shipley (p65)
70 Charing Cross Rd (Map 9 F3)
Centre/Covent Garden

Shipley Media (p65)
80 Charing Cross Road
(Map 9 F3)
Centre/Covent Garden

Silver Moon (*see Foyles*, p65)

Simon Finch Rare Books (p82)
61a Ledbury Road (Map 6 D3)
*West/Notting Hill &
Westbourne Park*

Travel Bookshop (p159)
13–15 Blenheim Cres (Map 6 C3)
*West/Notting Hill &
Westbourne Park*

Department Stores

Fenwick (p79)
63 New Bond Street
(Map 8 D3) www.fenwick.co.uk
Centre/Mayfair & St James's

Fortnum & Mason (p79)
181 Piccadilly (Map 9 E4)
www.fortnumandmason.com
Centre/Mayfair & St James's

Harrods (p79)
87–135 Brompton Road
(Map 14 B1) www.harrods.com
West/Knightsbridge & Belgravia

Harvey Nichols (p79)
109–25 Knightsbridge
(Map 14 B1)
www.harveynichols.com
West/Knightsbridge & Belgravia

John Lewis (p79)
278–306 Oxford St (Map 8 D3)
www.johnlewis.com
Centre/Marylebone

Liberty (p68)
210–20 Regent St (Map 8 D3)
Centre/Soho

Marks & Spencer (p85)
458 Oxford Street (Map 9 E2)
Centre/Soho

Selfridges (p71)
400 Oxford Street (Map 8 C3)
Centre/Marylebone

Fashion

202 (p80)
202 Westbourne Grove
(Map 7 F3) *West/Notting Hill &
Westbourne Park*

Agnès B (p60)
Floral Street (Map 9 G3)
Centre/Covent Garden

All Saints (p62)
5 Earlham Street (Map 9 F3)
Centre/Covent Garden

>> £££ **expensive** ££ **moderate** £ **cheap** (Price ranges: Restaurants, *see p25*, Hotels, *see p181*)

Intoxica! (p83)
231 Portobello Rd (Map 6 D3)
*West/Notting Hill &
Westbourne Park*

Phonica (p67)
51 Poland Street (Map 9 E3)
Centre/Soho

Ray's Jazz (p65)
Foyles Bookshop, Charing
Cross Road (Map 9 F3)
Centre/Covent Garden

Rough Trade (p81)
130 Talbot Road (Map 6 D3)
*West/Notting Hill &
Westbourne Park*

Prints & Posters

Artcadia (p87)
108 Commercial St (Map 11 F1)
*City & East/Spitalfields &
Whitechapel*

Rennies (p64)
At French's Dairy
13 Rugby Street (Map 9 H1)
Centre/Bloomsbury

Rock Archive (p90)
110 Islington High St (Map 4 A3)
North/Islington

Stage Door Prints (p64)
9 Cecil Court (Map 9 F3)
Centre/Covent Garden

Storey's (p64)
3 Cecil Court (Map 9 F3)
Centre/Covent Garden

The Tintin Shop (p60)
34 Floral Street (Map 9 G3)
Centre/Covent Garden

Vertigo (p60)
22 Wellington St (Map 9 G3)
Centre/Covent Garden

Vintage (p66)
39–43 Brewer St (Map 9 E3)
Centre/Soho

Shoes & Accessories

Anello & Davide (p72)
20–21 St Christoper's Pl (8 C3)
Centre/Marylebone

Anya Hindmarch (p76)
15–17 Pont Street (Map 14 B2)
West/Knightsbridge & Belgravia

Bill Amberg (p81)
10 Chepstow Road (Map 7 E2)
*West/Notting Hill &
Westbourne Park*

b Store (p67)
6 Conduit Street
(Map 8 D3)
Centre/Mayfair & St James

Erickson Beamon (p76)
38 Elizabeth Street
(Map 14 C2)
West/Knightsbridge & Belgravia

Georgina Goodman (p69)
12–14 Shepherd St (Map 8 D5)
Centre/Mayfair & St James's

James Smith & Sons (p63)
53 New Oxford St (Map 9 G2)
Centre/Bloomsbury

Jess James (p68)
Newburgh Street (Map 9 E3)
Centre/Soho

Jimmy Choo (p77)
169 Draycott Avenue
(Map 14 A3)
West/Chelsea & Fulham

Kate Kuba (p79)
22 Duke of York Square,
King's Road (Map 14 B3)
West/Chelsea & Fulham

Kirk Originals (p60)
29 Floral Street (Map 9 G3)
Centre/Covent Garden

Lara Bohinc 107 (p86)
51 Hoxton Square (Map 5 E5)
Ctiy & East/Shoreditch & Hoxton

Lulu Guinness (p77)
3 Ellis Street (Map 14 B2)
West/Knightsbridge & Belgravia

Oliver Sweeney (p79)
29 King's Road (Map 14 B3)
West/Chelsea & Fulham

Osprey (p72)
St Christopher's Pl (Map 8 C3)
Centre/Marylebone

Patrick Cox (p75)
129 Sloane Street (Map 14 B2)
West/Knightsbridge & Belgravia

Philip Treacy (p76)
69 Elizabeth St (Map 14 C2)
West/Knightsbridge & Belgravia

Poste (p70)
10 S Molton St (Map 8 D3)
Centre/Mayfair & St James's

Poste Mistress (p61)
261–3 Monmouth St (Map 9 F3)
Centre/Covent Garden

Rachel Skinner (p90)
13 Princess Road (Map 2 B2)
North/Primrose Hill

Tatty Devine (p88)
236 Brick Lane (Map 11 F1)
*City & East/Spitalfields &
Whitechapel*

Willma (p84)
339 Portobello Rd (Map 6 C2)
*West/Notting Hill &
Westbourne Park*

Art &
Architecture

Art Galleries

The Agency (p110)
Charlotte Road (Map 5 E5)
City & East/Shoreditch & Hoxton

The Approach (p110)
Approach Road
(🚇 Bethnal Green)
City & East/Bethnal Green

Camden Arts Centre (p106)
Arkwright Road (Hampstead)
North/Hampstead

Chisenhale (p110)
Chisenhale Road
(🚇 Bethnal Green)
City & East/Bethnal Green

Gagosian (p110)
www.gagosian.com
6–24 Britannia Street
(Map 3 G4)
Centre/Bloomsbury
8 Heddon Street (Map 9 E3)
Centre/Mayfair & St James's

Hayward Gallery (p109)
South Bank Centre (Map 9 H4)
South/South Bank

ICA (p96)
The Mall (Map 9 F5)
Centre/Westminster & Pimlico

Jerwood Space (p109)
171 Union Street (Map 10 B5)
South/Borough

Lisson (p110)
52–4 Bell Street
(Map 8 A1)
Centre/Marylebone

Matt's Gallery (p110)
42–4 Copperfield Road
(🚇 Mile End)
City & East/Bethnal Green

Photographers' Gallery (p95)
5 & 8 Great Newport Street
(Map 9 F3)
Centre/Covent Garden

Saatchi Gallery (p109)
County Hall (Map 9 H5)
South/South Bank

Sadie Coles HQ (p110)
35 Heddon Street (Map 9 E3)
Centre/Mayfair & St James's

Serpentine Gallery (p101)
Kensington Gardens
(Map 7 H5)
West/Kensington

South London Gallery (p110)
65 Peckham Rd (🚇 Elephant &
Castle, then 171 bus)
South/Camberwell

Stephen Friedman (p110)
Old Burlington Street
(Map 9 E4)
Centre/Mayfair & St James's

Vilma Gold (p15)
25b Vyner Street (Map 5 H3)
City & East/Bethnal Green

Wapping Project Space (p105)
Wapping Wall (🚇 Wapping)
*City & East/Wapping &
Docklands*

Whitechapel Gallery (p104)
80 Whitechapel High St (11 F2)
*City & East/Spitalfields &
Whitechapel*

White Cube (p110)
Hoxton Square (Map 5 E5)
City & East/Shoreditch & Hoxton

Wilkinson Gallery (p110)
242 Cambridge Heath Road
(🚇 Bethnal Green)
City & East/Bethnal Green

For markets, see p236

Index by Type

Tate Modern (p111)
Bankside (Map 10 B4)
South/Borough

Theatre Museum (p95)
Russell Street (Map 9 G3)
Centre/Covent Garden

V&A (p102)
Exhibition Road (Map 13 H2)
West/Kensington

The Wallace Collection (p101)
Manchester Square (Map 8 C2)
Centre/Marylebone

Performance

Cinemas

Curzon Soho (p120)
99 Shaftesbury Avenue
(Map 9 F3)
Centre/Soho

Electric Cinema (p123)
191 Portobello Road
(Map 6 D3)
*West/Notting Hill &
Westbourne Park*

Everyman (p128)
5 Holly Bush Vale
(Map 1 A5)
North/Hampstead

NFT (p130)
South Bank (Map 9 H4)
South/South Bank

The Other Cinema (p121)
11 Rupert Street (Map 9 F3)
Centre/Soho

Ritzy (p131)
Brixton Oval (◎ Brixton)
South/Brixton

Combined Arts

BAC (p131)
Lavender Hill (◎ Clapham Jctn)
South/Clapham

Barbican (p124)
Silk Street (Map 10 C1)
City & East/The City

Riverside Studios (p124)
Crisp Road (Map 12 A4)
West/Hammersmith

Tricycle (p129)
269 Kilburn High Rd (◎ Kilburn)
North/Kilburn

Comedy

Comedy Café (p125)
66–8 Rivington Street
(Map 5 E5)
City & East/Shoreditch & Hoxton

Comedy Store (p121)
1a Oxendon Street (Map 9 F4)
Centre/Soho

Hackney Empire
(See Theatres)

Jongleurs (p128)
Middle Yard
Chalk Farm Road (Map 2 D2)
North/Camden

Dance

Laban (p130)
Creekside (Map 16 A3)
South/Greenwich & Deptford

The Place (p122)
17 Duke's Road (Map 3 F5)
Centre/Bloomsbury

Sadler's Wells (p126)
Rosebery Avenue (Map 4 A4)
North/Islington

Music Venues

Borderline (p119)
Orange Yard,
Manette Street (Map 9 F3)
Centre/Soho

ENO @ The Coliseum (p119)
St Martin's Lane (Map 9 G4)
Centre/Covent Garden

Jazz Café (p127)
5 Parkway (Map 2 D3)
North/Camden

Mean Fiddler (p120)
168 Charing Cross Road
(Map 9 F3)
Centre/Soho

Ocean (p125)
270 Mare Street (Map 5 H1)
City & East/Hackney

Ronnie Scott's (p121)
47 Frith Street (Map 9 F3)
Centre/Soho

Royal Opera House (p118)
Bow Street (Map 9 G3)
Centre/Covent Garden

St John's Smith Square (p122)
Smith Square (Map 15 G2)
Centre/Westminster & Pimlico

Scala (p126)
275 Pentonville Rd (Map 3 H4)
Centre/Bloomsbury

**Shepherd's Bush
Empire** (p123)
Shepherd's Bush Green
(Map 6 A5)
West/Shepherd's Bush

606 Club (p123)
90 Lots Road (Map 13 G5)
West/Chelsea & Fulham

South Bank Centre (p129)
Belvedere Rd/South Bank
(Map 9 H4)
*South/South Bank
(For National Theatre see
Theatres; for NFT see cinemas)*

The Spitz (p124)
Old Spitalfields Market
(Map 11 F1)
*City & East/Spitalfields &
Whitechapel*

12 Bar Club (p119)
22–3 Denmark St (Map 9 F2)
Centre/Covent Garden

Union Chapel (p127)
Compton Avenue (Map 4 B1)
North/Islington

Wigmore Hall (p122)
36 Wigmore Street (Map 8 C2)
Centre/Marylebone

Theatres

Almeida (p126)
Almeida Street (Map 4 B2)
North/Islington

Arts Theatre (p119)
Great Newport St (Map 9 F3)
Centre/Covent Garden

Donmar Warehouse (p118)
41 Earlham Street (Map 9 F3)
Centre/Covent Garden

Hackney Empire (p125)
Mare Street (Map 5 H1)
City & East/Hackney

Hampstead Theatre (p128)
Eton Avenue (◎ Swiss Cottage)
North/Swiss Cottage

King's Head Theatre Bar (p127)
115 Upper Street (Map 4 B2)
North/Islington

Old Vic (p130)
The Cut (Map 10 A5)
South/South Bank

Royal National Theatre (p129)
South Bank (Map 9 H4)
South/South Bank

Shakespeare's Globe (p130)
Bankside (Map 10 C4)
South/Borough

Soho Theatre (p120)
21 Dean Street (Map 9 F3)
Centre/Soho

Pubs, Bars & Clubs

Pubs

Anchor Bankside (p152)
34 Park Street (Map 10 C4)
South/Borough

Black Friar (p144)
174 Queen Victoria St
(Map 10 B3)
City & East/The City

Bread & Roses (p155)
68 Clapham Manor Street
(◎ Clapham Common)
South/Clapham

The Bricklayer's Arms (p162)
63 Charlotte Road (Map 5 E5)
City & East/Shoreditch

Blue Anchor (p154)
13 Lower Mall
(◎ Hammersmith)
West/Hammersmith

Coach & Horses (p144)
29 Greek Street (Map 9 F3)
Centre/Soho

Crown Islington (p151)
116 Cloudesley Rd (Map 4 A3)
North/Islington

Index by Type

Pubs, Bars & Clubs

Pubs *continued*

The Dove (p154)
19 Upper Mall (🚇 Hammersmith)
West/Hammersmith

The Endurance (p138)
90 Berwick Street (Map 9 E3)
Centre/Soho

Fitzroy Tavern (p144)
16 Charlotte Street (Map 9 E2)
Centre/Fitzrovia

Founders Arms (p154)
Bankside (Map 10 B4)
South/Borough

Freemason's Arms (p153)
32 Downshire Hill (Map 1 C5)
North/Hampstead

French House (p139)
49 Dean Street (Map 9 F3)
Centre/Soho

George Inn (p163)
77 Borough High St (Map 10 D5)
South/Borough

Globe Tavern (p163)
Bedale Street (Map 10 D4)
South/Borough

Golden Heart (p149)
110 Commercial St (Map 11 F1)
City & East/Spitalfields & Whitechapel

The Grapes (p149)
76 Narrow Street (🚇 Wapping)
City & East/Wapping & Docklands

Greenwich Union (p155)
56 Royal Hill (Map 16 B3)
South/Greenwich & Deptford

Island Queen (p151)
87 Noel Road (Map 4 B3)
North/Islington

Jerusalem Tavern (p146)
55 Britton Street (Map 10 B1)
City & East/Clerkenwell

Lamb (p141)
94 Lamb's Conduit St (Map 9 H1)
Centre/Bloomsbury

Lamb & Flag (p137)
33 Rose Street (Map 9 G3)
Centre/Covent Garden

Market Porter (p163)
9 Stoney Street (Map 10 C4)
South/Borough

Nag's Head (p141)
53 Kinnerton St (Map 14 B1)
West/Knightsbridge & Belgravia

Pillars of Hercules (p144)
7 Greek Street (Map 9 F3)
Centre/Soho

Pineapple (p151)
51 Leverton Street (🚇 Camden)
North/Camden

Pride of Spitalfields (p148)
3 Heneage Street (Map 11 F1)
City & East/Spitalfields & Whitechapel

Prince of Wales (p155)
38 Old Town
(🚇 Clapham Common)
South/Clapham

Prospect of Whitby (p149)
57 Wapping Wall (🚇 Wapping)
City & East/Wapping & Docklands

Royal Inn on the Park (p153)
Grove Road (🚇 Bethnal Green)
City & East/Hackney

Royal Oak (p163)
44 Tabard Street
(🚇 Borough)
South/Borough

Spaniards Inn (p153)
Spaniards Road (Map 1 B2)
North/Hampstead

Trafalgar Tavern (p155)
Park Row (Map 16 C1)
South/Greenwich & Deptford

White Cross (p154)
Water Lane (🚇 Richmond)
South/Richmond

Windmill (p153)
Clapham Common
(🚇 Clapham South)
South/Clapham

Windsor Castle (p144)
114 Campden Hill Rd (Map 7 E5)
West/Kensington

Bars

The American Bar (p137)
Savoy Hotel, Strand (Map 9 G4)
Centre/Covent Garden

Apartment 195 (p142)
195 King's Road (Map 14 A4)
West/Chelsea & Fulham

Atlantic Bar & Grill (p137)
20 Glasshouse St (Map 9 E4)
Centre/Soho

Bar Kick (p162)
127 Shoreditch High St (5 E5)
City & East/Shoreditch

Bar Rumba (p138)
36 Shaftesbury Ave (Map 9 F3)
Centre/Soho

Blue Bar (p142)
Berkeley Hotel, Wilton Pl (14 B1)
West/Knightsbridge & Belgravia

Bug Bar & Lounge (p154)
St Matthews Church (🚇 Brixton)
South/Brixton

Café Kick (p145)
43 Exmouth Market (Map 4 A5)
City & East/Clerkenwell

Cargo (p146)
83 Rivington Street (Map 5 E5)
City & East/Shoreditch & Hoxton

Cherry Jam (p141)
58 Porchester Road (Map 7 F2)
West/Bayswater & Paddington

Dogstar (p154)
389 Coldharbour Lane
(🚇 Brixton)
South/Brixton

Elbow Room (p162)
97–113 Curtain Rd (Map 5 E5)
City & East/Shoreditch

Embassy Bar (p150)
119 Essex Road (Map 4 B2)
North/Islington

The End (p141)
18 West Central St (Map 9 G2)
Centre/Covent Garden

Escape Bar (p158)
10a Brewer Street (Map 9 E3)
Centre/Soho

Fluid (p146)
40 Charterhouse St
(Map 10 D1)
City & East/Clerkenwell

G-A-Y (p158)
30 Old Compton St (Map 9 F3)
Centre/Soho

Golborne Grove (p143)
36 Golborne Road (Map 6 C1)
West/Notting Hill & Westbourne Park

Gordon's Wine Bar (p136)
47 Villiers Street (Map 9 G4)
Centre/Covent Garden

**Hoxton Square
Bar & Kitchen** (p147)
2–4 Hoxton Square (Map 5 E5)
City & East/Shoreditch & Hoxton

Jerusalem (p139)
33–4 Rathbone Pl (Map 9 E2)
Centre/Fitzrovia

Lobby Bar (p136)
1 Aldwych (Map 9 H3)
Centre/Covent Garden

Lock Tavern (p152)
35 Chalk Farm Rd (Map 2 D2)
North/Camden

Lonsdale (p143)
44–8 Lonsdale Rd (Map 6 D3)
West/Notting Hill & Westbourne Park

Loungelover (p149)
1 Whitby Street (Map 5 F5)
City & East/Shoreditch & Hoxton

Mac Bar (p152)
102 Camden Road (Map 3 E2)
North/Camden

Market Place (p140)
11 Market Place (Map 9 E2)
Centre/Fitzrovia

Mash (p140)
19–21 Great Portland St (8 D2)
Centre/Fitzrovia

Medicine Bar (p150)
181 Upper Street (Map 4 B2)
North/Islington

Mother (p147)
333 Old Street (Map 5 E5)
City & East/Shoreditch & Hoxton

The Player (p139)
8 Broadwick Street (Map 9 E3)
Centre/Soho

Pool (p162)
104–8 Curtain Road (Map 5 E5)
City & East/Shoreditch

The Social (p140)
5 Little Portland St (Map 8 D2)
Centre/Fitzrovia

Townhouse (p142)
31 Beauchamp Pl (Map 14 A1)
West/Knightsbridge & Belgravia

Trailer H (p143)
177 Portobello Rd (Map 6 C2)
West/Notting Hill &
Westbourne Park

Vertigo (p145)
Level 42, Tower 42,
25 Old Broad St (Map 10 D2)
City & East/The City

Vibe Bar (p148)
Old Truman Brewery,
91–5 Brick Lane (Map 11 F1)
City & East/Spitalfields &
Whitechapel

Zeta Bar (p140)
Mayfair Hilton Hotel,
35 Hertford Street (Map 8 C5)
Centre/Mayfair & St James's

Zigfrid (p162)
11 Hoxton Square (Map 5 E5)
City & East/Shoreditch

Clubs

333 (p147)
333 Old Street (Map 5 E5)
City & East/Shoreditch & Hoxton

93 Feet East (p148)
150 Brick Lane (Map 11 F1)
City & East/Spitalfields &
Whitechapel

Fabric (p145)
77a Charterhouse St (Map 10 B1)
City & East/Clerkenwell

Fridge/Fridge Bar (p153)
1 Town Hall Parade (☺ Brixton)
South/Brixton

Heaven (p136)
Under the Arches,
Villiers Street (Map 9 G4)
Centre/Covent Garden

Herbal (p147)
10–14 Kingsland Rd (Map 5 E4)
City & East/Shoreditch & Hoxton

Madame Jo-Jos (p138)
8–10 Brewer Street (Map 9 E3)
Centre/Soho

Ministry of Sound (p153)
103 Gaunt Street
(☺ Elephant & Castle)
South/Kennington

Notting Hill Arts Club (p144)
21 Notting Hill Gate (Map 7 E4)
West/Notting Hill &
Westbourne Park

Substation South (p165)
Trinity Road (☺ Brixton)
South/Brixton

Turnmills (p146)
63a Clerkenwell Rd
(Map 10 B1)
City & East/Clerkenwell

Vauxhall Tavern (p153)
372 Kennington Lane
(Map 15 H4)
South/Kennington

Hotels

Expensive

Blakes (p185)
33 Roland Gardens
(Map 13 G3)
West/Chelsea & Fulham

Charlotte Street Hotel (p181)
15 Charlotte Street
(Map 9 E2)
Centre/Fitzrovia

Claridge's (p183)
Brook St (Map 8 D3)
www.savoygroup.com
Centre/Mayfair & St James's

**Covent Garden
Hotel** (p180)
10 Monmouth St (Map 9 F3)
Centre/Covent Garden

Dorchester (p183)
Park Lane (Map 8 C4)
www.dorchesterhotel.com
Centre/Mayfair & St James's

Dorset Square (p183)
39 Dorset Square (Map 8 B1)
Centre/Marylebone

The Franklin (p184)
28 Egerton Gdns (Map 14 A2)
West/Knightsbridge & Belgravia

Great Eastern (p187)
Liverpool Street (Map 11 E2)
City & East/The City

Hazlitt's (p181)
6 Frith Street (Map 9 F3)
Centre/Soho

The Metropolitan (p182)
Old Park Lane (Map 8 C5)
Centre/Mayfair & St James's

One Aldwych (p180)
1 Aldwych (Map 9 H3)
Centre/Covent Garden

Ritz (p183)
150 Piccadilly (Map 8 D4)
www.theritzlondon.com
Centre/Mayfair & St James's

The Rookery (p188)
Peter's La, Cowcross St
(Map 10 B1)
City & East/Clerkenwell

The Savoy (p183)
Strand (Map 9 G4)
www.savoygroup.com
Centre/Covent Garden

Moderate

**City Inn
Westminster** (p184)
30 John Islip Street
(Map 15 F3)
Centre/Westminster & Pimlico

The Colonnade (p185)
2 Warrington Cres
(Map 7 F1)
West/Bayswater & Paddington

Durrants (p182)
George Street (Map 8 B2)
Centre/Marylebone

Five Sumner Place (p184)
5 Sumner Place (Map 13 H3)
West/Chelsea & Fulham

Hamilton House (p189)
14 West Grove (Map 16 C4)
South/Greenwich & Deptford

London Bridge Hotel (p189)
8–18 London Bridge St
(Map 10 D5)
South/Borough

Malmaison (p187)
Charterhouse Sq (Map 10 B1)
City & East/Clerkenwell

**Mercure London City
Bankside** (p189)
71–9 Southwark St (Map 10 B4)
South/Borough

Miller's Residence (p186)
111a Westbourne Grove
(Map 7 E3)
West/Notting Hill &
Westbourne Park

The Portobello (p186)
22 Stanley Gardens (Map 6 D3)
West/Notting Hill &
Westbourne Park

Topham Belgravia (p183)
28 Ebury Street (Map 14 D2)
West/Knightsbridge &
Belgravia

The Zetter (p188)
86–8 Clerkenwell Road
(Map 10 B1)
City & East/Clerkenwell

Cheap

Abbey House (p186)
11 Vicarage Gate (Map 7 E5)
West/Kensington

Crescent Hotel (p181)
49–50 Cartwright
Gardens (Map 3 F5)
Centre/Bloomsbury

Dover Hotel (p183)
42–4 Belgrave Rd (Map 15 E3)
Centre/Westminster & Pimlico

La Gaffe (p188)
107–11 Heath Street (Map 1 A4)
North/Hampstead

Generator (p181)
Compton Place (Map 3 G5)
Centre/Bloomsbury

Mayflower (p184)
26–8 Trebovir Rd (Map 13 E3)
West/Kensington

Travel Information

London's Underground train ("Tube") and bus networks are extensive and easy to navigate, though frequently crowded and subject to delays. A weekday Congestion Charge for drivers has recently been introduced in the centre of town. This has freed up traffic flow, making bus and taxi journeys noticeably quicker, and improving the atmosphere for cyclists and pedestrians. Numerous guided tours are available, and riverboats offer a fantastic way to see the city.

Arrival

There are five international airports near London, of which Heathrow is the busiest. Waterloo is the terminal for trains coming from mainland Europe. From these international points of entry there are various ways to travel into central London.

Heathrow Airport

The **Heathrow Express** train is the fastest and most comfortable way to travel into central London. Trains depart every 15 minutes and take 15–20 minutes to travel non-stop to Paddington Station. The cheapest option for time-rich travellers is a Tube train (Piccadilly Line), which takes about an hour into central London. You can also catch the A2 bus. A taxi into central London is the most expensive option (about £45), unless you are travelling in a group of five.

Gatwick Airport

Gatwick is about 30 miles south of central London. The **Gatwick Express** train usually runs every 15 minutes and takes about 30 minutes to travel non-stop to London's Victoria Station. There are also slightly cheaper, standard stopping services into Victoria and King's Cross Stations. A taxi into London will cost about £100.

Stansted Airport

Stansted Express trains depart from the airport every 15–30 minutes; the journey to Liverpool Street Station takes 45 minutes. There is also a standard stopping train once an hour. The A6 coach into central London is a bit cheaper but takes at least 90 minutes.

Luton Airport

The **Thameslink** train service runs from the airport to a number of central city stations, including Kings Cross, every 5–10 minutes. The journey takes 30–40 minutes.

London City Airport

A shuttle bus runs between this small airport and Liverpool Street Station, via Canary Wharf, every 10 minutes during peak hours. Otherwise, you can take a taxi into town.

Waterloo International Terminal

Waterloo Station, on the South Bank of the Thames, is served by the Underground's Bakerloo, Jubilee and Northern Lines. There are also taxi ranks and numerous bus stops outside.

Getting Around

Tube trains, buses and taxis are plentiful. Overland trains serve the suburbs and beyond.

Advance Booking Option for Overseas Visitors

Visitors planning to travel to London from Europe, the US, Australia and several other countries can purchase a Visitor Travelcard in advance through **www.ticketonline.com**. This covers unlimited travel on all trains, buses and the DLR, and there's an option for the Heathrow Express. The card is not available in the UK itself.

London Underground

The Underground network stretches to 275 stations across the city. Trains run from about 5:30am to 11:30pm or 1am, depending on the line. This is the oldest underground train network in the world and usually offers the quickest way to get around town. However, the ageing system is prone to delays and over-crowding. Tickets are expensive in comparison with the cost of subway travel in other major world cities.

Journeys are priced according to zones radiating out from the city centre (Zone 1) to the far reaches of Greater London (Zone 6). If you have missed buying a Visitor Travelcard *(see above)*, there are various options, including the basic Travelcard, which covers unlimited travel on the Tube, buses and DLR (Docklands Light Railway). There are daily (available after 9:30am), weekend or 7-day options. If you're travelling sporadically within Zone 1, buy a so-called "Carnet" of 10 discounted single tickets.

If you are travelling around London for more than a week, consider buying a rechargeable Oystercard (**www.oyster card.com**). Holders of Oystercards need only touch the card to the yellow pad on the turnstiles, and can recharge at the pad on the ticket machines.

Buses

Buses are cheaper than the Tube and are a great way to get to see London, but try to avoid rush hours (7:30– 9:30am and 5–7pm).

The flat fare is £1. In central London, you must buy a ticket before boarding – look for a ticket machine at the bus stop or buy a booklet of six discounted Saver tickets from Tube stations and some newsagents. Night buses operate 11pm–6am with a separate scale of fares.

Car

Driving around and parking in London is frustrating and expensive. A **Congestion Charge** of £5 is levied on all cars travelling through the city centre between 7am and 6:30pm on weekdays. "C" signs mark the boundaries of the Congestion Charging zone, and cameras record every car. You can pay online (see directory), or at selected newsagents and garages. A hefty fine will be issued if you fail to pay before midnight. Speeding, using bus lanes and stopping in box junctions also attract fines.

Parking is restricted almost every-where. Read street parking signs carefully or you'll probably return to a penalty notice or clamped wheel. It's best to use NCP car parks (**www.ncp.co.uk**) if in doubt.

Taxis

Classic black cabs are plentiful in central London, but tariffs are high, especially after 8pm and at weekends. Licensed minicabs (from offices) are usually cheaper.

Other Forms of Transport

Pedicabs (or rickshaws) congregate in Soho and some other areas, offering short hops. They are unregulated, though, and can be expensive.

There are several riverboat services along the Thames (see pp12 & 113) – Travelcard holders get one-third off the fare on some routes. Canalboats are operated by **The London Waterbus Company**. Trams are making a comeback in some suburban areas.

Tours

A qualified Blue Badge guide can be booked for either a general sightsee-ing tour or something tailor-made – see the **Association of Professional Tourist Guides'** website for individual profiles or book through their recom-mended agency, **Tour Guides Ltd**. **Black Taxi Tours of London** offers qualified tour guides too.

The **Original London Walks** is a good one to try for themed strolls – actors, experts and historians lead tours such as Ghosts, Gaslight and Guinness, or Jack the Ripper Haunts in the East End. Wellbeing centre **Kairos** in Soho offers a historical walking tour of Gay and Lesbian Soho. **London Open House** runs Saturday-morning tours led by architects and historians. Consult Time Out magazine for other unusual themed walks.

Directory

Airports
www.baa.co.uk (Heathrow, Gatwick & Stansted)
www.londoncityairport.com

Association of Professional Tourist Guides
020 7505 3073
www.touristguides.org.uk

Black Cabs
020 7432 1432
www.computacab.co.uk
www.dialacab.co.uk

Black Taxi Tours of London
020 7935 9363
www.blacktaxitours.co.uk

Congestion Charge
0845 900 1234 / www.cclondon.com

Kairos in Soho
020 7437 6063
www.kairosinsoho.org.uk

London Open House
www.londonopenhouse.org

The London Waterbus Company
020 7482 2660
www.londonwaterbus.com

The Original London Walks
020 7624 3978 / www.walks.com

Tour Guides Ltd
020 7495 5504

Trains
Heathrow Express 0845 600 1515
www.heathrowexpress.com

Gatwick Express 0845 850 1530
www.gatwickexpress.com

National Rail Enquiries 08457 484950
www.nationalrail.co.uk

Stansted Express 0845 850 0150
www.stanstedexpress.co.uk

Thameslink www.thameslink.co.uk

Transport for London
The Tube, buses, DLR, taxis, riverboats & trams
020 7222 1234 / www.tfl.gov.uk

Practical Information

The information and tips here should help you have a stress-free visit to London. Some forward planning is often beneficial – start with the websites offering tourist information and listing events. Visitors with special needs, such as wheelchair users, are supported by a number of dedicated organizations, and gay and lesbian travellers are particularly well catered for in this city.

Disabled Travellers

Recent changes to the Disability Discrimination Act require anyone who provides a service to the public to make it accessible to disabled people, within reason. Equal-access campaigner **Artsline** has a constantly expanding online database listing over 400 arts and entertainment venues and their provisions for sensory-impaired people and wheelchair users. A factsheet from **Greater London Action on Disability** gives details of what to expect at well-known tourist attractions, and another lists accessible hotels.

Improvements to the accessibility of the Tube are in progress, but at present only 40 stations can be reached without using stairs or escalators. For a copy of *Access to the Underground*, call 020 7941 4600. Buses are better – over 90% of the bus fleet has wheelchair access.

Emergencies & Health

In the event of a serious accident, medical emergency, fire or criminal incident requiring urgent assistance, call 999 and specify ambulance, fire service or police. Calls from any phone, including payphones, are free. Citizens of the European Economic Area and countries with a bilateral healthcare agreement with the UK are exempt from hospital A&E charges.

See the **Hospital Charges** website for full details of exemptions.

If you require an emergency prescription or less urgent medical attention, the private **Medicentre** chain offers walk-in clinics. Branches are located in train stations, central London and the City.

If you need advice outside clinic hours, call **Doctors Direct** to arrange a home visit or refer to the **NHS Direct** website's useful self-help guide.

Pharmacies are a good first stop for minor ailments. For late-night prescriptions, **Bliss Pharmacy** is open until midnight, while **Zafash** is London's only 24-hour pharmacy.

Gay & Lesbian Travellers

Soho is London's pink mecca, with the highest concentration of bars, clubs and gay-oriented shops. There is an established scene in Brixton, and nightspots have also sprung up in Vauxhall. Free pink paper **Boyz**, available in gay bars and businesses and online, features London listings. **The Gay Times** website has useful links to services from arts centres and bars to shops and support, while lesbian magazine **Diva** offers online area-by-area mini guides. The **London Lesbian and Gay Switchboard** has a 24-hour helpline. For recommended bars and clubs, *see p134*.

Listings/What's On

Time Out is London's hippest and most comprehensive weekly listings magazine, covering new shops and restaurants as well as arts and entertainment. It has an online guide, **www.timeout.com/london**.

Metro Life, free with Thursday's *Evening Standard* newspaper, is a good guide to goings-on in the city. It is affiliated to **www.thisislondon.com**.

The Knowledge, in *The Times* on Saturday, rounds up London listings in a handy format.

Money

There's no shortage of bureaux de change in the city, but you may get a better exchange rate if you use your bank or credit card to obtain cash from ATMs. The practice of keying in your PIN number rather than signing a credit card slip at point of purchase is being introduced in some businesses.

Opening Hours

London closes early in comparison with cities such as New York or Paris. Most **shops** are open from 10am–6pm Monday to Saturday, staying open an hour or two later on Wednesday or Thursday. Many open from noon to 5pm or 6pm on Sunday. Some major department stores, such as Harvey Nichols and Selfridges, stay open until 8pm every week night.

Restaurants tend to close at 11pm or midnight (last servings 10–10:30), and **pubs** call "time" at 11pm, owing to the UK's licensing laws on alcohol (10:30pm on Sundays). **Bars** with extended opening hours usually offer some form of entertainment, such as live music or DJs. Most **nightclubs** close at 3am, though some stay open until 6am at weekends.

Banks are open from 9:30am to 3:30pm or 4:30pm Monday to Friday, and **post offices** from 9am to 5:30pm on weekdays. Some banks and post offices are open on Saturday morning.

Phones and Communications

Public telephones may be less plentiful than they once were because of the proliferation of mobile phones, but they have become more sophisticated. At BT Internet kiosks, you can surf the Internet, send and receive emails, or send a video text message as well as make a phone call. For long-distance calls, it's worth buying an international phone card, available from newsagents, which gives you an access number and code for a cheaper rate.

Most mobile phones in the UK, Europe and Australia operate on GSM 900MHz or 1800MHz frequency bands. Visitors from the US and Canada will need a tri-band phone to connect with a UK network – check with your service provider before travelling.

The **easyInternetcafé** chain (www.easyeverything.com) dominates the drop-in web-surfing scene, but the city is dotted with numerous small Internet cafés.

Security

Crowded pubs, train stations and shops are prime spots for bag-snatchers and pickpockets, so keep your bag close to the front of your body and your wits about you. Mobile phone theft is common, particularly from just outside Tube stations. Be alert when using ATMs, as they have been the target of various scams. Don't use a machine that looks unusual, such as any that seem to be fitted with extra attachments. Make sure no-one behind you can see while you key in your PIN. Unlicensed minicabs also pose many dangers, especially to single women. Never accept a lift from a driver touting for fares on the street.

Tipping

As a guide, if service has been good, give 10–15 per cent to waiters (unless a service charge has already been added to the bill), hairdressers, beauty therapists and taxi drivers. It is not customary to tip in pubs, even if you order food, but tipping is becoming more common in posh cocktail bars that employ expert "mixologists". In hotels, £1–2 is a standard tip for luggage porters.

Tourist Information

London's official tourist organization is **Visit London**. Its excellent website contains a comprehensive directory, including bureaux de change, Internet cafés and hospitals. There are also sections for gay and lesbian, and disabled visitors. The official **Britain and London Visitor Centre** is near Piccadilly Circus. The privately run **London Information Centre** in Leicester Square operates in tandem with **www.londontown.com**.

Directory

Artsline
020 7388 2227
www.artslineonline.com

Bliss Pharmacy
5–6 Marble Arch, W1 (**Map** 8 B3)

Britain and London Visitor Centre
1 Regent Street, SW1 (**Map** 9 E4)
020 8846 9000

Directory Enquiries
118 118 • 118 500 • 118 180 • 118 888

Doctors Direct
020 7751 9701
www.doctorsdirect.co.uk

Emergency Services
999

Gay & Lesbian
020 7837 7324 (24-hour helpline)
www.llgs.org.uk
www.gaytimes.co.uk
www.boyz.co.uk
www.divamag.co.uk
www.timeout.com/london

Greater London Action on Disability
www.glad.org.uk

Hospital Charges
www.publications.doh.gov.uk/overseasvisitors/index.htm

London Information Centre
Leicester Square, W1 (**Map** 9 F4)
020 7292 2333
www.londoninformationcentre.com
www.londontown.com

Medicentre
0870 600 0870
www.medicentre.co.uk

NHS Direct
0845 4647 • www.nhsdirect.nhs.uk

Visit London
www.visitlondon.com

Zafash Pharmacy
233–5 Old Brompton Rd, SW5
(**Map** 13 G3)

General Index

General Index

General Index

Acknowledgements

Contributors

Jonathan Cox is a writer, editor and photographer who has worked for a wide range of publications, including the *Sunday Times* and the *Time Out London Eating Guide*. He edited Time Out's guide to *Weekend Breaks*. For *e»guide London*, he wrote the **Restaurants** chapter.

Lisa Ritchie is an American based in London, and has written for various magazines and newspapers, including *Time Out* and the *Evening Standard*. Lisa was deputy editor of *Time Out Shopping Guide 2004*. For *e»guide London*, she wrote the **Shopping** and **Hotels** chapters, as well as the **Practical**, **Travel**, **Seasonal** and **Top Choices** sections.

Michael Ellis has written for a number of guidebooks and listings, including the *Virgin Guide to London*, and Time Out's guides to *London*, *Eating & Drinking*, *Pubs & Bars*, and *Weekend Breaks*. He has also reviewed exhibitions for *Frieze* and *Art Monthly*, and produces the annual *Londoner's Diary*. For *e»guide London*, he wrote the **Art & Architecture**, **Performance**, **Streetlife** and **Havens** chapters.

Andrew Humphreys is a regular bar writer for London's weekly culture and entertainment magazine *Time Out*, and for three years was the editor of the same company's annual *London Pubs & Bars Guide*. For *e»guide London*, he wrote most of the **Pubs, Bars & Clubs** chapter.

Peterjon Cresswell is a contributor to Time Out's annual *Pubs & Bars Guide*. He is regularly sent on assignment by the London-based HPI Research Group to assess nightlife and drinking trends in major cities across the globe. For *e»guide London*, he contributed text for the **Pubs, Bars & Clubs** chapter.

Max Alexander is a New Zealander by birth, but has been based in London since 1987. As a freelance photographer, he has worked on a large number of prestigious publications, travelling extensively to produce 15 travel guides for DK. He has recently completed a book on *Bordeaux & its Wines* for Duncan Baird Publishers.

Produced by Blue Island Publishing
www.blueisland.co.uk
Editorial Director Rosalyn Thiro
Art Director Stephen Bere
Editor Jane Simmonds
Editorial Assistant Allen Stone
Proofreader Val Phoenix
Picture Researcher Ellen Root

Published by DK
Publishing Managers Jane Ewart, Vicki Ingle and Anna Streiffert
Senior Editor Christine Stroyan
Senior Designer Marisa Renzullo
Cartographic Editor Casper Morris
DTP Designer Jason Little
Production Coordinator Louise Minihane

Acknowledgements

PHOTOGRAPHY PERMISSIONS

The publishers would like to thank all the churches, museums, hotels, restaurants, bars, clubs, shops, galleries and other sights for their assistance and kind permission to photograph at their establishments.

Placement Key: t = top; tc = top centre; tca = top centre above; tcb = top centre below; tl = top left; tr = top right; c = centre; ca = centre above; cl = centre left; cla = centre left above; clc = centre left centre; cr = centre right; crc = centre right centre; crb = centre right below; b = bottom; bl = bottom left; br = bottom right; l = left; r = right

Works of art have been reproduced with the permission of the following copyright holders:
Jerwood Space: © Trevor Appleson *Uniforms*: 109cr
The publishers would like to thank the following companies and picture libraries for permission to reproduce their photographs:
Atlantic Bar and Grill: 137cl;
Stephen Bere: 10cl, 11cr, 63bl, 94tl, 163clc, 169c;
Berkeley Hotel: 17bl, 142tr; Blakes Hotel: 185tl/tr/cl;
Lara Bohinc: 86cr;
Cargo: 17tl, 146b; Corbis: Gail Marie Orenstein 11bl;
Reuters/Peter Macdiarmid 10tr
Dorset Square Hotel: 183tr; Dulwich Picture Gallery: 112tl/cl;
Michael Ellis: 107t; The End: 141cl; Everyman Cinema Club: 128br;
Fabric: Tom Stapley 19tl, 145bl; Firmdale Hotels: 180br, 181cr; Freud Museum: 108tr;
Gate Restaurant: 41br; Great Eastern Dining Room: 48tl; Great Eastern Hotel: 187tl/tr;
Hackney Empire: 125tr; Hayward Gallery: 109bl;

Korres Natural Products: 79br;
Locomotiva: 147bl; Loungelover: 149cla;
Mandarin Oriental Hyde Park: 37cl; Mash: 140cr; The Metropolitan Hotel: 182t; Ministry of Sound: 153cr;
© National Maritime Museum, London: 112b; National Trust: 107c, 107b; Network London: 39br;
Ocean: 125bl; One Aldwych: 136tr, 178tr, 180tl/tr;
Redferns Music Picture Library: Nicky J. Sims 121tl;
Royal Academy of Arts, London: 100cl; Royal Borough of Kensington and Chelsea: 102br, 103tr; Rules: Gary Alexander 30cl/bl/r;
Sardo: 29t; Scala: 126cl; Selfridges: 71tc/tr/br;
Serpentine Gallery: 101cl; Dennis Severs' House: Deidi von Schaewen 104ca; M. Stacey Shaffer 104t;
Shakespeare's Globe: photo John Tramper production *Edward II* 2003 130cl; Sir John Soane's Museum: 97tr, 97cr; Somerset House Press Office: 94r; South London Gallery: photo Marcus Leith, all works courtesy Tomio Koyama Gallery, Tokyo, Feature Inc, New York and Stephen Friedman Gallery, London 110br;
Space NK: 80crb;
Tate Britain: 99crb/br, 100tl;
Walthamstow Stadium: 126tl; Whitechapel Gallery: exhibition: Gerhard Richter: *Atlas* 104br;
Zefa Visual Media: Masterfile/Lloyd Sutton 1, 6–7;
The Zetter Restaurant & Rooms: 179b, 188tl/tca/tcb.

Jacket images Front: Corbis/Pat Doyle (clc and spine); DK Images/Carrie Love (crc); Getty Images/Julian Calder (cl); Courtesy of the Trustees of the V&A Picture Library/Vivienne Westwood (cr); Zefa Visual Media/masterfile/Lloyd Sutton (background).
Back: Zefa Visual Media/masterfile/Lloyd Sutton (c); DK Images/Carrie Love (tr).

© Transport for London